Writing Home

POLLY DEVLIN

INTRODUCTION BY JOAN BAKEWELL

PIMPERNEL
PRESS LTD
www.pimpernelpress.com

For Carmen Callil

Pimpernel Press Limited
www.pimpernelpress.com

Writing Home
© Pimpernel Press Limited 2019
Text © Polly Devlin 2019
Introduction © Joan Bakewell 2019

Design by Becky Clarke Design

A catalogue record for this book is
available from the British Library.

ISBN 978-1-910258-33-0

Typeset in Amasis MT
Printed and bound in England
by CPI Books

9 8 7 6 5 4 3 2 1

Contents

Introduction

BY JOAN BAKEWELL

'I know there is a blessing in this somewhere . . .' a consoling saying of the Ames family in Marilynne Robinson's *Gilead*: their way of finding riches in the most untoward events. Polly Devlin's writing life is full of such benison, turning small events, unpromising landscapes – rooks, Irish bogs – into reading gold. Turn to any one of these chapters and you confront the tantalizing, the gossipy, the heartfelt, the passionate, the lyrical. Nothing fulfils expectations because you will have none. This is a totally surprising array of occasions and insights overflowing with Devlin's wit and love of language.

Here she is caught in a traffic hold-up on an Irish road: 'It is a fine Saturday in August and I am driving from Belfast to Warrenpoint . . .' (Her narrative impulse is sound as a rock.) 'At the entrance to the town I am stopped by two policemen . . . Then I remember: Lady's Day, 15 August, the Feast of the Assumption, is one of the two days the Hibernians march: I look forward to hearing the old tunes.' The Hibernians are an Ancient Catholic Order and the Devlins are an ancient Catholic Ulster clan. Polly's is a Catholic calendar. Instead of the little girls in white dresses she half-expects she is confronted by bowler hats, dark suits and orange sashes, the elite of the Orange Order. It is to be a hideous encounter.

Once the parade has passed she describes a tiny detail that is to cause trouble. Trying to restart the car, 'I slightly panicked, swore, tried again and then, remembering I was driving an automatic, put the gear into drive. The car jumped forward as though stung and lurched off.'

A hundred yards down the road, she is flagged down by a B Special – one of the notorious quasi-military reserve police force, since disbanded. Others join him and they subject her to sustained and voluble abuse for 'cursing and shouting at the marchers'. They bang on the car, examine her driving licence, confer on the radio, consult the police computer. She grows fearful, almost tearful.

Then the nastiness of the mood is suddenly transformed: they are benign, even friendly.

They have, she speculates, discovered on her records that she has an OBE, an honour from the Queen. 'From being one of Them I became one of Us.' Their tone mellows. They ask her occupation: 'I'm a writer.' 'That's some job you have there . . . maybe you'll put me in a book sometime.'

And now she has.

Polly Devlin's sensibility and warmth are fine-tuned throughout her writing life to the intensity of her childhood home, her parents and her six siblings. It was both warm-hearted and austere: 'No one born since the sixties in Ireland can know how dark everything was for a great many months of the year.' 'The lecky' only came to her area in 1957, when she was in her teens. Until then rooms were lit by oil lamps or gas lights with mantles – 'fragile white objects like wasps' nests or fretted meringue . . .' The child's eye does more than see, it enjoys. It has proved a valuable gift.

She grew up in a remote rural parish, Ardboe, famous for its ancient cross, near the great expanse of Lough Neagh in Northern Ireland, and its image haunts her all her life and creeps regularly into her prose. So does the brooding power of the Catholic Church: 'Night after night, we recited the five glorious mysteries, the five sorrowful ones, and I forget the rest because I don't want to remember.' There is a proud melancholy about the stories she tells of those years. Among them, a shocking but reticent revelation of sexual abuse. She tells it with discretion and pain. 'The wound is profound, the scar hurts on as a real historical unhappiness. I've never learnt to come to terms with it . . . But I embrace life and joy and love – I must, otherwise the perpetrator is forever the victor. You can't undo damage, but you can assuage it.'

Armed then against the hurts of the world, Polly Devlin takes flight on a dazzling trajectory. And we travel with her. Home in Ardboe she would regularly see an outdated copy of *Vogue* on special order from Sheehy's in Cookstown. In one January issue she comes across a talent contest, and she enters. She wins (Jackie Kennedy had been an earlier winner) and so begins her first job in 1963 as a writer at London *Vogue*'s headquarters in Hanover Square. Within six months of arriving – and, she says, without 'any rocket-like brilliance on my part' – she becomes features editor. She makes it sound as though with a bit of luck it could happen to anyone. And then she is poached by Diana Vreeland, legendary editor of American *Vogue*.

And Diana Vreeland – *there*'s a story! For Diana Vreeland, 'each issue of *Vogue* was like her newborn baby, and she behaved towards the finished issue rather like a father staring at his new baby: that its conception, by now a remote pleasure, should have resulted in *this*? . . . She set ground rules that were hard to pre-empt: "The first thing to do is to arrange to be born in Paris. After that everything follows naturally." I'd fallen at the first fence. Ardboe was the antithesis of Paris.'

Despite having been born in Ardboe rather than Paris . . . in no time Polly is interviewing a whole raft of celebrities, pinning each of them with her sharp wit. Bob Dylan looks 'a bit like Thomas Chatterton, only upright'. David Bailey is rude – 'that's half the point.' His girlfriend, Jean Shrimpton, 'looks as though she sleeps in cathedral pews and sucks artichoke hearts for sustenance'. This is a woman who has found her talent and is relishing, as do we, the extravagant world that opens up to her – 'it's like being a provincial at Versailles.'

Whatever happens, she finds 'a blessing in this somewhere'. And there are many blessings indeed: a happy marriage to a talented entrepreneur and generous philanthropist, three daughters named after flowers, Rose, Daisy and Bay. Homes in New York, Paris, Somerset and London. The security of this background nourishes her ideas and her pen. Her mind and curiosity are never idle: she was for years on the Northern Ireland panel of *Round Britain Quiz* (her lively mind making connections that might never have occurred to the rest of us). She taught writing at Columbia University in New York. This book garners the wealth of this lifetime, opening us up to her opinions and welcoming us as friends.

Joan Bakewell, 14 January 2019

Flight Path

There are histories where the beginning is still happening.

So it is with the event known as the Flight of the Earls. Over four hundred years ago, in September 1607, the news reached the native population of Ulster, the most Gaelic province of Ireland and the one that had held out the longest against the English, that the most powerful chieftain in Ireland, Hugh O'Neill, Earl of Tyrone, leader of the resistance during the Nine Years' War, had set sail in an unnamed French warship for Europe from Rathmullan on Lough Swilly in Derry, with ninety-nine others, including the nobility of the north, their wives and children and followers. The desperate centuries-long warfare with England was over, the native culture and order was broken.

His brother Cormac O'Neill wrote of his leadership, 'For all the Irish obey O'Neill as sails obey the wind. For they have as much love for him as sons do for their parents both for his own sake as for hatred of the English.' And with his departure the Gaelic dispensation of Tanistry and Brehon law that had lasted for millennia, a whole way of life and culture, was doomed. It was calamity for people like us, his henchmen, his clan, his soldiers. The waves behind his ship are still breaking on our shores.

The event was not called the Flight of the Earls until a century later and many think the term is misguided and loaded – that there was nothing fugitive about their journey but rather that the leaders of Ulster had left for Spain to get help and reinforcements to continue the bitter fight to the death. But nevertheless, a flight it was, leaving Ulster rudderless, open to the worst, to what was inevitably going to happen, to the storms ahead, to the wreck of a nation.

That benighted voyage is on an endless loop of what if . . . and if only . . . to those to whom the worst did happen. My family for a start.

A list preserved in the Borghese Papers in Rome records that as the ship at last reached the shores of France after a hellish crossing, which took twenty-three days when it should have taken four or five – there was one barrel of water left (though there were five gallons of beer). The sad fugitives – not unlike the ones we see now every day on our screens, pushed out of their homeland on to stormy seas to seek refuge where they may – landed near Rouen, exhausted and sick, and began their epic journey across Europe. Their hopes for further help from Spain were fruitless and The O'Neill died in Rome in 1616.

O'Neill had held together many opposing strands in Ulster – the chieftains quarrelled among themselves and cattle raids were a way of life, and he was arbiter of these quarrels; the English were always on the rampage, burning, killing, annexing territory and he negotiated with them and with their Queen. He knew that the war he was waging was between two wholly different civilizations, the one despising the other. So, the Flight is one of the most calamitous events in Irish history. Everything fell apart. *The Annals of the Four Masters*, written in the early seventeenth century, judged it thus: 'Woe to the heart that meditated, woe to the mind that conceived, woe to the council that decided on, the project of their setting out on this voyage, without knowing whether they should ever return to their native principalities or patrimonies to the end of the world.' With the leaders gone, the way lay clear for the agrarian settlement known as the Plantation of Ulster, a weasel description of illegal acquisition and theft. Our land was taken, brought under English jurisdiction and laws and parcelled out to Protestant settlers from England and Scotland and, as the historian George Hill wrote in his book *The Plantation of Ulster,* 'When the native gentry lost their homes and houses they received short shrift; anyone found lingering around their old homes could expect to be shot . . . The British settlers generally do not appear to have had any kind thoughts or sympathies; for that class who had been more respectable than themselves they naturally cherished a vague terror . . . We may imagine something of the agony and dismay of those who had occupied positions of comfort and respect throughout the several counties of Ulster but who were doomed to be outcast on their own soil.'

We may well imagine. I don't need to – the agony and dismay is in our DNA. My English name is Devlin but it is also Doibhlin (with prefix Ni because I am female; the male line is O'Doibhlin). It is an ancient Irish tribal name or more accurately it is the name of an Irish sept – a branch of a clan.

The O'Doibhlin had been part of the praetorian guard to The O'Neill. They were horsemen and what might now be called courtiers, though from the sound of it they were far from courtly, since their duties included the taking and guarding of hostages and collecting fines for robbery.

My grandfather was known as the Hatchet Man. I thought that it was a contemporaneous nickname given because he had a terrifying temper, and only years later discovered that the appellation was passed from generation to generation and comes from our breeding – to have a temper which rarely erupts but, when provoked, is upsetting all round, or, as cousin Willie said on seeing mine in action, 'fuckin' lethal'.

The clan lived beside Lough Neagh, near three sites of great significance in our history: Tullyhogue, O'Neill's headquarters (the name means Mound of the Young Warriors), and two settlements, small towns now called Dungannon and Stewartstown. Dungannon was from the Gaelic, Dun Eigeann. Stewartstown is a new name: it was originally known as An Craobh and is still called that by old local people. It too was an O'Neill stronghold. The O'Doibhlin had a castle near the lough, at Roughan, where our legend has it that in one battle a thousand of our sept were killed.

Tullyhogue, the crowning place of the kings of Ulster with its throne and its crowning stone, was the centre of the world for my ancestors. It was destroyed by the piratical Sir Toby Caulfeild – what a piece of work he was – who was appointed receiver of the rents of The O'Neill after the Flight and took thousands of acres of land as his own. There is a village near us called Castlecaulfield (the spelling is now changed). Not a welcoming place.

Tullyhogue is now only a wide, high circular mound in the middle of a field, with ruined traces of fortifications surrounded by trees and enclosing a depression covered in bryony, moss and sweet cicely. When I visited what is to me a shrine it seemed apparent that whoever has this land would plough it into the ground and grow crops over it if he could. I know from the rich look of the land that rich Protestants owned it. I would think that, wouldn't I? And with reason.

What all the clans who lived in the O'Neill territory realized as word of the Flight spread was that the future struggle would no longer have anything to do with battles and that this catastrophe was on a different scale. The calamity of the Flight rendered us outcasts – landless, homeless, powerless and paupers. It lies at the roots of the recent Troubles of the political entity of Northern Ireland.

One day when I was about fourteen years old I found in a bookcase a slim green volume with red lettering called *The Story of an Irish Sept: The Devlins of Tyrone* which I assumed was an Ancient Tome but had been written, with earnestness and scholarship, not long before by a professor from Pennsylvania called Joseph Chubb Develin, who had sent it to my grandfather as a mark of respect. All of the O'Doibhlin clan were listed and treated of there. We had a history! I read it with astonishment and disbelief and a dismay which turned to sorrow and anger. To read it was to open a door into the suffering of my ancestors. I see when I look back at that adolescent transcribing every word – I still have the little manuscript – I see her almost as poring over the Rosetta stone, trying to decipher a way into a lost world.

Something terrible and calamitous happens to a colonized people, apart from the original calamity of invasion. The brutality and cynicism which often accompanies colonization, and the disruption, denigration and disintegration of their culture which prevents a people from being proud in their own country, happened profoundly in Ireland. The Irish did not lead a life of material ease, of great houses and hierarchy. The chieftains ate in the same room as their servants, everything was shared and there was little husbandry – cattle were their main crop, O'Neill had hundreds of thousands of head of cattle. The way of life was ancient, almost pagan, and with dignity, ritual, custom and ceremony. After the Flight, when we lost everything and were driven to the fringes, we knew what it was to be abject and to be mocked. When I read of the Sioux or the Comanches, proud preservers of their great lands now herded on to arid reservations again, I do not need imagination to feel for them.

The history of every country begins in the heart of a man or a woman. I know when I visit Tullyhogue that history is alive. I stand in the enormous emptiness and know that O'Neill left behind no hope. The place is steeped in sorrow. You can almost hear the cadence of vanishing as a last cry is blown across from Lough Swilly. In writing about the history of O'Neill and of the events surrounding the Flight of the Earls I am writing my own history.

Some colonized people try more or less successfully to ape the ways and habits of those in power in order to get somewhere. The result is pathetic camouflage. Where that somewhere is, is a good subject for speculation. Every time we drove past Stuart Hall, with its great tower and gothic darkness, near Stewartstown, on the way to boarding school I yearned to be the grand person who lived there in its fastness. (Actually, it was mostly uninhabited, since Lord Castle Stewart was rarely there.)

Northern Ireland for us was neither one thing nor the other, neither here nor there, neither English nor Irish. We were taught English history as the record of our past, read English literature and recited English poetry without anyone ever making the point that many of the writers and poets we studied came from our country. We studied natural history in terms of the flora and fauna of Suffolk and Yorkshire, not of the great stretch of water beside which we lived. We warbled English folk songs, 'Greensleeves' and 'Scarborough Fair', whereas in the houses around I heard Irish music fiddled or played on the flute and ballads sung by men and women, often with cracked and off-key voluptuous voices. I never heard any of these as a distinct expression of a nation's voice and memory, but rather as valueless native music. Because my imagination was sparked by English (in every sense – the fabulous language, the written word, the stories), it became fixed on Englishness; and my idea of Englishness and the English, when I was far away in West Tyrone, held other, attractive, seductive qualities. I longed for that sophisticated world delivered by writers like Jane Austen, Evelyn Waugh, Nancy Mitford, Anthony Powell, Simon Raven, where one was witty, lived in divine houses, had countless love affairs and was heartlessly cruel.

It was a matter of credentials; and so, from my earliest years, I believed that to be English was to be good, right and acceptable.

I know now that obliterating a history is a fine suppressor and silencer of pride and grief. If you don't know what happened to you and something happened to you, who will you blame except yourself? The Flight keeps on happening and rage keeps its surge in the blood.

All my adult life I have fled from place to place, always on the move, constructing myself, under a different name, in my own demesne, in different countries, trying to create what I thought was an imaginative fancy when it was something much deeper and older. What I was looking for was the place that though I'd never known it I was nostalgic for. The place of our own.

The Road to King's Island

She drove to school every morning in all weathers and she hated it with a fearful anticipation. In the 1950s cars were not as reliable as we take for granted now and there were battles with a starting handle every frosty morning and roads were bad in the part of Northern Ireland where we grew up. We lived on solid enough ground, physically, though it was fairly shaky metaphysically speaking, reared, as we were, between the two warring dispensations of the political situation in that god-ridden place.

She taught in a school fourteen miles away. She could not get a job nearer – something about being married to a publican, plus the rampant sexist discrimination that riddled employment then – there were hardly any headmistresses in the primary schools. (We won't even mention the religious discrimination – but there – I've mentioned it.) So she set out on a journey across the small, twisting, narrow roads that traversed our back of beyond, some of them hardly tarmacked. It would be a formidable enough daily journey now, but then it was a major undertaking.

Hers was the only car on the road except for the priest's and occasionally the doctor's, out on a call from the tiny village of Coagh, and by this token there were few garages, no mechanics, no breakdown services – in any case there were no telephones to summon help. The telephone was only installed in our house (and we were very avant-garde) in the late fifties, and the neighbours often came to take calls at midnight from their relatives who had emigrated to the USA. If the car broke down or a tyre was punctured, she was on her own in the middle of the country, often in the dark and the cold.

The place she most dreaded was the Moss road that ran towards King's Island, where her school was situated. Although we took the strange, crisp English name for granted, it was an alien moniker, so candid and unsecret, King's Island, among the mysterious Irish names of the townlands that surrounded it – Killycavanagh, Tamnamore, Annaghmore, Killybegs, Ardtrea, Cluntoe. I always wondered who the King had been, and only learnt many years later that a man named King had lived on this piece of land, which had been a raised island in the middle of a bog (it was called the Moss in our district), so that the Moss road had once been, near enough, a small causeway.

So, although we did not attend the school she taught in, and did not do the journey often, it was on that straggly negotiation towards her school that I first recognized the phenomena of marshes and bogs, and moss roads, and on every journey the change in atmosphere struck me with intense, almost osmotic force.

You could almost sniff the change in the air as we got nearer the bog road: children (and dogs) are like barometers, constantly reacting to pressure and elements and atmosphere, and all three were elementally present in our Austin as my distracted mother drove white-knuckled along the pot-holed road. The line and air along the edges of the bog seemed different: even on dry days there was the hint of mizzle, of tension between damp and dry, the air lambent, full of condensation. Even though we were well used to water, having grown up by the great silvery shield of Lough Neagh, this liquid was more to do with secrecy than with reflections; this was the dew of ages soaking into earth's tissues.

We were, of course, infected by her fear. If the car toppled over it would be sucked in softly, plop, the soft earth closing over quietly, the matted vetches knitting up again, the soft wellings still again, innocent, no sign of us. It wasn't so far-fetched; there were a couple of mounds out at the edges which we knew were the remnants of sod houses melting back into the bog since they were abandoned, shards of a poorer time. And I'd read the graphic and thrilling account of Carver Doone sinking into the quagmire in *Lorna Doone*.

The little fields in the townlands around our house were productive, with cows and crops, and the places were peopled thickly, houses on every second field. But the bog was empty of produce, or domestic animals or humans; and yet filled with life – snipe and wagtail and weasel – and rich vegetation – bog cotton, sally trees and myriad plants, small birch trees along the edges and, of course, the rich black turf. For all my fears I wanted to stop, to venture through the grasses and whins, the milkworts, the ferns, the mares' tails, and the yellow flags which we called shaggins.

She drove as fast as she dared, to get away from that shifting stretch of land and on to dry, trustworthy, definite stuff where people gauged the sky for the weather and not the ground.

Again, it was only years later that I learnt the meaning of the Gaelic names for the townlands that she traversed towards safety, a whole landscape we had lost the skill to read. *Bordnamona*, edge of the turf; *Annaghmor*, great marsh; *Aneeterbeg*, little low-lying ground, *Cluntoe*, meadowy land, where she began to relax a little, within what she called a hound's gowl of home, and thence through *Farsnagh*, a wide roomy place, past the Old Cross – at least a thousand years old, and one of the great treasures of Ireland – and into *Sessiagh*, the sixth division, where we lived in Muintirevlin, the country of the Devlins.

Further along the Moss road, where the ground rose a little, a few scattered cottages lay at the end of hedgy loanings and one summer's day we drove up one of these loanings to the thatched cottage with its jamb wall, its front room, its single bedroom, housing a family of nine people. Some of the older children wove the sally rods into baskets and I wish I had one now, so intricate, sturdy and satisfactory.

While she was buying the baskets, I went around the side of the house and stepped out across the street, as we called it, and into the mossy hinterland. Into the bog. I once read that when we walk across bogland – across sphagnum – it may take a year or more before our footprints disappear. I want to think that somewhere that child's impress, so hesitant, so venturesome, is lying fifty years below the surface, waiting for her return.

A Family Christmas

Of course it meant trouble. Everything disrupted and that meant tempers short and the days out of kilter so that underneath there was that tension – the feeling of the knife edge without which nothing had much authenticity. A feeling of flare in the air, the atmosphere spiked, a taut line behind the dark, sometimes snowy, atmosphere, like a watermark in the old pages of the encyclopaedia that showed the simpering Victorian Holy Family. No hint of tension there, no siblings peering over the edge of the manger, which I thought was a haven for selfish dogs, no signs of distress or sweat on the brow of a fifteen-year-old virgin who had just produced a bouncing boy, and one who, it was manifest, was going to give her nothing but trouble.

There was peace in that illustration but nothing to do with the peace wrung from the boiling battles lost and won in our household. Peace was a form of barter, the cowrie shell of the day, which if we could give it to the adults, especially to their heads ('For God's sake, will yous give me head peace?') would give us credit or keep something at bay. Between ourselves we spilled in and out of the role of appeaser or aggressor depending on which space was vacant. And good will to men doesn't have the same heft when you are sisters. The men in our lives The Father, The Brother, had our easy good will, since they never tapped the venom. But, mercy, we all loved each other. No one but ourselves could begin to know how much.

Now I try to remember what we gave each other for Christmas and I can't remember a single thing, though the voluptuous pleasures of the garden of delights that was Sheehy's Walk-Around store in Cookstown has never been equalled – not in Neiman Marcus, not in Bloomingdales, not in the Avenue Montaigne. It gave me a real taste for luxury, did Sheehy's. with nothing more than half a crown and everything gimcrack.

We were always indulging in surpluses of gratitude and remorse and Christmas is a time for a surfeit of such surpluses. I do know we all gave each other things we longed for ourselves, which kept a nice little simmering pot of longing on the boil, over the following week or so, before the precious object was lost or broken or spirited away. And I remember there was a lot of talc. I don't know why we're all still alive.

There were various emblems of Christmas which increased in intensity as the days wore on and our emotional temperatures rose. The holly berries were the first, but in the soft climate by the lough shore the berries enamelled earlier so by early December the birds were gorged, the trees were empty and I was afflicted by the sense of loss that I carried around with me like a comforter. I wasn't so far gone in pre-emptive dolour that I didn't grudge the birds the berries, but 'Live horse and you'll get grass', Ellen, our maid, would say as I lamented over the empty glossy leaves, an utterance I could never fathom. I went to the oracle to have it explained. My father. 'It's an old, old saying. Like "Die dog or eat the hatchet",' he said, and smiled his smile. (None the wiser.)

One of the first real signifiers of Christmas was that the breakfast room door couldn't be opened unless you flung yourself against it. There's an appalling passage in *Jude the Obscure* where Susan leaves her house after a heartbreaking scene in which her children – whom she loves more than life itself – overhear their parents murmur that it might have been better if they had never been born. She returns home and tries to open the door and feels an odd resistance, something heavy and dangling, and she knows, knows to the pit of her stomach, what is hanging on the hook behind the door. Such emotional baggage is something I could do without, but there it is, tidily hung up in my head, through the art and anger of Thomas Hardy and when I read it, although I knew there was a diminishment and wrong appropriation in there, nevertheless it brought back with clarity that day when we would come back from school and go to the breakfast room (which kept its grand appellation although it had long since been relegated to junk room) and would find, on pushing the door, that something soft and heavy and fairly dreadful was hanging in there, staking out the room with its white vacancy.

'Mind the Burd,' Ellen would call. She knew from wherever she was in the house exactly what we were each of us up to. It became a fact of Christmas life, this white, plucked carcass hanging from the hook behind the door, its neck getting longer as the days passed, its comb flopping to one side, turning a pallorous purple as Christmas drew nearer.

It was hard to reconcile it with the magnificent fact of life it had been a few days before, strutting, swollen, cocksure, puffed out in a glory of circular feathers, its wings brushing the ground insistent and arrogant. We knew, of course, we all knew that, come the day, it wouldn't fit the oven though the old range would be white with heat and the air would turn blue with oaths as Ellen tied to cram it in, and that finally she'd start muttering about making Crippen of herself as she dismembered it. But that never deterred our father – a turkey had to be big to be beautiful and he would recite with pleasure a litany of its weight and dimensions.

The last great harbinger outside of the Plumping of the Puddings was the archaeological Dig for the Decorations. After all, we didn't live in so big a house – how could they have been so effectively lost? Every year there was a volcanic period when the decorations were not to be found. There were recriminations, each party accused the other of secreting them in some atavistic and distant place; there was wild surmise and speculation and suggestions – Long John Silver with his crinkled map and black spot wasn't in it when it came to our familial searches for a large brown box of tacky tinsel.

Then when it was found – always where it was all the time – and the air had healed there was the shock of the resurrection of the decorations. Buried and forgotten they now came festooning into the light with a drift, a faint and frowsty bloom of all the Christmases before clinging to them.

They'd not been the most beautiful decorations at the beginning of their tenure – flimsy coloured paper shapes cut into elaborate patterns, concertinas glued at each little end to form a chain; each year another couple of sections were left behind on their drawing pin. As we grew older the chains spanned less space so that by the time we were leaving home and loosening those other chains that forever span our lives, they were only a few coloured remnants over the doors.

Memory makes enormous the surrounding of our youth, we are astonished by their diminution on our return. Not our Christmas decorations. Their dwindling was real. But the Christmas of my childhood grows bigger every year. And then, at the bottom of the box, the trove, the decorations for the tree, of exquisite fragility and glamour – so utterly removed from the everyday hewn textures of our lives, these glass and glittery objects. One year a sister broke the silver trumpet. It was quite clear to all of us there, that when the disaster was uncovered by the grown-ups, Christmas would be cancelled. Yet when they were eventually told no one seemed to care – they didn't register the epic scale of the calamity in our small lives, how frightened we were by the breakage.

And then the point where all the shadows of Christmas met. Midnight Mass. Made wholly strange by having to go up to the parish church in Mullinahoe instead of to our own little chapel in Moortown; the parked cars stretched right back down to McConville's corner and we'd tread a perilous way between them, our faces and those of all our neighbours illuminated in flashes by other cars negotiating the narrow spaces. We were only two miles away from home but everything was magical, heightened, in this upper country, glinting with excitement and faith. The sky was always starry and inside the church the holly was dripping with scarlet. Then Master Ryder would open up the old harmonium and let her rip and Charlie Devlin's lovely voice would soar in 'Panis Angelicus' – no matter if it was an Easter hymn – he sang it so well, it must be sung – and we all stood for 'Adeste Fideles', the whole parish, cracked voices and young pealing together to the rafters, and Christmas had begun.

The Millstone

Once upon a time there was this little girl – she was lovable, as little girls are, but she felt unlovable and unloved. In photographs she stands with her head tilted to one side, the signifier of the placatory child. She did everything she could think of to be lovable, to feel the touch of a loving hand. She did things that others didn't want to do; cleaned out the guts of the plucked chickens and became overly familiar with giblets and gizzards and croppins and lights (words that have disappeared from poultry vocabulary but things which were used to make soup with then). The child gave away – always – the things that she loved and, of course, she lost anything that belonged to her which was valuable, and even now she is an old woman has continued to do so. People with low self-esteem lose their precious possessions and things of worth, and the art of losing is indeed not hard to master. *(Write it!)* Someone just has to master and abuse and degrade you at an early stage in your life.

There's a faded, almost sepia, photograph of her that I sometimes look at. It shows a privet hedge with a gap leading to a lawn and the child – head to one side – is standing beside a rhododendron whose branches over the years have spread so low that they trail the ground. When she crept underneath these drooping branches she was its living heart, under a green web of leaves and purple flowers for walls, the floor dry but smelling of earth; this sun-dappled lair was an escape place.

She brushed the floor with twigs and even when it rained the close leaves sheltered it so only a smattering of raindrops fell inside. I know so much about it because of course the child in the photo is me, but I did not know then what I was escaping from and I do now and so do many of us women.

I remember, as a child, sitting in the pews at Mass in that heavily segregated little chapel in our parish, where about once a year one of our priests, a rotund good man called Father Donnelly, would make a startling sermon which, young as I was, sounded sinister

– about what Jesus had said about sinning against children – that it were better for the offender that a millstone be hanged about his neck, and he be drowned in the depths of the sea than that he should offend one of these, his little ones.

The punishment had real significance for me because we lived beside an inland sea and often gazed down its unfathomable depths; the idea of a man with this huge thing around his neck falling, falling through the water was acutely visible. But as to what the priest was talking about, I had no idea. But I do now and so do all of us, and what's more one of the other priests who stood at the altar on Sundays should have had the millstone tied around his neck.

Child abuse is going on all the time, always has been, and we know now what happened in Ireland; but abuse was always widespread throughout families as well as institutions and the most shocking cases involved priests because of the position of trust they held in our society. That wicked priest Brendan Smyth abused – by which I mean raped – at least one hundred and forty-three children over a period of forty years in parishes in Belfast, Dublin and the United States, Every time he was found out he was moved on by his superiors . . . Superiors! But then again, he was called Father until his death in prison and his gravestone had the appellation Reverend on it. Reverend Father! Caliban, more like: 'a thing most brutish'.

But as far back as forever respected members of society and politicians (not the same) were child abusers and getting away with it. The scandal of the Kincora Boys' Home for working boys in Belfast has never been fully explored. Senior establishment figures including bishops and peers were alleged to be involved and the police had been informed over and over about the abuse but did nothing about it. There have been constant claims that MI5 allowed the abuse to continue during the Troubles in order to gather sensitive intelligence reports.

Such cases are legion. The stink of one vile man, Jimmy Savile, rose to cover England with its stench. The country reeled under the shock. Yet so many people knew about his behaviour when it was happening and did not do anything to stop it. Savile didn't give a toss. He once said he didn't care if allegations that he was a paedophile and necrophiliac became part of his legacy after he was gone.

Every time I read something about Jimmy Savile I am filled with a deep distress, not only because of revulsion, but because of what he did to each child he smeared and how he knocked their life out of true, skewed their vision and skewered their soul. I am not being wise after the event when I say I viewed him with a deep repugnance. His appearance was so ghastly for a start – that pallid dungy face – and the poverty of the vocabulary: 'Now then, now then . . .' Those dead eyes, that mouth always filled with a fat cigar, the slimy Wonka hair. One of my colleagues said, 'Something told us a long time ago that he was a creep and a thoroughly unlikeable man and most women would agree. Is it because of female intuition, a gut instinct?' Gut instinct has to do with morality, conscience, upbringing and experience, not some mystic feeling in the entrails, and for me it was not only a gut instinct but an aesthetic and intellectual response, and moral revulsion.

What is so terrible about child molestation is not just that it is going on all the time but that there is nearly always someone who knows what is happening and colludes or keeps schtum. Parents don't know who is approaching their children when they are outside their ken, and children don't know they are being groomed, they can't intuit when someone has bad intent. G. K. Chesterton once wrote, 'It would seem as though the living creature had to be taught the art of crying out when it was hurt . . . We learn of cruelty to children from journalists, from doctors, from inspectors, teachers . . . but we never learn it from the children, never from the victims.' More often than not they are frightened into silence by threats of further violence.

What child abuse does to its victims is profoundly terrible. A deep insecurity is born, a hunger that is never filled, a void that gapes and roils in your life. Fear and lack of trust become part of your character. The child has a flawed relationship with the outside world and with other people. The conviction of being loved and valuable *as we are*, that validation of our inner and intrinsic worth, is the beginning of the most fundamental kind of self-esteem, what psychologists call global or core self-esteem, and the lack of it is a crippling psychological disorder. One little-publicized result is that its victims often become overweight as a form of protection.

I know whereof I speak. That child in the photo beside the rhododendron tree had an STD – trichomoniasis – all her young life. She thought it was something she had been born with and it made her life a misery. She became anorexic and when she finally got help – the invention of Flagyl changed her life – she was told by the doctor she could have only have received it from penetration. She was an infant, vulnerable, unprotected when she was raped and infected. To put it mildly the assault, inflicted and endured, caused damage to my reproductive system and it did profound damage to my psychological system. It was a millstone round my neck, not round the man who gave it to me. I could not know who it was but whenever I met a certain man who lived half a mile away and sometimes worked for us, a squaljd, socially inadequate man dead these many years, I shied away from him though I never knew why. Now I know why.

It's easy to say you must not go on being a victim, but it's not easy to do. The wound is profound, the scar hurts on as a real historical unhappiness. I've never learnt to come to terms with it. All my life I have been restless, seeking somewhere else about to be, moving from place to place. But I embrace life and joy and love – I must, otherwise the perpetrator is forever the victor. You can't undo damage, but you can assuage it. As ever, I go back to poetry. Auden's words are always underwritten by common sense and though he wrote 'For poetry makes nothing happen', poetry can and does help. Auden's lines 'In the deserts of the heart/Let the healing fountain start' are consoling and Seamus Heaney's wisdom – 'The way we are living, timorous or bold, will have been our life' – has supplied me with courage and hope and order.

You have only to read Auden's poem about Sigmund Freud, where he writes that he 'merely told the unhappy Present to recite the Past like a poetry lesson till sooner/or later it faltered at the line where long ago the accusations had begun . . . and was life-forgiven and more humble, able to approach the Future as a friend' to know that you are in the company of a vatic healer.

So, I read and wrote and read and wrote and faltered and faltered until I met someone who held me up and held me straight, so I too could approach the Future as a friend. For if self is a location, so is love.

Tinkers

The best second-hand treasures you can discover, unearth and store are other people's memories, conveyed to us by whatever means. Things they saw that have vanished for ever, but which are preserved in and by writing and painting. A visual language that might have gone, a syntax so nearly lost, a remembering passed on, not just through generosity, but because of a human pressing need to enshrine, to say *this* is how it was, and thus honour things, customs, ways of behaving, old manners that otherwise would have disappeared completely.

Each year as a child I saw windowsills spread with kingcups, yellow and glimmering in the twilight, put there on the eve of the first of May to keep the bad spirits away for the rest of the year; I saw, oh when was the last time, a man standing high, high above me on a steamroller, a true juggernaut, the tar pushing and oozing out from under its vast inexorable roller, black as gravity, viscous and thick and sensuous so that we rolled it avidly in our hands between our palms, feeling its black sinful give. (Natch, we got it all over our clothes and were clouted on our heads for our pains when we got home.) I saw a woman weeping because a hare ran across her path and she knew her child would be born with a harelip.

When I think of what I saw, and took for granted without realizing that it was all vanishing, that an unremarked glimpse was the last time I'd see something special! If I'd only known, I'd have looked with such care. But then that's how life is. I try to remember when was the last time I saw one of those blue-clad nuns – were they the Sisters of Mercy? – who wore huge white edifices on their heads, bleached and starched and pleated and raised, like windmills, making an unmistakable silhouette on the Paris skyline. They were a commonplace sight on the bridges of the Seine and in Dublin until the middle of the sixties; then suddenly they weren't there anymore. Pope John Paul had decreed them religiously or politically incorrect (though that phrase hadn't been invented then) and suddenly all nuns were in a subfusc navy blue, a drab and drear habit, whereas that other blue and white one seemed a symbol of tenderness and longevity and a springing faith.

When I was growing up in a really, really, really, ultimately really, remote part of Ireland – well, it wasn't remote to us, it was our locus, our place, our being's heart and home and anywhere else was someplace else – we were visited twice or three times a year by a gaggle or a seepage or some kind of collective noun of tinkers. They came by stealth. One day there wasn't a sign of them and the next you saw a distinctive shape ahead of you walking down the road and you knew the tinkers – or travelling people, or as we often wrongly called them, gypsies – were camped somewhere in the district.

What I am going to describe everyone and anyone writing for the five hundred years – or maybe even more – up to the mid-twentieth century could have described in precisely the same way. But no one, no one except me and a few others, could describe it now. The shape I saw before me was female, and the image breaks my heart, though I never knew her as an individual. She – and all her kind – wore a heavy black shawl, fringed, pulled over her head and down her shoulders, or pulled across her shoulders, tied crosswise across her breasts and torso and then tucked into the drawstrings of her skirt at the back. This skirt was long, heavy, full and generally black, although sometimes it was a flowered print. Over this she wore a kirtle, a sort of long apron, tucked up at the sides. Both skirt and kirtle were gathered at the waist so that the whole shape was broad and bulky, pulled in at the middle. This figure bore no resemblance to the shape of the female figure today. There were no such things as bras so their breasts lay as it were on their torso – so that everything was large, rounded and layered. Generally within their shawls in the crook of their elbows there would be a sleeping or suckling baby. And before and behind them would run or walk at least two other children, dirty, with lice in their heads and always distinguished by their beauty. They would cling to their mother's shawl and hide in its folds when she knocked on the door selling clothes pegs or baskets. In our house, Sarah, who looked after us, would give them short shrift and I always prayed my generous father would meet them on the way out through our gate and take pity on them. I knew they had their own way of life, their own pride, their own systems and wouldn't thank you for pity. It was money and drink they wanted. They begged for alms, beseeching and imploring, and I felt then, as I feel now, sorrow for the children who watched this humiliation. Yet not so long before they would have offered to tinker our broken metal containers, or to put metal handles on to china jugs and mugs, and earned their money.

That was where the word came from – a tinker was a craftsman, usually itinerant, who mended pots, kettles and cans. Where I grew up it was another word for gypsy, although real gypsies were Romanies, dark-haired with their own language, and these people on the contrary were fair, often beautiful, freckled, what was called 'very Irish-looking'.

Some writers thought romantically of the tinkers as the aristocracy of the people of the roads, above the tramps, the drovers and the peddlers. The thing they all had in common was they were nomads or travellers. They owned no land, no houses. They lived in vans, what we, the people tied to their possessions, shackled and unfree, called caravans, pulled by horses. Life was unromantic and hard, but it was the life they had chosen and clung to.

All the same they were a romantic sight, grouped around a camp fire, their dogs, lurchers, greyhounds, or little mixed-breed dogs which looked half-dog, half-fox, wandering around, feral and gaunt, scavenging for food. I own one such dog, got from a tinker, and love her dearly and a clever, handy little animal she is. The horses were tethered on the verges, grazing what was called 'the long acre', the free grass along the sides of the road.

We believed in the lore about tinkers, including the belief that tinkers left a mark on or near houses, indistinguishable to us, the settled, shackled people, which told of the character and generosity – or otherwise – of the inhabitants. I would search for the mark but never knew what I was looking for. I would like to think that in those marks, those crossed sticks or arranged pebbles, was a message that we, in our house, were kind. But I fear not – they were regarded as nuisances and light-fingered and Sarah always ran out to take our washing off the line lest it be stolen. Old cotton knickers, darned sweaters, patched sheets; she gathered them up as though they were precious damasks.

It seemed, then, as though they would be there for ever, those trudging shapes. In that manifestation they were gone for ever within a decade. Now the travelling people of Ireland live in large mobile homes (fair play to them) and don't tinker or sell pegs. They are still moved on from pillar to post, disregarded and unwanted, these people who have wandered Ireland since – it is said – they were dispossessed by Cromwell, but now they have a more comfortable way of life.

I've written before and no doubt I'll write again, being such a fervent recycler, that almost my favourite object in the world is a blue and white delft jug I found in a ditch in Monaghan, with a metal handle tinkered on. Now, that word tinker has sunk and lost its esteem and has become a word for clumsy or inefficient mending, or interfering, but my jug is mended with skill. It is literally better than new.

Every time I look at it I see them, the women and the children ahead of me, shawled or bareheaded, those broad, often weary, abused, beautiful faces, begging a penny, beseeching for alms, wending their way through the back roads of Ireland.

Last year I drove through Asturias and Galicia in northern Spain and saw old women holding a cow on a piece of rope as the cow grazed the Spanish long acre. There they were, women with the same shape, the scarf, the skirt, the shape, ineluctably, of age and poverty. The tears were tripping me.

Initiatory Drawings

I saw in a friend's house a little Neapolitan watercolour. When I enquired of its provenance, he said he'd bought it at the selling-up sale of Glyde Court. I stared at it for the longest time.

In life you come across things that puzzle you, disproportionate to their importance or relevance. Well, I do; every so often, an old mystery slurps up out of the murk of the mind – not necessarily old-fashioned mysteries like the *Marie Celeste* abandonment, or the Bermuda Triangle, things that under rational examination turn out to be more or less explicable, nor those mysteries closer to home like why you constantly lose your keys or why you continue to behave in ways that damage you – these mysteries are dynamics in life; at best some sort of repair is going on, at worst, some repetition of early damage. Nor am I talking about those things which, in my childhood, were called mysteries of faith, to question which was to question the whole foundation of the bizarre system of belief by which we lived. Well, this is what faith is: credulity, unquestioning belief. Night after night, we recited the five glorious mysteries, the five sorrowful ones, and I forget the rest because I don't want to remember. It all seemed darkish to me and, in any case, I couldn't see anything so mysterious about the Crowning with Thorns or the Carrying of the Cross, they seemed all-too-clearly-fathomable examples of man's inhumanity to man.

I've always disliked mysteries; they added to the chaos that for years seemed ready to engulf me. I like things that are explicable, plain and withstand scrutiny. In De Tocqueville's *Letters from Ireland*, I noted particularly a sentence spoken to him by an old priest in 1832, 'The Protestants hold that we love the dark. They will soon see that we love the light.' But, over a hundred years later, we still lived in the dark or, at least, that is how I saw it in my childhood; life lay in an old squalid murkiness, an apprehension of this beautiful world given to us by the Catholic Church in Ireland.

Of course, another aspect of this general apprehension of the darkness is because the lights weren't switched on, literally. Until I was in my mid-teens, the rooms of all the houses I knew were lit by candles or oil lamps.

The rich, velvety, indecipherable darkness of the night has long since disappeared from the skies in the western hemisphere. Reflected light from the world's illuminations has rendered our night sky much lighter than ever in our history; that famous twinkle of the little star has disappeared under the onslaught of sodium lights from our cities, and it is an aesthetic and sensual deprivation.

The prevalence of artificial light is one of the greatest changes that has taken place in my lifetime. No one born since the sixties in Ireland can know how dark everything was for a great many months of the year. The nights closed in so early and the ritual of filling the little lamps with paraffin, trimming the wicks, fixing the fragile glass globes back on to their grips was a kind of triumph against the darkness, never equalled by the alarming, sudden incandescence of electricity.

In our house we were well advanced, in that all the rooms on the ground floor were lit by gas lights, with little dangly chains with 'Off' and 'On' filigreed into discs which had been put on the wrong way round. (I still have difficulty with didactic instructions on containers and labels since the reverse always appeals to me.) The mantles were fragile white objects like wasps' nests or fretted meringue, which shattered at a touch. They were the most delicate things I'd seen outside the artefacts of nature.

I was mystified by the idea that such a little confection could survive the journey from the factory to the shop to our house in its rural fastness, especially as the mantles were made of cotton or artificial silk, saturated in a chemical solution, and burnt to crispness and had been invented in Austria only a decade or so before they were installed in our house. I am surprised by the speed of its adoption and installation in big houses in Ireland, considering the bulk of the gas containers, the intricacies of installing the system; it burned with a lovely glow, much softer than the electric bulb. The lecky only came to our district in 1957 and, suddenly, there was illumination everywhere, as though a torch had been held up to an old fresco showing details and corners and aged webs, and aged faces.

The lights of the town of Lurgan had long been a kind of glimmering girdle on the opposite side of the pitch-black expanse of Lough Neagh, sometimes glistening in the path of the moon. But one night in that year driving back from Lurgan, we could see, for the first time, light on our side of the lough. So, as quickly as that, over the span of one day, we jumped from a medieval apprehension of darkness to one where, at the flick of the switch, not only was all darkness banished, but, at the flick of another, we entered the new, alien, outside world of television, a luminous, ectoplasmic, plague-spreading infection, destroying the recipe for being a community.

I wonder was it at that time that October Devotions stopped? We walked to the little chapel every evening of that month for special prayers and saw the quick brightness of the stars above us, the spilled stretch of the Milky Way and the Cassiopeia cluster. (Bad Cassiopeia! I was shocked by the idea of a mother chaining her daughter to a rock.) We watched for shooting stars, since this meant there had been a displacement in the firmament through which a soul had entered heaven. All along the road we could see the black outlines of couples or groups of people, walking towards the chapel, silhouetted against the silvered skyline. On each side of the dark hedges, in the middle of many fields, stood a fairy thorn undisturbed for centuries.

Life was indeed more mysterious then, people looked odder, things were kept concealed, there was no merit to frankness; book learning was easier to come by (though I knew old people who couldn't read or write), but there wasn't much street wisdom about, or, if there was, I could not tap into it. On the other hand, there was no street. I remember at boarding school, at the end of the summer term, a group of older girls began an endless whispering, but when any of us younger ones came near, they stopped. One of the older girls took pity and promised to reveal the secret at the beginning of the September term. It was unimaginable but true that, as we sang 'O Causa Nostrae Laetitiae', the holiday hymn,

I longed for the holidays to be over before they had started so I could know the dreadful secret. Alas, I never returned to that school and now the secret will never be revealed, like the one about Fatima which haunted all our childhoods and which the Pope was supposed to reveal in 1960. Then, when it came to the crunch, he didn't. So it hangs in there still like a rennet bag. (Or maybe he did and I missed it. Blimey.)

All this train of thought about mysteries was brought on by the Glyde watercolour; Glyde Court was a Georgian house (with nineteenth-century Jacobean additions to romanticize it up) in County Louth, where the Vere Foster family lived. In the National Gallery in Dublin there is a fascinating portrait by Sir William Orpen of members of the family – the epigone you might say, painted in 1907.

This portrait seems to reveal the absolute necessity of separateness as a means to sanity and, though it appears to be such a conventional rendering of an upper-class family, almost a piece of iconography, it is only a trace of reality, full of mystery, never mind the donkey which one of the daughters is holding. Vere Foster complained that 'the donkey and all of us seem to share the same expression', but with his red kerchief hanging out of his pocket, his rakish bow tie, the thin, etiolated face, he is style, accessory and anxiety. Beside him stands the ultimate accessory, his wife, looking like a contemporary *Vogue* model in pale green and taupe. Their two daughters are extremely got-up and ravishingly pretty. One is in lace and furbelows, the other, holding the donkey, is a dead ringer for one of the doomed Princes in the Tower, and indeed she always wanted to be a boy.

I love this picture on its own account, but I stare at it because I know so much more about the occupants of those painted bodies than the subjects themselves knew; my account is the final tally. I know for example that, long after the picture was painted, Mrs Vere Foster hibernated all winter – never got out of bed. I know that the nine-year-old girl who looks like the Prince, a dandy to her fingertips, went on to re-christen herself John, wore a tie and a man's hat, cropped her hair, wore breeches, perhaps to fulfil her mother's wish for a son and heir. I know that sometimes the donkey, with its burden of dead birds, had to be painted in the drawing room, as it rained every day of that summer when

Orpen was painting the portrait – which the Fosters at first liked but later grew to dislike. In that year, 1907, Orpen painted in the same chiaroscuro gloom in which we, fifty years later, lived.

I know all this, but, most of all, I know what they couldn't know, that another child, Anthony, was to be born to this gilded, haunted couple. He sounds like a character out of a Molly Keane novel – light-hearted, marvellous, with a capacity for joy, but with the undertow of melancholy pulling him down. He revived the Midsummer Festival of Pattern or Patrun in Tallanstown near Glyde. I can never look at this portrait without remembering what Mark Bence-Jones wrote in that invaluable book *Twilight of the Ascendancy* about the boy whose invisible future presence stirs beneath the surface of this picture. It invests the portrait with a sense of *lacrimae rerum*. 'Later that year [1934] his regiment moved from India to Khartoum, where, in September, he was found dead in tragic and mysterious circumstances.'

That elegiac sentence colours my view of the picture. What, I wonder, were the tragic and mysterious circumstances? Perhaps, like the secret in the playground, you know the answer in your bones; best to let it lie there. The other thought that crosses my mind is what I would have been like if, in childhood, I had been dressed up like either of those children. Could you ever get over it? A whole generation and class of children never got over their grounding in class consciousness through clothes, and in gender puzzlement. (Rilke's mother pretended he was a girl until he was five, called him 'Sophie' and refused to cut his ringlets. For ever afterwards, though he professed to love women to distraction, he could never abide living with one. His poem 'The Panther', which begins, 'This gaze those bars keep passing is so misted with tiredness, it can take in nothing more,' is stunning. For pure force only Blake's 'Tyger Tyger' can pad along with it.)

I was pondering on the Vere Foster portrait and wondering why the name was so utterly familiar when I remembered – how could I have forgotten? – it was indeed as familiar as my own handwriting. When we were children at Moortown Public Elementary School all our copying and drawing books were called 'Vere Fosters'. The letters of the alphabet were drawn at the head of the page, and our first attempts at joined-up letters were done by following his printed examples; our drawings –

Initiatory Drawings [I used to wonder what an Initiatory was] *in Domestic Objects* (*Simple*) and *Domestic Objects* (*Perspective*) – were done under his aegis. And, indeed, the Vere Foster of this portrait, thirty-four at the time he was painted, was the great-nephew of the philanthropist and educationalist who did so much for Ireland, not least inventing these copy books used by generations of Irish schoolchildren. One way or another, he taught us all how to write.

So I wish I too had been at the selling-up of the contents of Glyde Court. I would have liked something to cherish this family by, these mysterious people I know so well and know not at all.

Tumbleweed
at *Vogue*

Dear Val,

Well, it's a big building with **VOGUE** blazoned over the door in the same logo as the magazine, so you can't miss it – but I did. Then I got out into the wrong lift, went to the wrong floor and was faced by a glass door which I couldn't open and behind it were two ravishingly beautiful girls, one wearing those round specs and looking a bit like Dilly Dreem, The Lovable Duffer, only not, and the other the dead spit of Louise Brooks. I banged on the glass door to be let in and they pointed and shouted but I couldn't hear, so I ran down a flight of stairs. I was wearing that grey flannel suit I bought at Wallis and strappy shoes from Saxone. They cost 29*s.* 11*d.* – a lot out of the £10 a week I am going to be getting from *Vogue* – but they are worth it. When I got to the floor below, there was another glass door, like in Kafka, and the same two girls and it turns out that, as usual, I was pulling when I should have been pushing.

Anyway, the Louise B girl got me in. She is Georgina Howell – Gina for short – is beautiful and funny and a writer for the fashion department. She is tiny and was wearing this skinny sweater and little skirt and a ring with diamonds all the way around and it transpired that she is married. I couldn't believe it, she looks all of fifteen. When I admired the ring, she said, 'The stones are beginning to fall out; when the last one falls out the marriage will be over.' Did you ever hear anything so sophisticated? I think she was joking.

So first I met two editors – not *the* editor, she's hidden away in an office at the end of the corridor – but I met Eliza Kendall, who was wearing a real Chanel suit (you were right, you can tell) and a huge black straw hat and talks in a drawl and writes about how to make canapés and conduct your dinner party. I thought how useful that will be for you at home in Ardboe, Nor'n Ireland.

Everyone is skinny, except me. I saw someone swinging down the corridor, little pleated skirt above long legs, and thought it was Georgina and called after her but when she turned around it was literally an old girl (I always thought that was just an expression like in P. G. Wodehouse). It was Lady Rendlesham, one of the most famous fashion editors of all, apparently, so trim and groomed and clean-edged. One of the things here is that everything is glossy and shiny and outlined, about illumination in every sense; there seem to be no murky corners at all. It's like suddenly accessing the future.

You'd notice it too – think of the shapelessness of home and what shines there; the sun on the lough, the reflection of a brass harness on a horse's neck, the gleam of leaves in the chestnut tree. Here, it's the arc lights in the studio, the shine on the pearls that nearly all the girls wear, the gleam on their faces, the sheen on a satin ball dress . . . I feel very atavistic somehow, as if I were wearing a shawl.

All the girls in the fashion department know each other, and other girls who work either here or at Sotheby's, or at an interior decorator called Colefax & Fowler, and they meet at lunch and talk the same talk, which I can't talk at all; it's like being a provincial at Versailles. Who? Where? What is a *fauteuil*? It's chic talk, which is a new one on me. I've also worked out that they are rich, though they would die rather than let on, whereas we'd be shouting it from the rooftops, wouldn't we?

There are only three people in the features department: Frances Hodge, the features editor, Wendy, the secretary, and me; and we do everything. Frances commissions the articles and we all have to think of ideas and I write . . . imagine being paid to go to the cinema and theatre and read books!

That was good, but now things have changed and I work from morning till night. Frances asked me whom I would most like to write about and I said Bob Dylan. And it turns out that Bob Dylan is in London for a TV play (which, of course, the BBC did not record), and he said yes when I wrote to ask if I could interview him. I can hardly believe that he exists in reality, walking the earth within arm's reach (hah!), like I'm on a different version of the wobbly planet called home.

WRITING HOME

He looks a bit like Thomas Chatterton, only upright. Funnily enough, I'm not in love with him, which I thought I would be, but I am in love with Tom Wolfe, who has written a book called *The Kandy-Kolored Tangerine-Flake Streamline Baby*, is dressed all in white like Father Mullan at Easter and has invented the 'new journalism', so I'm on the human junk heap already at twenty-two. I don't mind about that.

Well that was the start, and though *Vogue* didn't get the point of Dylan they did like the interview, so I was asked to do more and now I write these big, long interviews and don't get paid extra. They're simply treated as part of my work but if Frances had commissioned someone to write them they'd be paid a lot. It makes me flaming mad but I can't do, or rather don't know how to do, anything about it. The photographers I work with, or rather accompany humbly on shoots, who are mostly thick as shit in the bottle, take a mug shot and get fifty times my pay.

I've started working with David Bailey. He has a Rolls-Royce and an E-type Jag and we went up to Yorkshire in it to photograph a naive painter – I mean, he paints naive pictures but he is also naive – and we drove at 100 mph on the motorway. I've never been on a motorway before now, never mind in an E-type – it's a far cry from Dad's Austin A40 – and it's all true, it is sexy. I had to let on I wasn't frightened – if I showed any fear he just went faster. His girlfriend is Jean Shrimpton. You won't believe it but she is even more beautiful in real life. She looks as though she sleeps in cathedral pews and sucks artichoke hearts for sustenance, doesn't talk the chic talk, drives a Mini very fast, has a little dog that Rover would think was lunch and you couldn't help but love her.

Life is much the same old boring routine as in County Tyrone. I flew first-class to Crete to talk to the wife of a writer called John Le Carré, who has written an amazing book called *The Spy Who Came in from the Cold*. And one morning I went up to the studios on the sixth floor where Bailey was photographing Mick Jagger, in lips and an enormous fur hood, and in came Jean Shrimpton and they all did a little dance. Jeanne Moreau has been in and Catherine Deneuve and Jane Fonda and Oskar Werner, who stamped out saying Bailey was rude. Well, Bailey is rude, that's half the point. I think.

You asked about the clothes: that other girl I saw the first day with the glasses is called Marit Allen. She has started a feature called 'Young Idea' and she is the epitome of it. I can't tell you how wonderful she looks, half startled and half amused, and with the kind of style you just want – striped dresses and tucked shirts and strappy shoes – and wonderful clothes from Paris by someone called Emmanuelle Khanh. I got a pair of white crepe trousers from her, and a chiffon jacket – wait till you see.

But there have been amazing changes at the last minute. The old editor and Frances, my boss, have suddenly gone, whoosh, so I've become features editor as there's no one else. The new editor, Beatrix Miller, keeps her door open all the time. This is where you should sit down. After I got back from Crete, she called me in and asked had I read *The Wilder Shores of Love*. Well, you know me and Lesley Blanch are like that, so to speak. Many's the long adolescent afternoon we've spent together, me dreaming that the expanse of the lough was the desert and I was by the oasis, and riding towards me on a camel through a cloud of sand, scimitar gleaming, smiling cruelly, was the beautiful sheikh. And then I knew I had to stop, otherwise imagine the embarrassment in confession! Father Mullan wouldn't have known where to put himself.

She asked me about the wilder shores of love because it transpired that the ruling sheikhs of Abu Dhabi, a tiny Bedouin country, had just arrived in London and I was to do the VIP interview. The fate of our future oil supply turns on it, apparently. Crikey, and I have to write about them.

The first thing was that the sheikhs were living in a penthouse in the Hilton and they were as wild and untamed and black-eyed and black-bearded as you could wish, dressed in white djellabas with daggers about their persons and a million mad servants rushing around. Bailey took a centrifugal photograph of the sheikhs which made them look as though they were spinning into space, which in a way they are, poor lambs – well, not poor lambs but actually very, very rich lambs who have not been in London before, nor out of the desert I shouldn't wonder – and, of course, not as poor as the lambs they were eating up there on the fourteenth floor. I felt for them; in fact, I felt they were probably just like me when I arrived. The noise! The people! And not knowing the language.

Everyone is after them because, apparently, Abu Dhabi is going to become the richest country in the world and there are about five people living there.

Anyway, after the photograph they asked me to stay on and we all sat smiling fiercely at each other and they pushed bits of lamb into my mouth as part of a feast. There was a sort of government inspector there (who kept looking at me as if I were the Mekon from planet Zog) and press people from oil companies, and the sheikhs insisted that I must go with them to Abu Dhabi and the PRs all looked terrified at this. I felt more and more as if I were wearing a Tenniel hair band and falling down a hole. When I finally got away, in a huge limousine, I looked in the atlas and it's part of something called the Trucial Oman States. Crucial, more like.

So my trip was all arranged by *Vogue* and the government person. I think I am the first pink woman to visit Abu Dhabi and I had to have a chaperone (who had to be a man) and he turned out, imagine, to be Irish, but not like our Irish. He is called Sir Desmond Cochrane. He is the Irish consul to the Lebanon and the Lebanese consul to Ireland, so he spends half the year in a palace in Lebanon and the other half in a palace in Wicklow – and talk about social caressing. Just speaking to him you feel stroked all over.

You fly to Beirut, which is the prettiest city, and then to another sheikhdom called Qatar. I was given a gold pen – I mean, solid gold – from the sheikh I'd met for half an hour at the airport and then we climbed into this minute plane to Abu Dhabi, where they had to clear the horses off a strip of sand for us to land. The sheikhs live in a Beau Geste type of tumbledown white fort surrounded by palm trees and the desert is as sandy and rolling as we imagined, mixed up with scrub, and it borders the sea, and a huge yacht that I think once belonged to Prince Rainier just lies rotting at the jetty.

The town hardly exists, so we had an excursion across the desert to Buraimi oasis where I saw gazelles and many camels scooping up water from small streams. Riding a camel isn't a laugh a minute. Well, it is, since I fell off all the time and this made everyone very happy. And laughing.

I stayed in a sort of guest house, horrible little place with a soldier with a gun sleeping outside my door and in the day was taught falconry. At night, such starry skies! I visited the harem, which seemed truly hell on earth, and sat on the ground for absurd feasts spread out in great tents and wondered how Lady Jane Digby could have borne the life for more than two minutes. I think I was invited to join the harem but I fled in tears.

So I am not going to be the richest woman in the world, after all. Too high a price just to have a lot of money, and I came to realize in the flaming desert that I am not a romantic heroine at all but a person who likes damp mornings and gothic northern men and people who can talk the hind leg off a goat.

And now. How to tell you that I flew to Ireland but couldn't get up to see you. An entirely different Ireland from ours. John Huston's house in Galway.

He has a Romanesque face and a rumble for a voice. His house is serene grey stone in a landscape that makes time trickle to a stop. There were vast cigars staying, with small Hollywood producers attached. Huston was unassailable and charming and everyone adores him. And we ate, now sit down, surrounded by the biggest *Water Lilies* by Monet you've ever seen. Well you've never seen. A yard away. If I put out my hand I could touch it.

But when I got back, there was a cablegram (the glamour, Val, a cablegram!) from Diana Vreeland, the goddess of American *Vogue*, saying she'd read a transcript of an interview I'd done (with John Osborne! Imagine!) and wanted to publish it and would I accept $500? And could I go to Paris to interview Barbra Streisand, who is a big new star in New York and who is doing the Paris collections with Avedon? Gina said, 'Lucky you, lovely Avedon – though I hear she's a right madam.' So I made a Molly Bloom of myself: and my heart was going like mad and yes, I said, yes, I will, yes yes . . .

Diana Vreeland: Wrists, Mists and Poets

'I suppose there *is* an Irish style,' she said, looking around as though it might be misplaced somewhere within the red heart of her exotic but always impeccable office.

'Long necks,' she said, 'swans, wrists, Yeats. And, of course, the poetry. The po-et-reee. The Irish open their mouths and poetry comes out.' She looked at me expectantly. I tried to lift my head further up from between my shoulders but fear had me in its hunch and the long Irish neck remained hidden. 'Wrists?' I thought frantically, 'Wrists? Perhaps she means mists.' I couldn't open my mouth as it was filled with rye bread and tuna, a deadly combination when you're sitting only a couple of feet away across a bridge table from one of the most extraordinary human beings you're every likely to meet, whose every line looks as though it has been drawn by a Higher Draughtsman, Blake or Fuseli perhaps, certainly someone not quite right in their mind, but absolutely at home in the further reaches of unhinged imagination. This woman, Diana Vreeland, the editor of American *Vogue*, who lived a life predicated on line, style, cut, was not the easiest with whom to share a working lunch, and I use the term 'share' loosely. She ate practically nothing, always more or less the same sandwich, and downed a slug of scotch.

She may have believed her office wasn't exotic: 'I hate exoticism, it's so silly; my office – just a big black lacquer desk, a leopard-skin carpet, leopard-skin upholstery and scarlet walls.' But then she believed whatever she wanted to believe. If this wasn't exotic then what would exotic be? I wanted to clutch my neckless head. Anyway, exotic or not, her office and lunch table were an education in formality and exactitude. Here was a woman who had a map of her desk so that everything on it would always be exactly in the same place. Not me, though. I seemed to spread like Asia over the map, and whenever we had lunch I tried to think of something to eat that would somehow be *tidy*. My taste buds were predicated on tidy. I didn't care about nourishment or taste. I just wanted not to have to dribble, or chew, or rescue things from about my face. Food took on its own crazed space-life in her room; at her card table, yoghurt dribbled, tuna splatted, hamburger fed my frocks, crackers crumbled down the cleavage, a BLT made me look as though I had just been prodded out of a pen with a well-warned vet in attendance. But she and I had this Eat-fest forum on the eighteenth floor of the Graybar Building on Lexington Avenue, in order for Mrs Vreeland to tap into my arcane knowledge of what the trendy young were doing.

I had absolutely no idea; but terror, though it made me draw in my neck, loosened my tongue, and a fair few of the items in that famous *Vogue* column 'People Are Talking About . . .' sprang straight from my crazed verbal inventions as I sought to unclamp my teeth from a piece of pastrami without her noticing.

'What does beady mean?' An old fashion baron was in the office with her; not old-*fashioned*, you understand. Old in the ways of fashion and infinitely old in age, like something that wandered out of Shangri-La. 'Now this word that's all the rage in London, beady, Nicky here has no idea about its meaning, have you, Nicky? Nicky's heart is in his icons. But Polly will know.' She bared her wonderful teeth at both of us. Nicky couldn't have been less interested in a twenty-three-year-old Irish female. He was hoping Bailey would come rocketing into the office. My ignorance was so wholesale that I knew that in a million years she could have no conception of how little I knew about her world, and equally how little she knew about a lost world that I knew: the world where I had been born and where I grew up, a world which she would have been amazed to know still existed. She might well have sent Irving Penn to photograph it as a witness to a culture on the brink of extinction. Then she wouldn't have used the pictures, since we weren't the mud-people of Lough Neagh but merely the ragged ends of a dispensation that had lasted for centuries, the world of the horse and cart and silence and lapping water and goodness and inbred madness. It was about to become extinct – but then so was her world, if she'd but known it.

That extraordinary symbiotic world of *Vogue* in the 1960s was her creation. Eclecticism, freakishness, style, hysteria, erudition, invention – and narrow to the bone. The world I had come from knew nothing of invention – everything was organic, decaying and the fatter the better. There were a lot of freaks – inbreeding tends towards that – but we didn't, as they say, remark on them. I was, though, inventive. I had to be to survive and so I invented myself and my identity like mad in that office which has now taken on a legendary status like Chanel's drawing room in the rue Cambon or Schiaparelli's Brown Study.

Whenever I came to lunch I brought with me a copy of her latest memo:

To Miss Devlin
RE: JANUARY 1 PREDICTIONS – URGENT
Each year we have a potpourri of things that are coming up . . . Last year we had the marvellous sun-bathing tub. The year before, a marvellous picture of a surfing movie and one of Ira Furstenberg . . . sketches of Courrèges as he was then behind a curtain and not showing, etc., etc.

What we need is a kick – a new thing – a thing we predict for 1968. It could be a sport – a game – a point of view – a new word – anything . . . but we need it and we need it fast . . .

Do ask the girls around you for something that we could either write in the Predictions – or we could photograph . . .

They could be small pictures – this is not a thing of great importance – but it is to delight the reader . . .

It may be a new discovery in the Orient . . . anything . . .

'Now, beady – this new word the young are using,' she said. 'Now, the last time that divine Jean was here she said that Bailey was looking beady. What exactly did she mean?' Bailey's eyes were small, dark and bright and were born beady; and when Jean thought that anyone was looking at her oddly in the street she'd whisper uneasily, 'Why are people being so beady?' 'They're being beady because they can't believe they're seeing *you*,' I'd say, but she'd dismiss that. Jean Shrimpton was the most famous model of her time and the most modest woman you could meet and never really took the impact of her looks on board. At that time Vreeland was in love with both of them, Bailey and Shrimpton, as she was in love with so much that was beautiful, and new, 'I loathe nostalgia,' she said. 'I don't believe in anything before penicillin.' Yet when she went back, after her husband's death, and looked at the house in Chester Square in London where they had lived as newly marrieds, she desperately wanted to have the knocker on the door. She'd bought it on their honeymoon. Perhaps such impulses are not nostalgia, but rather emotion and sensibility. Certainly, even when she became an old, almost blind woman, running the Costume Institute at the Metropolitan Museum and making the most tremendous go of it, she was surrounded by the young and the talented, who admired her, who recognized how unique she was, how her life and art ran in ornamented channels.

She had no simplicity and little amplitude. But you don't need these qualities to be editor of *Vogue*. And she wasn't interested in the dark swirls of the unconscious. She was surface, surface, surface. But what a surface.

'I want you to go and talk to the swan-uppers of England. All the property of the Queen, of course, and if you kill a swan you can be beheaded. Absolutely as it should be.'

'What *is* swan-upping?' I was faltering fast.

'Well, I believe it's turning the swan, that sublime creature over, upsy-daisy, and marking it, tenderly, I hope; the divine right of kings or queens and its wonderful flurry of white, white feathers and long necks and costumes like beefeaters. On the Avon, I believe. I want wonderful text, wonderful photographs.'

Swan-upping? Where do you start?

She had first come into my life, like a genie, via a cable to British *Vogue*, where I had just started work. It was my first job and I was absolutely penniless. I had come straight from Ardboe, a tiny almost medieval place on the shores of Lough Neagh in Northern Ireland (loosely and erroneously called Ulster), where a copy of *Vogue* was a fairly recherché object. My mother contrived to get it on special order from Sheehy's in Cookstown, and I read it as I might read an archive from the future. In one January issue there was a talent contest; the prize, a job in *Vogue*. Jacqueline Kennedy had once won it, the legend said, and Penelope Gilliatt, who had married my hero, John Osborne (and who was to hit me hard across the face in a theatre foyer; but that was later). The closing date was three days away by then. I wrote the answers sharpish (one task was to write an autobiography, a fairly hubristic endeavour for a twenty-year-old), and I won it.

I started work at *Vogue*, in Hanover Square, London, in 1963 and my salary was £10 a week regardless of how much I wrote or published. *Vogue* owned all rights. I didn't realize this. But then I didn't know much about rights of any kind.

Within six months of arriving at *Vogue* and due to a series of sackings rather than to any rocket-like brilliance on my part, I became features editor; also caption writer, commissioning editor and features writer. In those days the feature department consisted of me, a secretary shared with the travel department (one person), and an assistant. We worked till we dropped. And then one fine day soon after I had arrived, a cable came into the office from American *Vogue*. It said simply: 'Osborne/Devlin text superb. $500 for first American rights. D.V.'

The John Osborne text was my first published piece. His play *Look Back in Anger*, first staged a few years before, had changed the course of English theatre history, blah, blah, and to many young people he was a hero and champion. I had absolutely no way of seeing it, a teenager marooned in Northern Ireland with not a penny to my name. He had made himself public enemy number one to many more conservative people when he'd written an angry polemical letter to *The Tribune*, an English newspaper now defunct: 'This is a letter of hate. It is for you, my countrymen. I mean those men of my country who have defiled it. The men with manic fingers leading the sightless, feeble, betrayed body of my country to its death. Damn you, England, you're nothing now and quite soon you'll disappear.' I loved his letter. Just what I'd have liked to have said myself, though from other motives. But after its publication a storm erupted, he was threatened with death by mad majors and had gone to ground. So when I wrote asking for an interview from my idol I didn't have much hope he'd give one. Might as well expect the blue and white statue in the chapel at home to suddenly flounce down on to the altar. So it was a fair old turn-up when I got a sweet note suggesting we meet for lunch.

He talked all afternoon. He was a wonderful talker, witty and biting, no holds barred. And funny with it. Talking about his early career, he said 'I got sacked from a lot of places – I seemed to have the knack of getting on people's nerves. Englishmen are not physically brutal . . . that went long ago. They are emotionally brutal. Perhaps brutal is too kind a word; they are vicious and barbed. Altogether I wrote five plays – this was when I was between eighteen and twenty-five, before *Look Back in Anger*, most of which I wrote on the pier at Morecambe and when I was writing it I thought it was the best thing I'd done. I would hate just to be remembered for that one play.' He is.

I wrote the article. And then the magic cable, trailing stardust, arrived. My stock rose within the office, since American *Vogue* was jealous of its commissioning originality and rarely lifted pieces from other magazines in the Condé Nast family. I was puffed up with pride, but the pride was as nothing compared to the prospect of $500 for those mysterious first American rights. $500 then was the equivalent of six months' salary, but it was much more than that to me. It was a recognition that I could write, that my writing was worth something, that people would pay to read it. The managing director of English *Vogue* cabled back and told them that they already owned All Rights so I didn't need payment. But that first enabling cable was from Diana Vreeland and I loved her for it. And now here was the reality in front of me. Using the word 'reality' loosely, you understand, because she was as fantastical as a unicorn, as flash as a kingfisher on that cold grey day in 1965, when London was in mourning for Winston Churchill.

Our offices at *Vogue* were open plan with partitions and bookcases about shoulder height and I was sitting sucking my teeth when this extraordinary apparition came bobbing or rather gliding along above the level of the filing cabinets – the wonderful carved head of a totem pole perhaps, or an Aztec bird woman, or a Kabuki runaway. It's a famous image now, that cassowary head, lacquered hair, high, rouged cheeks, the arched nose – but when it first came, disembodied, into my life, along the line of a grey London corridor, it was like a religious visitation. And its voice was booming, ricocheting around, a boomerang going back to its sender, only to be spun away again bearing another sibylline pronouncement. Then she appeared through the gap in the cabinets and threw up her hands. Now, there's a word not much used nowadays, 'limned' – to illuminate, to edge in colour. She was always limned, set in shock against her background. You could hardly see her for the dazzle: the huge mouth, the high, bright red cheeks, the burnished black-on-black lacquered hair, the edge and cut and glitter of her chic, the slanting knowing eyes, like a fox terrier's, that missed many a thing to do with the soul and nothing, nothing to do with the body. To me she was so ugly, I couldn't believe it. Five minutes later the ugliness had vanished under the fascination. The way she stood was unique. Cecil Beaton famously described it: 'the Vreeland medieval slouch, pelvis thrust forward to an astonishing degree and the torso above it sloping backwards at a forty-five-degree angle'. She was offering me a job on *Vogue* in New York and while doing so talking non-stop and examining me with her twinkling eyes. And twinkle they did, and glitter, like tiny light bulbs flashing, taking an infinite series of shots, and editing down into what *she* wanted to see. In the process she missed a lot, but what she missed, she didn't want, or thought she didn't.

Her vision ignored the ordinary but, of course, one of the things that made her extraordinary was that she never tried to be fantastical, or larger than life. It was all natural to her, if the word natural could ever have been used within her aura. She said: 'I figure that if I like something, the rest of the world will like it too. I think I have an absolutely solid ordinary point of view.' True eccentrics do think that what they do and how they think are perfectly normal. Perfect, yes. Normal, no.

Her account of the last evening she spent in Paris in September 1939, when one of the world's greatest calamities was beginning, and when she knew she was leaving it perhaps for the last time (and she loved Paris as others love lovers), reveals a mindset that is almost frightening in its deliberate disregard for horrid reality. She was on the Champs-Elysées. 'We must have walked ten miles that night . . . and hundreds of people were strolling but they hardly spoke, only this unearthly silence . . . I can remember exactly what I was wearing. A little black *tailleur* from Chanel, a little piece of black lace wrapped around my head and absolutely exquisite black kid slippers.' Verbal textures, strange priorities, nothing rough. Anyone else might have spoken of their emotions, about their sense of despair, of apprehension, or being part of a historic moment. But what she *wore* informed her memory of occasion. There is no right or wrong in chic.

Her refusal or inability to turn her back on anything that seemed chic or stylish, no matter how mendacious, was what made her, in my eyes, an amoral woman. She thought that Coco Chanel, an active anti-semite who betrayed her friend and *éminence grise*, a Russian Jew, the man who had helped her invent the scent that made her rich beyond belief – betrayed him and took the money and ran – was for her one of the greatest women of the twentieth century (which, of course, as an unparalleled designer who transformed the world of fashion, she was).

She would ask me to go and interview people who smelled of badness, a rank smell of horrid sex, money and mendacity, chicanery and foolishness, but they were stylish, so she admired them. And I would go. I would go. I would register my displeasure. 'Oh, you just want to ride the tiger's back,' she said. But I had bought into the deal; virtue was not necessarily something to be admired, and style was. 'Be stylish, young maid, and let who will be good.' Nothing was allowed to interfere with her idea of style: she hated liars but she herself invented the truth.

Listening to her talking about clothes was to hear voluptuous pleasure, delight in the art of clothes, of textures and sheens and fabrics. She talked about colour like no one else: 'When I say orange, I don't mean yellow-orange, I mean red-orange, the orange of Bakst and Diaghilev, the orange that changed the century.' Or: 'The best red to copy is the colour of any child's cap in any Renaissance portrait.' She returned from South America and crooned . . . 'a world of youth with long oval faces, long waving arms like the palm trees along their long waving coastline'.

She set ground rules that were hard to pre-empt. 'The first thing to do is to arrange to be born in Paris. After that everything follows naturally.' I'd fallen at the first fence. Ardboe was the antithesis of Paris. Fashion there depended on how the priest wore his biretta. So, I clamped my teeth over my sandwich and kept mum about my background. But in any case, she wasn't interested. She filleted people for what they could give her, not for what they were. She invented me for herself. 'She sprang from nowhere, the wilds of Ireland,' she told Nicky, who stared out of her window down Lexington, where there wasn't a pretty boy in sight. 'I discovered her writing this prooooose, you know, about Osborne and the poets, one of the great playwrights of England.' The wilds of Ireland, tiny farms, hens in the rampar, ceaseless rain, the rushes along the lough shore, the misery of school in Magherafelt, the fashion as revealed in the Drapery in Cookstown, the realities of a world where there was no such word as elegance or luxury. I thought about her practical early DIY tips in *Harper's Bazaar* and how useful they would be in my own dear family life in County Tyrone. 'Why don't you . . . sweep into your drawing room on your first big night, with an enormous red fox muff of many skins . . . knit yourself a little skullcap . . . turn your old ermine coat into a bathrobe . . . tie black tulle bows on your wrists . . .' Thinking about it I burst out laughing and the old baron turned around just in time to see me choke into the Dixie cup.

Over the two years I worked for her I lost my terror of her, and what helped was that I knew that this woman, whose style was in the cut of her vision, who was also ridiculous and often unintentionally funny, could miss the point by a mile and still arrive on target. She was also a fashion genius and utterly chic.

She was determined that no one would think she wasn't serious or hard-working: 'Never be deceived into thinking that the life of fashion was easy. It was exhausting. After a day of fitting you crept to your dark room.' (A dark room that contained a highly trained maid and often a manicurist and a masseur to restore herself to herself.) I thought of the dark rooms at home lit by oil lamps and grinned with pleasure that it was all behind me, and I thought perhaps next time I had lunch I could order something I could suck through a straw, or bring a bullet and bite on it when she started to praise some pretty, druggy layabout who wasn't worth a hill of beans, but had a lot of chutzpah and a good line in cross-dressing.

She was funny, sharp, with a tongue quick as a lizard's; she rolled up words to create images and once set her fashion editors searching for a new miracle fabric called Chelanayzee or thereabouts. Defeated in their search, the fashion editors did a bit of lateral thinking and came up with Celanese. 'Don't you adore the look of white silk slippers with the dark hem of a velvet dress? The Eskimos, I'm told, have seventeen different words for shades of white. This is even more than there are in my imagination.' I once told her that there was no word for 'No' in the Irish language and a thousand ways of saying 'Yes', and she was enchanted. (I think I made that up.)

She became editor of American *Vogue* in 1962 after twenty-eight years of working for *Harper's Bazaar*. ('They gave me a raise of $1,000. Can you imagine? Would you give your cook that after that many years?' My cook? Hello?)

I once asked her how much she thought she'd changed *Vogue*. She said, 'By the time I hit the place everyone looked great. The boys inspired the girls, the boys were nuts about the girls. The girls were nuts about the boys. I don't say it was great photography but it was the photography of the hour.' All the same she did change *Vogue*, sending it into a spin of extravagance, exaggeration and fantasy. She loved the whole youth thing to a fault, and the aloof *soignée* beauties of tradition in *Vogue* disappeared, to be replaced by something called the Youthquake, a word she coined to describe new movements and trends. She was unembarrassed in her invention of labels and names like this. Thus, the Beautiful People became a cliché for a certain style of *mondaine* and would-be *mondaine* life in the 1960s. 'I hate to see the term misused,' she complained. 'We mean people who are beautiful to look at. It's been taken up to mean people who are rich. We mean charmers (but there is no harm to be rich).'

Each issue of *Vogue* was like her newborn baby, and she behaved towards the finished issue rather like a father staring at his young: that conception, by now a remote pleasure, should have resulted in *this*?

Her bosses at *Vogue* seem to have been equally startled and less pleasured. It made for exciting times. Alexander Liberman, for years the *Vogue* supremo, wasn't a great fan. The crux of the matter was whether *Vogue* was a magazine of record and fashion, showing what women might wear in their ideal and perfectly groomed lives; or, as Diana Vreeland conceived it, a place for the wildest of dreams. He said: 'Vreeland was one of the editors who really struggled with photographers, to make them bring out what she thought was fascinating in fashion. And the photographers would consider that they were taking a picture. It made for great conflict.'

There were photographers who adored her, but others were driven into hysterics. 'She'd look at the clothes and then drift into a sort of trance,' one said. '"I see white," she'd moan, swaying about like Madame Arcati. Or she'd wind a length of hair around a girl's neck, around, around, nearly strangling her, and she'd be saying "It's Undine, water, naiads" – and the girl's eyes were popping.'

Those who did not know her often thought that she was affected, but her affectations were intrinsic and, paradoxically, normal to her, and that her observations and behaviour had a startling effect surprised her, or so she pretended, since surprise wasn't a reaction high on her agenda. Honesty was.

It would be easy to make her sound like a snob but the famous names in her lexicon were all her friends. 'I believe totally in romance, love, pleasure and beauty,' she said. 'Anyone who's afraid and does not search and give as much as possible to the world of pleasure is a totally ingrown person.' Well, for such a thing to be said to a convent-educated Irish girl, who had been taught that pleasure made your private parts drop off, fairly made the world rock on its hinges.

After a while she stopped sending me to interview Eurotrash and sent me into the homelands, as it were: to Barbados to talk to Oliver Messel, to Maryland to talk to Eunice Shriver, to Paris with Avedon and Barbra Streisand to do the collections, to Iran to talk to Empress Farah Diba, to San Francisco to talk to Janis Joplin, to 14th Street to listen to Aretha Franklin, to Houston Street to listen to a group of hairy people rehearsing a strange, anarchic, joyous musical tentatively called *Hair*. At lunchtimes we would all troop up to a fashionable East Side doctor to have a massive injection in our bums to give us energy. B12 I think it was called, and I thought it was great. A far cry from Dr Brown's brown and buff surgery in Coagh.

'The sixties were an extraordinary period,' she said. 'It was the Youthquake, it was the pill, and that released a whole different association between the boys and girls and created an entirely different society. Everybody, everything was new, and you were knocked in the eyeballs. For the first time youth went out to life instead of waiting for life to come to them, which is the big difference between the sixties and any other decade I have ever lived in. And don't forget we were at war all the time – and the horrible truth is that people thrive in war, industry, money, spirits and fortunes. It's invigorating, but it's terrible, it mustn't happen again.'

She had a fantastic beckoning eye for the *immediate* future . . . the future of two or three issues away. And one of her secrets was that nothing was unattainable – you just had to streetttch to get it. And just saying a word like 'stretch' would lead directly to a feature on Martha Graham. She created the needs of her readers and then fulfilled those needs. Looking back at that marvellous series of *Vogue*, four, five hundred pages in each issue – high-rolling, ridiculous magazines with their irresistible snobbery, their own passwords, their exclusively beautiful people – one sees that she created a monument, albeit a folly, to a certain time in New York, a time in which, in the pages of *Vogue*, no matter what reality was doing outside, the denizens danced in the ethnic temples that were their homes, in flowing chiffon pyjamas and chain mail and hairpieces a foot high and a foot wide and jewellery like treasure trove from under the sea. And the women looked good too. The Vietnam War was ripping the US apart but she lived in a place where the young were about to conquer everything, where the best season ever for exciting colours, new styles of living, was just around the corner. 'It was a very theatrical moment, everyone was theatrical. We had every pretty girl in the world, don't you think?'

For me Diana Vreeland was the Imprimatur, the Governor, the arbiter of style. So it was with some bemusement that I discovered that this was not necessarily everyone else's view. At about this time I married an Englishman, a man whose godparents and their friends had great dynastic American names, like Pell, Bigelow, Witney, Drexel. And once, staying in Hobe Sound, or lunching at the Knickerbocker Club, or somewhere where the publicity-shy (Yes!) wives of these quietly, enormously rich 'old money' Americans gathered in their beleaguered herds, I launched into a eulogy of Diana Vreeland, and saw something I'd never seen before, never even considered a possibility. These women not only did not like her, they did not rate her; and they hated what had happened to *Vogue*. Later I spoke of these women to Diana Vreeland (without, of course, mentioning their opinions). 'Dinosaurs, darling,' she said. 'Dinosaurs. Their day is over if they ever had a day, which I am incliiiiiined to doubt.'

Soon afterwards, not just a day but a whole era was over. Diana Vreeland was sacked, *Vogue* became more prosaic. Her extravagant style was seen as inappropriate for the seventies. Devastated she might have been, but, indomitable as ever, she went to the Metropolitan Museum of Art in New York and embarked on a spectacularly successful career as special consultant to the Costume Institute. Shows of period costumes from Russia, from Paris, from Hollywood, which she conceived and organized, were the social events of the season – 'Four hundred thousand people in the basement of the Metropolitan Museum. You've got to say it's quite something.' She was quite something.

I never did solve the problem of what to eat when I was with her. Years and years later we had supper in the Plaza Athénée in Paris. I ordered fettuccini. Half an hour later, almost paralysed, I was still rolling the pasta around the fork and the plate. 'I've always said it,' she said, 'but I'll say it again. The Spanish are dervishes compared to you Celts. No sense of time.' She laughed, that big loud lovely laugh that rang down the halls of fashion and style of the twentieth century, and lifted it in a way it has never been lifted before or since.

Portrait of the Artist as a Young Interviewer

I brought being an interviewer on myself. Talked myself into it. Fool. When I went from college in Belfast to my first job at *Vogue*, not knowing what to do, and needing to fill my pages, I started to interview people. Famous people, mostly writers and actors. And that became my thing, as it were, and I went on doing interviews for magazines and papers all over the world. Hated every minute of it.

I'd rather be boiled in oil now than do another interview.

The very idea of earnestly questioning celebs, finding out their thoughts (hello?) and feelings leaves me aghast. And although most of what the famous told me then wasn't worth a hill of beans, their thoughts seem Socratic wisdom compared to what I read now. Plus, everything now is so focused and monitored that if, when interviewing a star, you deviate from the submitted questions or write the truth as you see it and it isn't wholly admiring, you, personally, are blackballed and the piece can't be published since the magazine would lose access to other stars. A writer I know interviewed someone very famous who told her of their enduring love for their partner, of how they were eternally linked, had been linked in a life before and would be for ever, and in the midst of this declamation segued without a pause into the words 'You wanna fuck?'

And few magazines I think would now publish my opinion that watching a certain young actor on set, labouring under many handicaps including that 'he bristles angrily, lacks grace of bearing, has little charm, doesn't know his speeches, drops lines and uses words ill' was not a laugh a minute. (At the time only John Huston, the director of the film he was in, came to his defence. And he would, wouldn't he.)

To be fair, some of those I interviewed taught me much and spoke interestingly, but they were always older people, or writers. Ivy Compton-Burnett remarked, 'I don't know why people write autobiographies . . . All kinds of subtle and important things have to be left out, can never be said. There is so much in people's minds that they can never reveal. I don't think that they can give themselves their own pictures.' (One of the things that couldn't be said then was that her lifelong partner was Margaret Jourdain, renowned expert on English furniture.)

Salman Rushdie told me that he spoke Urdu, a lyrical language with an enormous metaphorical content, until he was fourteen. And he said, 'If *Midnight's Children* were translated into Urdu it would disappear . . . All the strange use of English would go. For example, in Urdu calling a child a piece of the moon is a normal endearment, not flowery language.' I've always wanted to speak Urdu to my children since.

I find it hard to believe, now, how far back I reached into deep history when I met the strange, fey, cross-dressing Prince Felix Yusupov, who helped kill Rasputin. That interview never was published. He was old, ill and tired, and there was legal trouble looming, after all those years, about what was, after all, murder.

One year I interviewed all the great couturiers, the most interesting of whom – not that that's saying much – was Yves Saint Laurent (also the most modest). What I did get from meeting these men was wonderful glimpses into what houses could look like, given a great eye (and endless money), and it coaxed my smouldering interest in interiors into passionate flame.

I remember the superb simplicity of YSL's dining room – white lacquer from top to bottom, with a fat white bunch of voluptuous cabbage roses on a shimmering ivory dining table.

Hubert Givenchy's apartment? Be still, my beating heart. A bronze mini-palace atop a spectacular building in the 7th, with a wonderful Miró hung like a patch of rippling blue sky above a drawing room that was so luxe, polished and civilized, so burnished, that it practically turned over and purred when you looked at it. From the ceiling small stars looked down. Tiny holes had been pierced in it so that minuscule gleams of light glimmered through, illuminating shining objects any museum would have been thrilled to acquire, black lacquer and shining glass, gold turtles under textured shells, an amazing Picasso hanging opposite a carved double door. (His most interesting quote was 'I am not always thinking of Audrey Hepburn.')

These designers' rooms were a far cry from those of the Russian-born French fashion illustrator and designer Romain de Tirtoff – his parents were so appalled at his wanting to be an artist that he had to use his initials, Erté, as his pseudonym. He was also a brilliant set designer for Paris music halls and theatres; but when I visited him in his hideous small Parisian flat I entered a squawking aviary – every room was filled with birds. The smell was overpowering, as was the noise.

The house that most lived up to what I imagined it might be was that of Eunice Shriver, John F. Kennedy's sister. Large, congenial, comfortable, commonplace, overlooking rolling white-fenced country near Washington, its rooms were full of light and noise and children, people coming and going, doors always open. The house hummed with energy – a friend of hers said wryly, 'Lord knows where the energy comes from. Perhaps because everyone there goes to bed so early . . . certainly not many people have seen the Shrivers on foot after half past ten. If you go to a party in their house you leave early else they'll be halfway up the stairs.' Eunice Shriver was a formidable woman – the only person I've been nervous interviewing.

I tended to interview people I wanted to sleep with – well, not Eunice Shriver, of course, but in general that seems to have been the dynamic. One of my first interviews was with Bob Dylan, and I write about it a lot, as it's not so often you mingle with geniuses who sing the backdrop to your life. *Vogue* wouldn't publish the interview and I was so green I didn't offer it to anyone else, and then I lost it, and there's hardly a year goes by when I'm not asked to send it to some magazine, or to some aficionado. (His life is so tracked that it's known what he was doing on what day in any year, and to whom he was talking.) Well, I spent a long day with Dylan – it went fast – and it's not everyone can say that.

Nor that they spent day after day with John Lennon and Yoko Ono, in New York, in Schenectady, and in Tittenhurst Park, their *haute bourgeoisie* home outside Ascot, fully staffed and set in a hundred acres of parkland with an arboretum – anything less suitable for this radical couple could hardly be imagined. Lennon was surely one of the great men of the twentieth century, but he was also foolish enough for anything, in the way that very bright people who haven't assembled an infrastructure often are. Yoko Ono was a phenomenon: I was fascinated by her art, by her haiku-like instructions to do your own thing (well, mostly her thing) her way, by her upfrontness, but most of all by her bravery – she wasn't afraid of ridicule, of criticism – she did what she wanted.

The first day I was in the Ascot house John and Yoko (she in white antique lace) were doing something involving a hearse and a helicopter. The second time the famous white piano arrived and John played and sang his new composition, 'Imagine', while Yoko drifted around the room. She was straightforward and honest. 'Being in love is an exactly equal thing. I don't want to find myself alone again. I wasn't happy before I met John – I had moments of happiness, but I was lonely and was beginning to feel that I'd never meet a man I could live with. Because I was getting to be thirty-four or five and I asked myself is this life? I lost my faith in men. I hated so many men – they were dumb and unintelligent and I'd never met a man who could do as much as I could do until I met John. There's an abundance of emotion between us. Why do we love each other so endlessly? Shall we cool it a little? But cooling is the hardest thing of all.'

The thing that worried her most? 'Which of us will die first because that's the one thing we can't control.'

So in many ways being an interviewer was an exciting way to earn a living, a daily adventure with wonderful recompenses. Pity I hated it.

One of the rewards was that I got to work with almost every outstanding photographer of the time (I went on to write a history of fashion photography). And sometimes I got top tips from them. Once when I was having difficulty with Janis Joplin – well, she simply wouldn't speak to me – Richard Avedon whispered, 'She's like plugged-in sandpaper', and she heard and our laughter triggered the interview. (One thing Joplin did say, with perfect gravity, when I asked her how different her life was now that she was a mega star, after her earlier existence bumming around from hand to mouth. 'It means I get an allowance now – but I got more when I was unemployed.')

When I was trying to fathom Mia Farrow (she was being photographed by Irving Penn, which didn't make it easy: 'How do you feel about your profile, Mia?' 'Not very strongly.'), a *soi-disant* friend confided, 'She was born cynical and thinks she was born wise.' Mia wasn't best pleased.

Modest George Harrison said, 'I'm beginning to know that all I know is that I know nothing.' Jean Shrimpton: 'I'm secure enough not to worry about whether men think I'm sexy or not as long as the man I'm with thinks I am.' Catherine Deneuve: 'I read that I am the most beautiful girl in the world but I do not believe it.' (Oh, la, la, la, Catherine.)

I once watched Estée Lauder – there was a piece of work – test new aftershaves for men; there was a cross-looking Frenchman there who I think had concocted the smells. Every time La Belle Dame Sans Merci uncorked a bottle, his face contorted with anxiety. After a few sniffs, she announced, 'This is the only possible one, the rest smell of soap. I want sex.' You never saw a happier Frenchman. The other cosmetics tycoon I had to interview was Charles Revson, one of the founders of Revlon, and one of the nastiest, most humourless men I ever met.

'I called my yacht *Ultima*, and can you believe that people said that I called it that for publicity purposes?'

'Well, yes,' I said.

He glared. 'I was going to call it the *John Charles* after my sons, but I thought, that's pretentious, not in good taste and I am sensitive about things like that. Then I bought another one, called it the *Ultima II*, and it's a scary little thing having two yachts.'

You may imagine how I sympathized.

I interviewed politicians. The sharpest was Barbara Castle, Secretary of State for Employment at the time, who said something eye-opening for innocent me – 'I'm trying to teach myself to be as irresponsible as my male colleagues.'

The one I admired most and still do was the heroic Bernadette Devlin, who was catapulted into prominence almost by accident. On her twenty-second birthday, while still a student at Queen's University, she became the youngest woman ever to be a Member of Parliament –'The whole thing just happened,' she said, 'and it's a bit bewildering and a bit amusing, all this heroine stuff, as I'm an ordinary person. I can tell you this –

come the next general election I'm not standing for re-election. I don't want to be public property.' She became public property. She was also shot nine times in her house in front of her children by Ulster Freedom Fighters (freedom fighters!), while the army stood by.

Most comedians were lugubriously unfunny. Frankie Howerd made me want to gnaw my hand off. But Morecambe and Wise were great. Eric Morecambe said, 'We have a major ambition, to become a classic part of British comedy so that years later we are used as a standard, are remembered as the *great* comedy team. We want to be so good that years from now people will look back and say, "Ah but you should have seen Morecambe and Wise."' I wish they knew how their wish has come true.

I listened to theatre directors – Peter Hall on opera was worth a guinea a box ('I think there is too much of the idea that a director is some sort of creative lunatic who expresses his own ideas'). I talked to artists (the first picture I ever bought was a David Hockney, for £30), sculptors, pop stars, opera singers, film directors – I liked Roger Vadim, was impressed by John Huston (and even more by his house in Ireland), and also amused. He brooded over my questions and then said, brightly, 'You ask Gladys, my secretary. She knows far more about me than I do myself.' I hated Orson Welles. (Big bully, so appalling that I lost the run of myself and cried – very professional, Polly. I was told later that he enjoyed being brutal to young blonde women, but what do I know.) I was delighted by Federico Fellini drawling, 'With all my limitations, with my laziness, my lack of money, my lack of time, I do what I want exactly. I am a lucky man and a happy man.' The most impressive actor I interviewed was John Hurt. 'Nothing is original,' he said. 'When people say "*What* an original performance", all they mean is they haven't thought of it before.' But he was original.

The most difficult meeting was my first with Andy Warhol. He was probably the cleverest of all, but when I met him then, in the sixties, I thought he was a freak.

'All this art is finished . . . Squares on the wall. Shapes on the floor. Emptiness. Empty rooms.'

'But that makes you redundant.'

'That's what my art is all about.'

When I next met him, twenty years later, I felt privileged, since by then I revered him as a genius, one of the hinges in art, like James Joyce or Duchamp, who make the doors of perception spring open. He was able to slip ordinary images upstream into the flow of collective memory, but they were also photo-documents from some place of his own imaginings. You are not conducted, as you are, say, in any Rembrandt self-portrait, into the workings of the human heart. Quite the opposite. You will not find comfort, or patience, poetry or redemption in Warhol's images. But you will get a slice of the twentieth century.

The people I really enjoyed interviewing, as it were, weren't being interviewed at all – I just wrote it all down (remember Joan Didion's remark, 'Writers are always selling somebody out'?) I was asked to lunch by a friend and the other guests included the Sicilian Duca di Verdura, writer, painter and maker of exquisite jewels, and Lady Diana Cooper, the legendary living symbol of an almost vanished world, though she had managed to retain a very tight clutch on the present one. Because of her famous and undisputed beauty (her likeness was even sold on cigarette cards), she got away with anything she chose to do. She still had the famous remarkable white enamelled complexion, like the description of Queen Elizabeth I's skin . . . 'Two thousand milk-white sheep I have in fold. But none so white as is thy lovely face.'

'Talking of widows,' said the Duke, 'have you read Ernest Hemingway's widow's book? I thought Hemingway was just awful. But as for the wife!'

Lady Diana said, 'I remember once when I was in Paris and not feeling well really and I was in bed, in Pauline Borghese's bed, and he said he wanted to come round. And I said to someone who was with me, "For heaven's sake don't leave me." Not that I was frightened of assault or anything like that, far from it. No, it was the tedium – I knew I couldn't bear it.

'He stayed and stayed and stayed, massively egocentric, and it became dinner time and my other visitor *had* to go. She'd come for tea and by now it was past eight o'clock, but I'd made frantic signs for her to stay while he was there. She said – she was as desperate as I was by now – "I *must* go, it's almost dinner time – how could it be?" But he just stayed there. I thought, I'm here for ever, that's all, trapped in Pauline Borghese's bed and I'll probably die from boredom and *he* won't even notice!'

'Did he write anything good?' the Duke asked.

'Well, his wife hasn't,' I said. 'This book is like that afternoon in Paris – you're bombarded by boredom, a tedium only broken by remarks that you can hardly believe – like when Hemingway first introduces her to his neutered cat he says, "Poor little pussy cat, he doesn't like women, Miss Mary, you see, because he thinks women took his balls off."'

(I thought, Jesus, how *could* you have remembered that quote?)

I interviewed normal women who were quite out of the ordinary by dint of circumstance – the American Hope Cooke who by marriage had become the Queen or Gyalmo of the little Himalayan kingdom of Sikkim; the beauteous Omunakai aka Princess Elizabeth of the little African kingdom of Toro (somewhere I have tucked away an invitation to her coronation); Farah Diba, the Empress of Persia, the big Iranian kingdom. Various other queens, of course, but none more queenly than Barbra Streisand of Middle Hollywood Kingdom. Streisand was Diana Vreeland's crush at that time, in the late sixties, and so was the celeb model for American *Vogue* at the Paris collections, and I spent four exhausting nights in studios in Montparnasse with her and Richard Avedon. She treated me as though I had been dragged in by the cat and I felt humiliated. It did no harm towards getting a good interview. Too high a price though. She had the grace to write and send flowers to me afterwards, but I was past caring.

Then, one day I was in the back of a Rolls-Royce, interviewing Ursula Andress, who had arrived at Heathrow and was graciously fitting me into her schedule. In a traffic jam at the Hogarth roundabout, the first major stop on the road into London, I thought, 'Why? Why am I here?'

I opened the car door and stepped out. The car moved smoothly on, into the evening traffic, and I walked away.

An Oddity

Another voice: this is my husband's account of our first meeting.

. . . I arranged a small party in Limehouse for [various] friends, including Michael Briggs.

On the day of the dinner, Michael had to go to Paris for a midday meeting. He sat in the next seat to a dishy blonde girl on the outward flight and then next to her on the homeward journey in the early evening. She said she had been to Paris for lunch, interviewing Orson Welles for *Vogue* magazine. It was natural that they should make friends and he asked if she would like to join him that evening for dinner with some friends.

After an interval of months, Mireille, my French ex-girlfriend, had telephoned me to say she had become keen on me, or the idea of me, and that she was coming to London to do some serious talking. She had arrived in London earlier in the day and I arranged for Michael to collect her on his way to Limehouse. He picked up his travelling companion and Mireille and in the car Michael asked Mireille what she was doing in London.

'I've come to London to ask Andy if he will marry me. We love each other but we were both foolish and I realize I was at the bottom of our misunderstandings.'

Michael arrived to find seven or eight of us about to sit down to a table spread with Charlie Cheong's delicacies. Mireille came in first and I had got to my feet to welcome her when I saw the girl whom Michael had met on his Paris trip, following her. Wham Bam Boom Wow. I knew I was going to marry her in the instant of seeing her. It was not a question of falling in love at first sight; it was a feeling of absolute certainty. Michael introduced us, 'This is Polly. We sat next to each other going to Paris and then coming back. I knew you would be happy about her joining the party for dinner.'

Towards the end of supper Mireille tapped her fork against her glass. There was silence. She stood up. 'I have come to London to ask Andy to marry me. Andy?'

I was taken aback and, playing for time, said: 'What a lovely question, Mireille darling. Let's talk about it later.' But Mireille had seen my eye for Polly, and she already knew. At just the right moment Andy Meyer's large comforting Texan arm circled Mireille's shoulders.

I had to get something from the kitchen and Polly was alone with me for a moment and she whispered,

'Are you going to marry her?'

I replied, 'No. I'm going to marry you.'

Guess Who's
Coming to Dinner

It's odd how fascinated republicans are by the British royal family. I'm not going to use a capital letter, it makes my keyboard choke. French, Irish, Americans don't seem to be able to get enough gossip about them.

My encounter with possibly the most spoilt member of this family, Princess Margaret, or PM as she was called – though not by me – was not auspicious. She came to have supper with Andy, who was my lover and who had been at school with Antony Armstrong-Jones, as he then was, and they remained friends. She was returning to a special place, a sort of sentimental journey, because before they were married they had rented a little flat on the Thames in the East End of London where they could pretend they were an ordinary couple in anonymity. After they were married going to such a hideaway was impossible.

Andy (who became my husband) also had an escape place in the heart of the East End, and they were having a reunion. I was, funnily enough, unaccustomed to meals with royalty and indeed was a natural stranger to the behaviour and morals of the English upper classes, though I was beginning to learn the secret codes and to perceive the network that connects them and which makes such an exclusive and overreaching community above the rest of the vast population of England. (Evelyn Waugh wrote of Sir George Sitwell, gazing from the terrace of Renishaw across the teeming, densely populated coal-mining valleys of the Black Country and remarking; 'See? No one between us and the Locker Lampsons.') Anyway, I was pretty keen to join in.

Everyone seemed to know everyone in that society, or they knew of each other, and the extent of the social network was a revelation to me. There were two (paradoxical) systems with their own hallmarks. One defined itself as a deliberate lack of ostentation, beautiful manners, no dissembling, certain modes of behaviour (I think Andy would have quietly died rather than wear his old school tie except when travelling); the other – arrogance, rudeness, richness, a love of killing things, the slight stench of non-caring. Both included an absolute deadly precision as to who was who in the hierarchy.

Evelyn Waugh, great and envious chronicler of class, described middle-classes aspirants in his adolescent manual *Brideshead Revisited*: 'I went full of curiosity and the faint, unrecognized apprehension that here, at last, I should find that low door in the wall, which others, I knew, had found before me, which opened on an enclosed and enchanted garden, which was somewhere, not overlooked by any window, in the heart of that grey city.'

All this was tosh, of course, and was still taking place at the time Philip Larkin wrote of in 'Annus Mirabilis': 'Sexual intercourse began/In nineteen sixty-three . . . between the end of the Chatterley ban and the Beatles first LP.'

In Ireland, as a yearning adolescent, I had read the gossip columns about the goings-on of young grand tearabouts – the Chelsea Set as they were called. At that time celebrities weren't pop stars or movie stars or models – titles were the flame that drew the publicity moths, and the celebrated were the sons of peers or the daughters of this lord or that, and they had all been to public school if male or if female were debutantes. I read about their arcane doings, especially in the *Daily Express*, with an avid interest (the same interest, I realize now, that so many people have about the young royals and TV stars and which sells so many magazines like *Grazia* and *Hello!*). Andy's name was often there as a giver of bohemian parties (though his name then meant nothing to me).

A little time later, from reading about these people from another planet I was meeting them. This was because one of the first people I fell in love with when I arrived in London was grand and he introduced me to people and to places to which and to where I would never had access on my own (though working at *Vogue* had been an entry into another kind of world: fashion and style and a certain amount of rock 'n' roll). I was a good observer and a quick learner and I was fascinated by the whole thing, so unlike our own dear home life in Ardboe, where no one had ever heard of the word class except in a different sense in Moortown School.

I was also fascinated to observe what Evelyn Waugh (him again!) called the sly, sharp instinct for self-preservation that passes for wisdom among the rich.

Tony Armstrong-Jones and Andy had been in the same house at Eton and forged a lifelong friendship based largely, I believe, on both of them being outsiders there and both being unhappy. Neither was good at sports or cared about being popular – Andy was the first boy ever to become a Catholic, which didn't make him top of Pop (there were many Catholic boys there, of course, but no one had actually gone so far as to convert), and Tony was a sort of genius – he loved inventing and creating and made a crystal wireless set at school, and his own camera. (He was small and slight and when he coxed the Cambridge boat to win the Boat Race in 1950 he weighed in at 8st 8lb. He had also designed a new rudder for the boat.)

When I first met Andy he was living in Paris, but he also had this apartment in the East End. The whole area was derelict, in the grip of the death throes of the docks and before its gentrification. I was taken to a dinner party he was giving and overheard him telling another guest of how he had begged outside his school gates. I was so touched by the deprivation that I went to sympathize with him and was mortified and amused to discover that he had stood in his top hat and tails outside Eton College with the other chancers to have their photographs taken by tourists.

I learned, too, that he had always been fascinated by the East End – which, for all its decline, was still a close, almost Dickensian, community of dockers and workers, with many surviving beautiful old houses and the Thames as its High Street. He explored the whole area on his Black Vincent motorbike and when Tony A-J was commissioned to do a book of photographs he rode pillion as Andy showed him the secret beauties of the place. My husband remembered other, more brazen occasions when they would pull up at a red light alongside, say, an open-topped two-seater sports car. Very glamorous. These cars had the rear-view mirror fitted far forward on the front wing, and Andy would inch the motorbike alongside, Tony would lean over, turn the mirror round and, with his nose a couple of inches from it, would squeeze an imaginary spot and adjust the parting of his hair, occasionally jiggling the mirror as if to get a better view. Sometimes the driver would join in the fun, but more often he'd get into in a rage, especially if his girl was laughing at him too – in any case the motorbike was off before he had a chance to retaliate. The upshot of these exploratory excursions was that Tony rented the little room in Rotherhithe as a bolt-hole and it was there that he courted Princess Margaret.

Eight Georgian houses had been preserved in Narrow Street where Andy rented his apartment, each with balconies beetling out over the Thames. Police motor launches tied up at the balcony supports and sometimes PC Water-Plod would climb up for a chat. Looking across the expanse of water at night to the glittering lights on the other side, the city almost had the look of Venice. It was an enchanted place.

One morning Andy called me to ask if I would join him in his East End hideout for supper with Tony, whom I hadn't met.

'And his wife,' he added.

'What will I wear?' I asked. (I wonder what I was thinking of? A tutu? A tiara?)

'It doesn't matter,' he said, soothingly. 'It's completely informal, just the four of us. They'd like to see again where they used to live. And Tony would like to meet you.'

There's no use denying it, I was all a-quiver. (But that was in another country and, besides, the wench is dead.)

Looking back, I think the evening was an unmitigated disaster. They arrived in a little Mini and first thing was: I didn't curtsey. I wish I could say it was because of my integrity to my republican sentiments but the truth is I didn't know I was supposed to curtsey. Princess Margaret was a real madam – she was acutely aware of her royal status (the thing is, these people believe they are different from you and me – really, truly, believe it). So I had a black mark against me from that moment on. We went out to the balcony with our drinks to look across to where they had spent their happy early days together. The man who lived next door, a (then) well-known writer, was on his balcony but shot indoors when we appeared.

PM ate very little, smoked a lot and was fairly rude about everything and everybody. She had an icy hauteur and kept wiping her hands as if something sticky was on them, and then washed up, which I gabbled she didn't need to do. She looked at me frostily and the royal hands went back into the Fairy Liquid.

I wanted to be a success for Andy and knew I wasn't being and became more and more inhibited. I can talk the hind leg of a goat, but there was no chance – I was too nervous, she wasn't interested in anything I had to say, and while the two men had their whole lives in common (if that is the word I am looking for), Princess Margaret and I had nothing, nothing. Plus, I was Irish. Anathema. (Thank God I didn't know until later that she referred to us as the stinking Irish.)

At last the nightmare evening was over and we went down to where the Mini was parked. Hanging from every door handle, from the windscreen wipers, from the bumpers, were odd transparent containers filed with liquid. Water, I hope in retrospect. 'What on earth are those?' the Princess piped from the doorway. 'Balloons?' I ventured. 'No, darling,' Tony said, 'they're French letters.' And he jauntily removed them. I liked him from that moment on. I was completely mortified that such a thing had happened. (We didn't confront the writer next door but when, years later at a party, he began to apologize I walked away, still angry at the gratuitous rudeness of his behaviour.)

Later that night we stood on the balcony looking over the still water. I was beating myself up about what a disaster I had been and when Andy said, so loyally, so sweetly, 'Darling, I thought you were a great success,' I thought, yes, I must marry this lying toad. Reader, I married him.

The Quality
of Women

All my life I have had the luck of knowing astonishing women. Their quality knocks me out. Besides the manifest pleasures of their company, I love the way their houses look, their concern with others, how, in their busy lives, they can find the time and energy to look after their friends. These women do much the same level of work as men but their surroundings reveal a love of beauty and a care for their environment that I don't *as a rule* see in the lives and surroundings of their male counterparts. The standard was set early, of course, since I grew up among women out of the ordinary. This is not mere and fond prejudice. Perhaps as a result of this high benchmark, I gravitate towards magical women, hoping the magic will rub off. Not that it should any longer be called magic, or intuition, or whatever words have been used for so long, to cloak the idea of women's power so that it either seems arbitrary and crazy or operates on some other planet situated down there.

The course of my life has been enriched by women and and has been changed too. However or wherever they live or lived, they showed a way or opened doors and heightened life into an adventure. The obverse side is that one is spoiled for anything else. It's hard to be patient with slowness of wit and language having been brought up on the verbal pyrotechnics of my sisters (and brother) or the magnificent style I witnessed when Diana Vreeland was alive and ruling her roost in Manhattan, and I'd be sorry to be in London and not visit Carmen Callil in a house filled with the books that might never have seen the light of day again if it hadn't been for her and for Virago, the company she founded.

I'd love to go back to Venice and stay with Peggy Guggenheim again. She is dead and her house is now a museum. She opened my eyes to a good deal more than the art on her walls. She lived in what sophisticates called the only bungalow on the Grand Canal; I called it a palace, the remarkable white stone vine-covered palazzo Venier dei Leoni, started in 1747 and left unfinished for lack of money. In it she found a magical house for her collection, with a pavilion and one of the largest gardens in Venice (she bought it for less than $60,000 just after the war – but that would surely convert to many millions of dollars now). She loved Venice more than any place on earth and she shared it. I spent my honeymoon there, with the waters of the Grand Canal lapping outside, and our bedroom had an Alexander Calder mobile overseeing any high jinks and a wonderful Picasso on the wall opposite; her drawing room was all white, in the style of Elsie de Wolfe, with white furniture and Arp glass and Brancusi's *Bird in Space* hanging fabulous there; and of course her collection of paintings and sculpture, the art of the first half of the twentieth century.

Her taste was formed by diverse influences: her acquaintance with artists, her love for some of them, her involvement with artistic life in New York, London and Paris. Though she always said she was poor, wealth is relative. She had luck on her side too – if the word luck can be used in connection with the terrible timing: the start of the Second World War, when she could buy more or less what she wanted before she fled Paris. But her knowledge and flair in the forming of her collection made it unique.

Her stormy relationship with Jackson Pollock has been well documented. She was sometimes represented as an exploiter of the tortured artist, but – she put him under contract, tried to instil some kind of discipline into his life, and undertook to buy and sell his paintings.

There were other aesthetic bonuses to staying with her – not least setting out in her gondola (one of the last private gondolas in Venice), decorated with carvings of her little dogs, the gondolier wearing brass armbands by Max Ernst. (When we sat on the terrace to watch the spectacle of Venice *en prince* Peggy would unscrew the remarkable penis from Marino Marini's sculpture of a man on a horse, so as not to offend the sensibilities of any passing swimming nun.)

I was first introduced to her in Venice in 1968, by my husband, who was a friend both of her and of her daughter Pegeen, who had died in Paris that year. My first sighting of Peggy was as she turned a corner in a street near the Zattere by San Gregorio, diagonally across the Grand Canal from St Mark's Square; over the years I came to know her distinctive silhouette outlined at the end of a dark *calle*, and followed by a flurry of small dogs, Shih Tzus and Lhasa terriers, those little Tibetan shepherd dogs which tumble around like thistledown and look somewhat like the charming dogs in the beautiful Carpaccios which are among the greatest treasures of Venice.

She walked like a dancer, toes turned out, elegant, careless, in vividly coloured mules which she had made and which were the only footwear I ever saw her wear (except in England and New York, where she wore boots). She was an addict of life, had a high level of adrenalin and curiosity and excitement – a vivid life force. She was not in any conventional sense a generous person – in fact mean as get out – but she delivered extraordinary experiences. One starry midnight we piled into her motor boat to cross the lagoon to Torcello. Ruskin's words about Venice being a ghost with nothing but her loveliness to protect her were never more true than on that ravishing night.

She was sexy, with bird-like bones, fantastic legs and a face dominated by an extraordinary squashy-tipped nose, the creation of a plastic surgeon in Cincinnati in the early days of plastic surgery. Her account of the operation and its result is typical in its insouciance. 'I was bored. I could think of nothing better to do than to have it changed. It was ugly before, but after the operation it was worse. I always knew when it was going to rain because my nose became a sort of barometer and would swell up in bad weather.'

When she was eleven she fell passionately in love with her Irish riding teacher, and continued to fall in and out of love for years. When she decided to have an affair with Max Ernst (whom she had rescued from France at the beginning of the war), he, somewhat bewildered by her advances said, 'When, where and why, shall I meet you?'

'Tomorrow at four, in the Café de La Paix, and you know why.'

She always knew the way to bohemia, at least since she came to Paris in the early 1920s to find a romantic alternative to life as a member of one of New York's richest Jewish families.

One of the galleries she opened in the course of her life was called Guggenheim Jeune, an ironic title to distinguish it from the famous Guggenheim Museum in New York built by her uncle (which she was wont to refer to as The Garage). In the 1960s she finally allowed her collection to be shown in her uncle's museum. By extraordinary synchronicity the house we lived in on East 88th Street shared a party wall with one side of the Guggenheim and, staying with us, she would bang on her bedroom wall every night to let her pictures know she was near. She was never in the least surprised by coincidences like these, they had happened to her all her life. Late one night after dinner we slipped through a service side door into the museum for a private view of her collection in its new unfamiliar setting and there, highlighted by a single spotlight shining into the surrounding circular darkness, was the *Bird in Space*, which she had always coveted and had finally acquired just before she left Paris for ever.

When she returned to Venice after the show in New York, and before her paintings were sent back, she wrote to me: 'The house here looks so empty after your neighbour so full of my children.' Referring to her pictures as her children was not merely sentimental. She felt they were her connection with the future and posterity.

She gave me a shabby copy of her autobiography *Out of This Century – Confessions of an Art Addict*, published in 1946. It had then long been out of print (and one legend had it that the rest of the Guggenheim family was so scandalized by its uninhibited frankness that they had bought up every available copy; there is another, longer, unexpurgated edition now).

She had an indomitable spirit that I only once saw let her down. In 1979 she came to stay with us in England after a foul operation on her eyes and one tired and pain-filled night she said she wished she were dead. The next day she came downstairs in purple dress and purple tights. 'I wish I hadn't said what I said. I have *never* talked like that and I don't want to start now. I've never suffered from self-pity.' Day after day I listened to her talking and never wrote a word down, not even when she was talking about Samuel Beckett, whom she called Oblomov after a character in a Russian novel. (I do remember her saying that after she met him they stayed in bed in a Paris hotel for four days and sent out for sandwiches.)

Last year my daughter Bay, who was her god-daughter, and I went to the Venice Biennale and as I walked along the little streets towards the house I felt I would see that silhouette, hear the click of the turquoise mules, see the tumble of dogs turn from the light into the dark; but those intricately wrought iron gates studded with fat coloured glass globules and rocks made for her by Clare Falkenstein ('Clare's knitting') were tightly closed; there was a function being held and we could not be let in.

A Child of Dominica: Jean Rhys

I first began to interview her in 1974 when she was eighty-four, and this loose interview continued, cursorily, off and on, over the next four years. Eventually we forgot we were 'doing' an interview and just talked, sometimes in London, where she spent the winter months and sometimes in Devon, in Cheriton Fitzpaine, where she had lived for nearly thirty years. She herself wrote:

> I am sorry for any journalist landed with the job of interviewing me. To begin with, I am not at all lucky on these occasions: it so often happens that the last thing I want on that particular day is a stranger's questions. If I lived in London, it would be easy to cancel or postpone the interview. In Devon, by the time that I have decided that I really can't go through with it, it's too late, he or she is already on the way.
>
> As usual several things have gone wrong. Perhaps somebody has turned my lucky horseshoe upside down. Blue eyeshadow. Too much? Too little? There is no one to tell me. But after all, this is something I have always insisted on deciding for myself . . . It will have to do.
>
> I wait to be questioned. What are you to say when they ask you, 'Were you glamorous in those days?' That all depends, doesn't it? Should it be: 'Oh yes, I was, very. People used to push little notes into my hand – "I love you." Fun!' Or: 'Good heavens, no, not at all!'

I never used the word glamorous, although I did think her wonderfully glamorous, and beautiful. I don't think I tried to push her into appearing sad to fulfil my own idea of her. But I thought she *was* sad. It wasn't my idea, her sadness seemed a reality. As did her sex appeal, her erotic presence. The French have, as always, a word for it. *Allumeuse* – the ignition element, a person who flames other people's sense into awareness when they enter a room, or even walk down a street; they might not be spectacular but they're alight. She had great allure.

Is the sitting-room all right? Fairly, I think; shift a vase and try to decide which chair I ought to sit in. Some say back to the light on back-to-the-light days, others no, sunlight, unlike glare, is very becoming; face the light on sunny days. Just as I have decided, there is a knock, the interviewer has arrived. 'Please sit down,' I say, when I have opened the door and we have reached the sitting room and the interviewer plonks down in the chair I've chosen. I sit in the other, already feeling exhausted There's not a thought in my head, not a word. I can only wonder if she (or he) will describe this place as a cottage, a semi-detached, or a horrid little bungalow with creepers and things all over it. I know already, it jumps to the eyes, as the French say.

I never thought of it as a horrid little house or bungalow, although perhaps it was, but I did think it a strange house, out of context for her. Now, this is doing what she had accused us of doing – pushing her out of her own life into the context of our imaginations. Removing things we don't find satisfactory about her. I do remember, though, noting as I first came through the door of her cottage in Devon, how she had made an arrangement of herself against the light.

The question-and-answer game goes on. I realize that I am being gently pushed into my predestined role, the role of victim.

I have never had any good times, never laughed, never got my own back, never dared, never worn pretty clothes, never been happy, never known wild hopes or wilder despairs. In short, I have never been young or, if I was, I've forgotten all about it. Wailing, I have gone from tyrant to tyrant; each let-down worse than the last.

She wasn't what you'd call a sympathetic personality. In fact she seemed hell-bent on destruction. But she could be enchanting when she chose. She exhausted one's compassion deliberately since she'd never wanted it in the first place, although it was always being lavished on her, as one of her own heroines. She was suspicious of this easy emotional welter which flowed from admiring devotees who felt she'd chronicled their own disconsolate voyages. They longed to love her for it. She became almost a totem for women who felt hard-done-by by the Tyrant, Man. She recoiled sharply from such voluptuous devotion, and set about finding out what happened when easy sympathy was punched in the gut by her sharp little fists. Some people just left, bewildered and hurt, and talked about her appalling selfishness. Others stayed with her until she died, taking abuse and taking care. (I particularly remember the writer Diana Melly's patient care.) They knew who she was. Jean found out by the test of tenure who *they* were, and whether or not she could trust the proffered nurture; which never meant she wouldn't damage it, if she could.

Interviewers were, of course, anathema to such a winnowing nature, although she greeted them/us with gratifying expectations. The chaff flew later. As she wrote, she supposed we'd get it wrong before we even started. On the other hand, we often did get it wrong by the time we'd finished. Interviewers read her books, and read her 'up', and thought they were privy to her psyche, thought, perhaps, that in her exploration of the state of those disconnected, forlorn abused and loving women whom she so brilliantly created she had also produced a series of shockingly revealing self-portraits. 'People always seem to make me so unhappy,' she said once, deliberately ambiguous. 'I hope you won't make me sound unhappy.' But I am compelled to write that she seemed to me to have sadness seeping out of every pore. Once I was trying to tie a scarf around her beautiful head in a new way, and the result was worrying her and she cried, tears gushing.

'A photographer just told me my head was too big for my body,' she said crossly. 'Photographers are so awful.' She got into a fine fury about them and their cameras and she said she could hardly bear to look at photographs of herself, because they showed the lines which she blotted out when looking in the glass. She glazed her sight deliberately, through diffusion and drink. Old age was hateful to her.

When I went to see her I always brought scarves, lipsticks, eyeshadows. She loved cosmetics of all kinds, loved painting her face. We'll eschew symbolism. The scarf and the colour of the lipstick were matters of far more real import than answering my questions, which were often too persistent. I wanted an apprehension of her earlier reality, I wanted to know how she appeared as she swung around the corner of the rue de Rivoli in that summer after the First World War when everything was golden and she was bursting with joy.

'Why do you want to know?' she asked, but she said it dreamily, not in the way she described. 'That all depends, doesn't it?' (But people *did* push notes into her hands saying, 'I love you.')

I wanted her to tell me because it would have been a step forward in our mode of talking. People in old age don't tell younger people that they oozed sex, that they were beautiful. I think they're afraid of meeting with amused incredulity in the listener's eyes. But I thought she was amazing, full of sex, and beautiful with her white skin and Parma violet eyes; and I've rarely met anyone who gave off such intensity of emotion, the utter opposite of resignation. She looked at me sideways: 'I was a very loving person,' she said, 'and they want now to make me unhappy. I loved in that way that takes all the heart's blood. And I don't, and didn't, do that easily. I wouldn't like to do that now even if I could. It was all terrifically exciting; but it's too tiring. I'm past it. The fact is that I've cracked up physically but not mentally – some choice. But I was . . .' She leaned forwards and smeared some more lipstick on her mouth (I watched, the interviewer finding significance); she hesitated . . . 'I was one of those people who *look* good.'

Oh, she enjoyed ambiguity all right.

I'm always being made into a victim, a passive person . . . but the fact is I was active. God knows I hardly think I should be copied in the way I lived my life and loves: but I didn't always make a mess of them, and I wasn't always the abandoned one, you know. My affairs ended mostly because I wanted them to end or I wanted to leave the place where they'd happened, or just wanted to get away.

One day she said:

> The reason I've run away so often is that I'd always rather run away than stay if I didn't like anything. I sometimes think the reason I ran away was because my father ran away to sea. He was the son of an Anglican clergyman; the first time he was fourteen and was caught at Cardiff; then he did go to sea and suffered under a brutal captain. He was a ship's doctor, came to the West Indies, loved Dominica, and just stayed . . . I've inherited his character I think. My grandmother was Irish; my brother was senior wrangler at Cambridge. But I didn't inherit the brains. One day my father found me weeping over a perfectly simple lesson. I didn't have any talent.

Be that as it may, she had a virulent gift for writing that sprang from within her being. She had the most fluid of personalities: she trickled it away when you tried to grasp it, like scooping moonlight off water. She used to rage about people getting her wrong. But she often tilted the mirror herself, through boredom, or because of whim or a new flash of illuminating memory. 'There are a lot of things I didn't – and don't – understand about myself,' she said, 'a great many things.'

> It's strange that I should have had such a passion for myself. I'm one of five children, two brothers and three sisters, yet everyone thinks I'm an only child. That's why I'm writing my autobiography, really, in order to put the record straight, because everyone says I had such a terribly unhappy childhood and was very lonely; but they don't know anything about my childhood and heaven forbid that they should . . . I wasn't unhappy and I wasn't isolated. I was fond of books; there were a lot of books at home and I was allowed to read what I like, which is far from being deliberately isolated. What is odd, though, is that for years after I came to England I didn't and wouldn't open a book. Not for years.

She said: 'It's often said that I don't like women and don't trust women. I don't know why people should think that.' But she often was the 'other' woman, constituting a threat, and she knew how cruel and Balzacian the respectable sisterhood could be in their dealings with those who prowled (or who had strayed) outside the stockades of marriage. Another time she said, 'I was jealous of other women, and I think I know when that started . . . I remember seeing my mother on horseback, looking very pretty, and I was furious and couldn't bear it.'

The one thing she never tilted the mirror about was her writing. She was puzzled by her thraldom to it: indeed, if ever talent lived up to Sylvia Plath's description as 'the rare random descent' it surely did in Jean Rhys's case. Sometimes it seemed as if her genius had ricocheted heavily on to her head when she was nineteen and she'd been blindly staggering about under the impact ever since.

> All my life I've tried to escape from writing. I'm too lazy for it and it's a lonely, beastly business and sometimes ugly, too; but always I have been dragged back to it not once but over and over; and sometimes I've thought I have escaped but I haven't. So I know it isn't chance, you see, it's more than that. I never got away from it, I wish I had – I think writers are dreadfully selfish people. But you have to be . . . you have to be. They're sad, beastly and lonely but I don't see how you can be otherwise, because the words go away. And I'm damned if I know how you can write about deep things and what's happened to you, if you're not alone.

The story of how she began writing has been chronicled in detail but it still makes a moving parable. She moved into a small bare London room with an empty desk and a bed. Walking down the King's Road she saw some coloured quills in a shop, bought them and some books and pencils. She went back and wrote, wrote demented, for days, without stopping, needing to get something secret down and out about her life that she could only fathom by writing. Her writing was a search for herself and for sense, but she never found the answer, although she knew well enough where and how to look.

'After I had written it I put it away and didn't look at it. But I lugged it around with me for years and years; wherever I went, it went, and it became *Voyage in the Dark*.' That's a famous story. What isn't so famous is what she said to herself when those frenzied notes exploded her life. 'What did you say to yourself when you'd finished?' I asked. 'I don't remember,' she replied. 'I was relieved to get it done, and surprised, and surprised that I could write at all. And it's still my favourite book.' Then she said – and her voice was like feathers – 'I do remember: "Oh God, oh God, I'm only nineteen. And I've got to go on living, and living, and living."'

Sometimes it wasn't as bad as all that and sometimes it was.

I've been so happy in my life, you know, although always followed by sadness. Living in Paris after the First World War with my first husband who was partly Dutch I was so happy. I felt for the first time absolutely free. It seems funny to say that it didn't matter that we had no money and that we slept on people's floors and that it was a beautiful autumn, and everyone was lovely and I was happy. Then my husband got into the Inter-Allied Commission and we went to Vienna and it was there that I became interested in clothes and loved dressing up, being elegant. And I felt, this is all too good to be true, it can't last, and it was and it didn't. I had a son and he died when he was three weeks old and I went back to Paris and everything went wrong . . . .

Inaccuracies occur, for people must be entertained. So now I read calmly of my dark dreadful life, extraordinary versions of my first marriage, that I worked on the stage for ten bob a week (this last annoys me) but as a rule I don't turn a hair.

She returned to England and went to live in Devon and didn't write at all. Her books went out of print. Only Francis Wyndham, a passionate admirer of her work, continued to campaign to have them republished and in the late 1950s *Good Morning, Midnight* was broadcast as a play on the Third Programme and interest in her work was generally revived.

I read an advertisement in the *New Statesman* asking did anyone know where I was, and I thought: 'Yes, I do', and a publishing firm wrote and offered me a small advance for a book and what came out was *Wide Sargasso Sea*. It had been lying inside me since I was a child in Dominica; and I had thought while reading *Jane Eyre* 'poor Mrs Rochester'. I thought I'd put the record straight.

I wish I could do the same for Jean Rhys. Perhaps her autobiography, *Smile Please*, will. But I doubt it.

Jean Rhys died in May 1979.

Stacking
the Linen

I'm in the wig room. For those of you who don't have one, it is a small room where footmen powdered your – or, more likely, your husband's – wig. This house was built in 1588, so there are many nooks and crannies, just perfect for me, the spy. So many young mothers are spies: they have to be, watching their child covertly, for clues, for signals, for some way to comprehend what is going on in that secret new bundle of nerve ends, tender flesh, brains and biology that we almost inadvertently create over a long nine months.

I'm in the wig room, putting away linen – it might be a charming image, a young matron, keys at her waist, but in fact I'm in a froth of rage about the whole business of being a baby mother. What I want back is what I was, as archetypal mother and writer Sylvia Plath put it, 'Before the bed, before the knife, before the brooch pin and the salve fixed me in this parenthesis'; so I stack the linen much as Lady Macbeth might have done, after she had washed Duncan's sheets.

I have three babies at this time and I love them. At first they were adorable, noisy blobs who, somehow, worryingly, are fast growing into people with wills of steel, and there are times, and this is one of them, when I want not to be a mother ever again. For a start I didn't realize that they were going to be there for ever. I thought in my innocence that you could as it were, dip into babies (and I remember once, at the very beginning, driving into Bath and remembering as I parked that I had a tiny baby and she was sleeping in an empty house some twenty miles away).

The wig room is off the nursery, which has a big old window seat, like in *Jane Eyre*, and Rose and Daisy, two of my three daughters, are sitting there. I know this not because I have seen them, but because they are in there together, talking, intimate,

WRITING HOME

and something about their tone, the urgency of their words, has made me freeze. Rose is six, Daisy is five. I know in my mind's eye how they look on the seat, their earnest, beautiful faces turned each to each, two philosophers with fat little lips. Sometimes I want to eat them, in order that they'll be safe again. I am famished by love of my daughters. How did this happen?

Motherhood had always been an uninviting prospect to me. I'd had enough of the receiving end. The word 'mother' carried a message I didn't want to hear – or repeat. Trammelled lives, little cruelties, a turntable of defeating busyness and no joy in sight. I watched my mother to make sure I would not become like her – and yet I loved her obsessively. I was sure there was a dark angel ahead waiting to drop her integument over me, turning me into a Mother. How many of us take our mother to pieces to make sure we will not become like her? It seemed to me there was no way of escaping the destiny of repetition. So, easy answer: I would not become one.

And here I was, a mother of three, stacking up fine linen, and feeling a wedge bring driven into my heart so that I could almost feel it creaking apart – I didn't know at the time that these wedges are necessary, to widen it up, since it has either to widen or to break. I was in a rage, because I wanted to have my life of such a short time before back, to go back to when I was a free woman, an adventurous spirit, in a society where a heart was a Chanel motif, to be worn on the sleeve, a bauble outlined in diamonds.

Then, suddenly, I was married and soon after, from having a future that belonged only to me, it became irrevocably linked to three solipsistic baby beauties who had no idea that I existed outside of their needs. Leaving apartments in Bloomsbury and then on the Upper East Side in glamorous New York, I found myself in deepest Gloucestershire with a husband and three babies. without practice or training. (They had no practice and I had no training.)

I am silent in the small room. I hear Daisy ask Rose, her elder sister by a year, therefore an oracle, and Delphic in her pronouncements – 'Rose, what would you do if you had a mother like mine?' I carefully, carefully, close the old door and try not to rustle with laughter, with love, with the understanding that I have heard a profound question. But I have also heard for the first time the word 'mother' used by my children in connection with me as a reality, as a definition of myself. And for all my laughter and my understanding that I have heard one of life's great truths (every child in the same family has indeed a different mother; I know I am irreconcilably different from each of my sisters and my brother and that brings its problems), I know too that whatever else has happened to me in that journey, short in time but infinite in compass between me on the eighteenth floor of the *Vogue* offices on Lexington Avenue and me here in my children's nursery, I have broken the motherhood pattern laid down for me, or at least enough to have given Daisy the power to think she could do 'something' about me.

In that earlier dispensation, adults, parents, were mono-lithically immutable – children were powerless. That went without saying. You suffered in silence or in sobs. Yet here was Daisy talking with a hint of brisk killer instinct that warned me I'd better change my ways.

My ways, it transpired, principally involved the amount of time I still devoted to writing and filming, and that this necessitated my leaving home. They weren't having any of it.

Those children grew up in a flash that still dazzles my perceptions and illuminates my life. I devised a fairly simple method of memorizing particular moments. I would look hard at three blonde heads bent over a book, or a four-year-old Rose in yellow sou'wester and little else running through the rain, Bay in a tutu that didn't fit, Daisy solemn in a lilac negligee. And register the mental snapshot. The next day it would have gone, overlaid by new realities. But I have only to close my eyes and those images are there, my lost children, running away from me. I know those children. I know all about them. Where are they?

Well, Daisy is working for *Vogue*, forging her own future, living the circle that binds us together in its lovely and ratifying spin. I believe in magic. We all have extraordinary powers if only we could access them. One way of accessing them is to be happy. *Mutatis mutandis.* One of the signs of magic, of happiness, is how things connect, of how you do one thing which seems arbitrary at the time and then turns out to be the first and most necessary step in a process that leads to fulfilment. So much is circular. *Vogue* lay in my past, I thought, but it was streaming through my future and that child who was pondering on the vexed question of what to do about me was already connected to *Vogue*. I see Daisy now and yet continually also see her as she has been through all the stages of her life; I see her at different ages, different sizes, image superimposed on image, growing up in an endless shadow play, always herself, in all her different manifestations, one melding into the other, a magma, an archaeological dig that only I can turn up instantaneously. And yet she could always escape me. The child who asked what could one do with a mother like mine saw that I was a spy and took her own measures. She silently slipped away, withdrew from the tempestuous encounters endemic to the rest of the family. Do you know that poem by Seamus Heaney about the hare?

> Choose one set of tracks and track a hare
> Until the prints stop, just like that, in snow.
> End of the line. Smooth drifts. Where did she go?
> Back on her tracks, of course, then took a spring
> Yards off to the side; clean break; no scent or sign.

Daisy was like that; all the evidence was there. Room like an ice palace, possessions in place. But the impeccable girl had sprung.

I think about her all the time.

Does she remember what it was like to cry passionately over a sad story, to mourn a dead bird, to lie awake dreaming of hunting with her pony? I go upstairs to the small bathroom where she, for one long, hot summer, meticulously laid out her syringes, bandages, medicines, home-baked pills, and see her there, in her nurse's uniform with the red cross on the white nurse's cap, in all her small and earnest reality mutilating her dolls so she could mend them. She's so real to me, I can reach out and touch her, both of us anxious-eyed. But she's not there, she's run into her future, into this beautiful New Yorker e-mailing me home, and working for *Vogue* and laughing at the idea of Nurse Bobbitty.

What goes around comes around. I remember showing a beautiful, limned, big-eyed, silent young girl with hair like a polished blade around the *Vogue* offices in the Graybar Building in Lexington Avenue. Her name was Anna Wintour. She is now Daisy's editor. I doubt if she would remember. But the fact that the circles are so clean and fitting is a sign of hope to me, a sign that we are all linked, that the magic that is coincidence and synchronicity works, that the world is not an arbitrary place.

And I remember that there is a grade of human character connected to the quality of perception of the external world. Saul Bellow once wrote, 'Not everyone sees the same world. Some people when they see the sun in the sky see something resembling a gold coin. Others see a chorus of angels crying "Holy, holy, holy". As you see so you are.'

Daisy sees more than most. I came across an article she had written for a newspaper. The toad hadn't bothered to tell me. In it she wrote, 'I wonder at our shared blood. I pore over photographs of her not just at the way she looks but to try to gain some sense of her. It still mystifies me that she bore me, that we are of the same ilk.'

I'm glad that I am no longer the oracle or the know-nothing, neither the solution nor the problem, neither the dispenser of justice nor the very opposite. Where once I went ahead and they followed, I now follow in their footsteps, an old page to their young Wenceslas. I have all the time in the world and all the space I could need. And at a deep and wistful level I want to be back in the wig room, to see them on the window seat discussing what to do about the most important person in the world.

Sunday Morning in the Country

Only Johnny, reading the posh Sunday papers, could find innuendo after innuendo, which he read out with raised eyebrows and a hurt, astonished look, his brown eyes full of mischief. He knew that fear is the enemy of love; but he had lived half his life unloved, in a state of fear, manifestly homosexual when it was against the law to be so. He fell in love with the man he went to work for, who fell in love back.

He used to come and stay with us at occasional weekends, especially after his partner died. My children adored him. So did I, and so did Olive, who was over eighty and ran the house with a rod of putty. I loved listening to Johnny. Coming from Ireland (where, of course, there were no gay people, none), I had never met that cast of mind. He was bereft but he was never miserable and he had innocence and unquenchable gaiety and a sense of life's silliness, but give him a book or a newspaper and he became a dowser, his mind a divining rod: quivering over good, clean, often boring articles on poetry, cookery, travel, he could delve into a magma of scatological references and double entendres. 'One track mind, dear,' he would say. 'No terrible diversions like you have, with these poppets.'

We're in the drawing room. It's Sunday morning just before lunch and two of my children are absorbed in a book, golden heads soldered together as in a Kate Greenaway illustration, and I am bewildered by this sudden, good, strange silence and speculate on what they can be reading to rivet them so, but hold my peace. Johnny is impressed.

'Penises,' Rose says loudly. 'There.' A finger stabs at the book. 'Spelt like peanuts only with the T out.' Daisy is *bouleversée* at such learning. I don't look at Johnny, who is slowly lowering his paper to goggle over at the two nymphets and then at me. I see they have found a copy of a manual called *Where Did I Come From* which a well-meaning godmother had given them.

'Where did *it* come from you might ask,' Johnny says.

'It tells you here,' Rose dimpling at him. 'You've got one of those peanut things, haven't you Johnny?'

'Last time I checked I had,' he says, and looks across at me. I lower my face slowly on to the table. Ostrich syndrome.

'It's you,' I say, my voice muffled into the tablecloth. 'It's your influence.'

'Not me, duckie,' he says. 'I've never seen that book before in all my life. It was here before I got here. But I must look at it. It might teach me something by the sound of it. Better than *this* anyways.' He rattled the newspaper. 'And this is supposed to be the saucy one. Let's see, girls,' he says. 'Show and tell.'

'No,' Rose and Daisy say firmly. 'we're using it.' They titter horribly.

Unfazed, he returns to his paper and I look at the children who, pleased to have my attention, pounce.

'What's c-l-i-, Mummy,' Rose begins. I raise my head from its pillow of shame and meet Johnny's eyes, gazing at me with interest.

'Go on, dear, *do* tell. Cling film perhaps?'

'No,' Rose says firmly. 'Not cling, it's c-l-i-t-.'

'Say no more,' says Johnny, equally firmly. 'Spare your mother's blushes. There are but two words in the English language beginning like that so it must be the raised band encircling the body of earthworms towards the middle.'

'Oh, come on, Johnny,' I say, 'You've made that up.'

'Streuth,' he says.

Rose wrinkles her nose in disgust: '*Worms*,' she hisses at Daisy.

'Stop it, Johnny,' I say. 'Think of the appalling word-associations you're giving that child.'

'Talking about encircling the body,' Johnny says, 'why don't we go upstairs and try on that shantung jacket you say you're chucking out, I can't think why.'

'It will suit you,' I say.

'It will suit my florid complexion more like,' he says.

Underneath his face and body, the lineaments of the young unhappy boy he had been years and years before were almost perceptible. He tried the jacket on and said, posing, vamping it up, 'I knew I was, well, gay you call it now but there was nothing gay about it then I can tell you, queer it was called and queer you felt – when I was fourteen. I didn't admit it until I was about twenty-two, of course; and I still think it's a fairly hideous joke on the part of Nature.'

'How did you know?' I asked.

'Well, all the boys were after girls, they never stopped talking about it and I hadn't the faintest interest. Didn't know what they were talking about.'

'What did you do?' I asked.

'What could I do? I thought I was sick, wrong, gone mad. It was so different then. Everything was closed, fearful, inhibited. There was no one to ask then, and nothing to read, nothing to do except worry yourself sick. Then I became a Bevin Boy. You don't know what that is, I can see, shows your age, you're so young.'

'I'm not, Johnny,' I said. 'I'm not.'

He looked at me consideringly. 'Well, then I'm so old. It was during the war. Bevin Boys were conscripts sent to essential industries . . . docks, mines. I'd been on the colliery anyway, the wages desk, and then I was called up and went into the Pay Corps. I was sacked from that – suspected TB – and I thought after the colliery there simply *must* be more to life than this, and I thought perhaps I could be a factotum of some kind. So I put an advertisement in the paper. It was extraordinary how many answers I got. I only answered one. A doctor who'd gone blind: I honestly thought I could do some good. He was a poppet. She was a real bitch – kept a coat of arms in the hall showing she was descended from William the Conqueror, well, weren't we all. Although I was very unhappy I stayed there quite a long time because I thought I was helping. But it got too much and by chance – well, not chance, call it fate – I'd kept one address from all those letters. I wrote and the man asked me to come for an interview. It was too long a journey for a day so I stayed overnight. There were flowers in my room and cigarettes and I thought it was perfect heaven.'

'It is perfect heaven,' I said – a most beautiful house with Johnny at its happy centre, but his friend had died and Johnny was a walking metaphor for bereavement. But he was so gallant in his grief, it was one of the reasons we all loved him.

He came downstairs wearing the jacket, went over to the piano and played and sang 'Linden Lea', quite without pathos in his jauntiness.

'I hate being alone. For all the clichéd reasons. There are always good reasons for things being cliches. The coming home at night to an empty house. Not being able to turn to someone and say "Look" when there's something beautiful you want to share . . . all that. But I knew I'd end up alone. Always. I believe in fate. Predestination. I don't know how to reconcile it with my Christianity: I go to church every Sunday – drive seven miles because the pastor there is a human being. His sermon last Sunday – he was saying how he'd been swimming off the coast, at Formentera – my dear he's eighty-four – and he was swamped by a wave – well to look at him a bit of foam would knock him over – and he lost his teeth. There he is in the pulpit, describing the loss of his dentures. He searched everywhere and eventually gave up and went back to his hotel: toothless and *minding*, you could hear how he minded and wouldn't you? On holiday? It takes ages to replace them at the best of times, and eighty-four or not you don't want that awful sudden sag – and he couldn't eat: he went out for a walk and when he came back there they were, in a parcel, on his place. If that isn't a miracle, what is?'

He pushed aside the paper and lifted a book by Harold Acton.

'When I was younger and with someone who knew the man who wrote that,' I said, showing off, 'I was taken to lunch at his villa outside Florence. Villa La Pietra. Astonishing garden – and house.'

'Well, fancy,' Johnny said. 'Not that I ever met him.' He opened the book and began to laugh.

'Shall I read this?' he asked. 'Or does it madden you – being read at?'

'Not the bits you read,' I said. 'I'm only amazed at how you instantly seem to find extraordinary innuendo wherever you look.'

'Well this is harmless; oh, hold hard, as the bishop said, maybe it isn't – it's about an old American bird called the Marchesa Lulie Torrigiani, whose conversation apparently according to this was so coarse that Max Beerbohm was once sick into a majolica basin at her dinner table – now why would you specify what type of basin he vomited into, beats me anyway, this story she told, it's about two policemen on the prowl for indecent behaviour in a public park. They hide behind a bush and hear a female voice implore, 'Oh do let me take a last look before you put it in.' Leaping forth to catch a couple in flagrant delight they find two old women burying a cat. The judge ruled that the arrest was exucontian. He'd want to watch his spelling on that.'

'I don't believe it,' I said. 'Let me see,' I saw. 'How out of a large book full of decent literary material do you alight on that? Anyways what does exocuntian mean . . .'

'Careful, dearie,' he interrupted. 'Mind where you put that "o". It means out of nothing, I believe. And the double meanings spring out quite by chance.'

Olive appeared in the doorway, her hat squashed down hard on her head.

'If any of you want to go out for a walk you should go now. 'Tis stopped raining. Only just, mind, and I shouldn't wonder but it will start up again . . .'

'Put on your bikini, Olive, and let's go.' Johnny said, lumbering to his feet and kissing her.

'Olive,' piped up Rose, 'what's v-a-g-?'

I seized her book and hid it before she could finish the spelling. The children squealed with rage.

'V-a-g-u-e, darlings,' Johnny said. 'Best thing to be around here.'

'Whatever's wrong with these children?' Olive said. 'Good as gold like the white hen's chickens when I came in, reading.'

'Mum's took our book,' Rose wailed. 'And it was all about pees . . .'

'And Q's,' said Johnny. 'Where shall we go for a walk?'

'You could go up to Nibley Knoll,' Olive said, 'afore it rains again.'

'Then our nibblies *will* be knolled,' Johnny said, prancing into the hallway.

The children dribbled off into the hall to climb into their sou'westers. Johnny said, puffing out his cheeks, 'She's worth a guinea a box.'

'She's worth what?' I said.

'Told you you were young,' he said. 'It was everywhere . . . a something . . . a hen and a Waverley Pen . . . they're worth a guinea a box. It was an advertisement. Enamel signs. They'd be worth a mint now. Those were the good old days, weren't they, Olive?'

'Not for me they weren't, sir,' she said.

'Nor for me, neither" Johnny said, and kissed her.

Now I look back I think I was young and I know I was lucky. I'm not young any more and there's less luck and laughter now that Olive's dead and now, so is Johnny.

On Blondeness

The mellow gold of honey, the sun-kissed colour of a field of wheat, the golden flecks in the eyes of a loved one. What is so special about blonde – that silken shade gentlemen have always preferred?

It is early summer 1679 and across the great civilized landscape of Versailles the hunt is streaming. At its head, the Sun King is galloping, keeping abreast with the girl with whom he is about to fall in love. She is Mademoiselle de Fontanges, a romantic lunatic, 'mentally pathetic, physically gorgeous, flower of a creature', and as she gallops under a low-hanging branch, her hat is swept off and her golden hair falls on her shoulders. Stopping only for an instant, she binds the cascade of hair up with a borrowed silk and gallops on. The King is as enchanted with the gesture as he is with the look and, besotted, he makes her a duchess. Within a week, the hairstyles of the fashionable women of France are affected by both the style of the gesture and the felicity of its result, and blonde cascades appear on heads everywhere, just waiting to be untied at the end of the day. Oh, gentlemen have always preferred blondes; and so have kings and cads. They have kept drowsy emperors awake when nothing else could.

And artists. When Picasso was walking down a street in St Paul de Vence in the summer of 1953 and saw Sylvette, with her long gold hair tied at the very tip of her head, like a circus pony, he was sufficiently ravished by her charm to make her his muse, and he produced a famous series of drawings that etched a look on a decade.

It was Brigitte Bardot who untied that silk ribbon, liberating not only herself but the image of the blonde, changing it from one of a cool and waiting turbulence into a sultry tawny creature tangled by sex before the event. The blonde as the explosive; the blonde as the erotic. At about the same time as Bardot was changing the look of young girls all over Europe, Marilyn Monroe was sliding her way into the American memory stream as the blonde to end all blondes. And to further this end and to keep her roots glittering, she was flying a little old lady on a round trip of hundreds of miles each week from San Diego to Beverly Hills because she had once tinted the shining cap of Jean Harlow, the platinum blondeshell, the torpedo of sex. And Marilyn Monroe, at first the Mark II blonde, although finally the ultimate, the number one, liked that link with Jean Harlow.

Marilyn Monroe . . . the one Mailer called 'the sweet angel of sex, a blonde who became a blonde, which is to say honey-blonde, golden-blonde, ash-blonde, platinum-blonde, silver-blonde – the blonde will be on call; and the sugar of sex came up from her like a resonance of sound in the clearest grain of a violin.' Monroe was the best of her kind of blondes but there is a different best in Marlene Dietrich, who flashed out the image of the cruel Ice Queen, with a smile like a scimitar ready to slice your face with a glance and terrorizing anyone who cared to listen (and of course everyone did), with husky songs like 'Blonde Women' ('those charming, alarming blonde women'). Her Lola was a threatening slit in the lovely world of the wraparound blonde.

The blondeness of blondes is so variable. The women behind this pale warmth are not just the Marlenes and Mermaids and Marilyns, the Lolas, Loreleis and Ledas; they are also the tired old tarts with the hint of Stilton cheese about their hair, they are the women whom Dorothy Parker said made men click their tongues and wag their heads roguishly. It is a potent and infected word, ready to smit and smite men as John Osborne knows. His Bill Maitland in *Inadmissible Evidence* has been smitten. 'I have an extraordinary thing about Blondes. They're like plague carriers to me. Even dyed blondes. My first wife was blonde, really blonde. Blonde, blonde. It was beautiful – I've never known hair nicer.' And Handel was surely in love with a blonde if he also wrote the lyrics to his great aria 'Where'er you walk', in *Semele*:

Surely you see My Lady,
Out in the garden there
Rivalling the glittering sunshine
With a glory of golden hair.

What is so extraordinary about this word is that it is not just a colour or a shade or anything as subtle as nuance but rather that it is a state, a luxurious suspension of colour. Blonde takes flight from definitions. A thousand different lights and emanations, a hint, a movement floating up through the mind and through the air, like pale smoke through wooden doors or sunlight squeezing around a rafter. A paradox of blondeness, containing and spilling out, spanning within its declensions whole continents of colour and temperatures, from the icy beauties of the north to the sunny freckles on the nose of an Australian beauty.

It is as much the extraordinary icon of Botticelli's Venus delicately using her Niagara hair to shield her body as it is the biscuit-coloured inside of my daughter's elbows. It is the form and shape of a golden Labrador bounding across autumn, as it is D. H. Lawrence's snake slithering across the heated noonday flagstones of a Mediterranean courtyard. It is Seamus Heaney's sun stood like a griddle cooling against the wall, while the water honeys in the slung bucket. It is what I saw as I walked home from school alongside flax fields that were the colour of a summer sky, when linen was an industry in Northern Ireland, and when that flax was scutched it was so golden that it burned and glimmered as if the sun and moon had mixed and fallen on it.

But no matter what filters of similes, of metaphors you push blonde through, it comes out unaffected, shining like spun gold, old as sand, fresh as daffodils, ripe as wheat, as light as champagne bubbles.

I admire the black hair of dark beauties, which Thomas Hardy described as closing over foreheads like nightfall, extinguishing the western glow, or T. S. Eliot's sweet brown hair over the mouth blown, but it's outshone by the 'careless yellow hair that seemed to burn' that Robert Lowell loved and by the extraordinary imagery in W. B. Yeats's poem to Anne Gregory:

Never shall a young man,
Thrown into despair
By those great honey-coloured
Ramparts at your ear,
Love you for yourself alone
And not your yellow hair.

Blondeness betokens ripeness, and ripeness is all, as Edgar affirmed in *King Lear*. The coagulations of honey within the hive, the sprawl of Breughel's stooked fields, the beaker full of the warm south that Keats lauded, with beaded bubbles, winking at the brim, and whoever, like him, seeks abroad to find Autumn sitting careless on a granary floor, her hair soft-lifted by the winnowing wind, will surely see that her hair will be golden.

Once on a beach I saw a child bury her arms in a castle of fine sand and then unselfconsciously raise those arms, and the sand fell back, slightly anchored by the tiny gold hairs on her arms, and there was a cloth of gold if you like. And when I was young, I looked into a covered china bowl and saw a coil of thin gleaming hair lying there, like Rumpelstiltskin's weavings. There was something sinister about it because the hair itself had a dead quality and yet the colour itself was electrically alive. I showed it to my mother and she said casually, 'It was your hair as a child.' I could only stare at this relic of the blonde I had been before I was a person. 'If I have only one life to lead let me live it as a blonde' was a brilliant advertising slogan.

But of all the blonde images that I carry about, there is one more perfectly golden than any other. I was sitting in a terrace in Tuscany, on a somnolent afternoon, and it's more than forty years ago, but if I half-shut my eyes, I can see that place as clearly as though that extraordinary landscape were still stretching, shimmering before me, covered in that most felicitous combination of crops, the olive, the wheat and vine. Two white oxen were toiling up the hill opposite. Everything was sleepy except for my handsome companion, whose hair had the thickness and colour of ripe barley. He was translating *Paris Peasant* by Louis Aragon, as one does. I looked at one of the translated passages and this is what I read.

So one day, in the Passage de l'Opéra I found myself contemplating the pure, lazy coils of a python of blondeness. And suddenly, for the first time in my life, the idea struck me that men have discovered only one term of comparison for what is blonde: flaxen, and have left it at that. Flax, poor wretches, but have you never looked at ferns? I have spent months on end nibbling fern hair. I have known hair that was pure resin, topaz hair, hair pulsing with hysteria. Blonde as hysteria, blonde as the sky, blonde as tiredness, blonde as a kiss . . . this concept of a blondeness which is not so much a colour as a sort of spirit of colour blended with the accents of love. From white to red through yellow, blonde keeps its mystery intact. Blonde resembles the stammerings of ecstasy, the piracies of lips, the tremors of limpid waters.

And that is why every six weeks or so I spend a fortune, and a good many hours, Becoming a Blonde.

Deceived by Ornament

Never underestimate the power of things to console. The old men knew that, with their chalices and chasubles and copes and tabernacles to help us through the vale of tears.

Spare me. I'm consoled by more secular things.

There are, on my desk, among a bevy of beautiful objects, three fairly hideous ones but which are nonetheless the ones I love the most and which are to me the most valuable, though they are worthless in worldly terms: a cream-coloured fat china pig covered in blue squiggles with a wobbly slit on its back for money but no opening anywhere to get said money out; a small ceramic model of a girl with her hand between her legs and her head to one side with what could be a bonnet on her head but is more likely a bad hair day (she has a look of intense pleasure on her goofy face); and an unusual paperweight. Stand back there while I describe it. It's a gruesome detailed terracotta depiction of an execution: a bloody axe lies beside a decapitated head in a basket. Friends are inclined to start back when they see this grisly object.

Above the desk hangs a needlepoint picture which is a bit of a botanical puzzler (unless you know the names of my daughters), since it depicts a huge Bay tree from which a Rose and a Daisy have fallen.

Each of these things was made for me by said daughters when they were little. Daisy laboured over the pig and the lady, whose hand, as she carefully explained, 'had fell into her lap when it was fired'; the execution scene was by Rose, who was always well into metaphor; and the needlepoint was stitched in solemn secrecy and heavy breathing by Bay. I longed to help her, but since I was not supposed to know what she was doing I could not. The fact that over and over again I bandaged up her fingers where she had pricked herself with the needle was never remarked on by me, nor were the tears of rage and the shouts of 'Bloody knots!' coming from the corner where she was sewing. It was a lesson for both of us: her in what it can cost to give; me in what it takes to let your child get on with it by herself.

My girls are all long grown up, and they look on these objects with a kind of retrospective pity tinged with amusement; but I know that at some level they are glad they are still there, still cherished, still endowed with the love and effort that went into their making.

My friend Lavinia remembers laboriously and obsessively embroidering – with the help of her nanny – a set of table mats for her mother for her birthday. The same afternoon she went, with the nanny, to a fete in the village and found on the sixpenny stall the set of napkins. Such a small thing but so epic; she never got over it.

There's a passage in Shakespeare (there always is) which struck me with peculiar force: in *The Merchant of Venice*, that passionate play about the weights and measures of the heart, 'The world is still deceived by ornament,' Bassanio sighs, and goes on, 'thus ornament is but the guiled shore to a most dangerous sea.' Indeed, indeed, and I was beguiled from the very start and hoisted my sail and set out on that dangerous sea years and years ago and have now lost sight of the shore; but it was the saving of me.

For as long as I remember, ornament and collecting has meant credibility, extras which added authenticity to my life, whether it was filling a tree house with broken shards of china or getting myself up with kohl and jangling metal belts and gold lamé. (And that was only last year.)

Decoration and acquisition can teach you important lessons: they allow stability to those who cannot easily be stable, because decorating yourself and your surroundings has to do with improving; with self-worth; with allowing yourself to live in surroundings that speak of your own grace and importance. Squalor or ugliness in your rooms is symptomatic of how you view yourself or your life.

But collecting and possessiveness has an even more serious side. It is symptomatic of deep-inlaid anxiety. Babies and children need constant touch and warmth and the knowledge of being wanted. If this is missing a deep insecurity is born, a hunger that is never filled. The child has a flawed relationship with the outside world and finds more reassurance in objects than in people, who have shown that they cannot be trusted. Acquiring things is a soothing and necessary device and is a mood regulator, and makes you feel special and clever. Look, mummy, at what I found. It's the opposite of complacency though; it reveals a passionate craving to be valued and to be loved.

Certain pieces that I bought gave me more than a collector's satisfaction. They gave me revenge of a kind. Once, at an auction, I bought some objects from the house of Lord Brookeborough, a bigot who was the prime minister of Northern Ireland when I was growing up; and although I hated him, I was fond of them. After all they couldn't be blamed for who owned them.

And why did I hate him? I'll tell you.

I hated him for the damage he did to the Catholic minority by deprivation, discrimination and political neglect in Northern Ireland. Under his remit we Catholics, the aboriginals of Ulster, were kept down, denied proper representation and treated as second-class citizens But I also hated him for more personal reasons. When I was a young woman I sat beside him at a dinner party in a grand house in Northern Ireland. I was there because I was writing a story for a magazine, and so I felt in the position of a governess – neither with the servants nor with the guests, but posed uneasily between the two. (I understand the priggish Fanny in *Mansfield Park*.) It is perhaps to my hostess's credit that she put me beside the guest of honour. She may only have seen a *placement* that needed to be done and imagined, I suppose, that any young woman eager to please and ready to sing for her supper would make an agreeable dinner companion for the old man. I was alarmed and amazed to find myself next to him.

The dinner progressed. He treated me with a heavy-handed flirtatiousness. I tried to regard him objectively, this man who personalized bigotry for me, who by his actions and attitudes had exacerbated the divisions in the community of which he was the leader, and who had contributed to the ruination of the prospects of many of my contemporaries' lives. At the end of the meal he said: 'Tell me, Polly – I didn't quite hear your name?'

'Devlin,' I said, looking at him; and seeing his face shiver and pinch inwards I said again, more clearly, 'Devlin.'

I might have hit him across the face. The name could only be that of a Catholic. His long head swivelled away, his hooded eyes grew more blinkered.

'Devlin,' he said and fell silent. And then he turned back. He said, with an intense viciousness, 'You've come far.' And turned away, nor spoke to me again that evening. I hadn't come far enough if I had arrived at a seat beside him.

Anyway, back to collecting. You can see why.

And it doesn't have to be paintings and objects, though they were always my tipple; the consoling stuff can be fashion, clothes, shoes, bags and though I never was into Louis Vuitton or Chloé or Hermès, when I look at their products I see that there is a fabulous eye behind them and much of what they sell is as beautiful as any antique object. The eye is what matters.

Once, years ago, in Cambridge, I followed signs to the mysteriously named Kettle's Yard, and found the most beautiful series of little houses (which had been four condemned cottages) connected into one living magical place where a saintly pair, Jim Ede and his wife, Helen, had solved for themselves any moral dilemma about the habit of acquiring possessions. In the unpretentious and charming arrangements of his much-loved collection he showed there was dignity to possessing, that what mattered was the inner worth of the outward show. His collection of pebbles was as impeccably shown as were the Barbara Hepworth and Henry Moore sculptures.

Collecting is not an arbitrary disconnected series of events – each one unique, not to be repeated. It is for many a linked chain that helps hold a fragile life together. For some the saturation point is never reached.

I have stopped collecting, though the evidence is still around me. Even as I cull, somehow my rooms don't seem emptier. But no matter what I get rid of, I will always keep the guillotined head, the fat pig and the dreamy girl; every time I look at them I see small starfish hands working to make something precious for someone who was once the most important person in their lives.

Camping It Up

Out on the lawn I lie in bed
Vega conspicuous overhead
In the windless nights of June;
As congregated leaves complete
Their day's activity, my feet
Point to the rising moon.

Picture this. It is a late summer evening in the gloaming, the curlew is calling and the hedges are dense, smelling, lit by the glow of woodbine. Our meadow field lies silent; the flying life that turns it into the Heathrow of the insect world has gone to rest. From the woods that surround the fields come the last strains of the nightingale. All is still. Down the lane, between the hedges, come two lunatics, trailing a motley selection of things. They are carrying spindly steel chaises longues (the uncomfortable ones, the ones that close up like a mousetrap when you lower yourself on to them, or snap and break your fingers). From about their persons drip blankets and sleeping bags and pillows. The man is making muffled whining noises in his head which the woman can hear by divination, and sometimes the noises break through the sound barrier and become audible as a resigned low grizzle; she is silent save for the odd snorting noise which anyone who has ever tried to suppress laughter (say in church) would recognize as stifled, verging on hysterical. Following the pair are five dogs, completely agog about what is going on, barking and yelping fit to bust, grabbing each other and fighting a bit, and between times rolling excitedly on badger droppings so that a smell rises from them that is pale and livid. The sheep on the other side of the hedges stir and rise as the odd procession passes onwards.

This odd group turns into the meadow, to its beautiful middle, where the flowers jostle each other, and begin to pitch camp. Or rather I, The Woman – Me, yes, 'tis I – and my husband, begin to try to put up the camping beds, which of course collapse and crush our fingers and crash on to the dogs, who have by now become demented by excitement. It is nearly dark and we can't quite see what we're doing but finally we get the bloody things up, arrange the sleeping bags artfully along their length and slither into them. As soon as we wriggle down into the bags the beds jack-knife. The dogs watch with grave and silent interest as our heads rise up and hit our knees, high in the air.

We climb, cumbersome, out of the bags, out from the vicious grip of the chairs, straighten them, arrange everything and very delicately try again. This time, by dint of movements that would put you in mind of Noh theatre, we get settled; but we are afraid to move, so we lie side by side looking upwards to where a few crows, disturbed by us, are circling on their way back to the wood, cawing their displeasure. I remember the lines from Macbeth – 'Light thickens and the crows make wing to the rooky wood. Good things of day begin to droop and drowse' and think not to go there towards night's black agents and instead try to remember the lines from Philip Larkin's poem – about the couple, tum, tum de tum, how does it go side by side, their faces blurred,

> The earl and countess lie in stone
> Their proper habits vaguely shown
> As jointed armour, stiffened pleat
> And that faint hint of the absurd –
> The little dogs under their feet –

But they're not exactly the lines I want to remember and, in any case, all poetic thoughts are flung out of my head as the dogs, who by now have almost swooned with pleasure as they finally realize that they are going to be sleeping outside for the night, suddenly come to their senses, remember they have a job to do, and start to bark; and bark; and bark. One stops, another starts; a leaf rustles, they bark; an owl hoots, they howl; a fox cries in the wood, their voices become unhinged with excitement; a pheasant rises with a squawk, they fall into a frenzy. The noise goes on, and on, and on. I turn my head to try to see my husband, to try to read from his face what he is feeling, what the state of our marriage is going to be on the morrow. He hadn't wanted to do this in the first place. It was only because I badgered and fossicked about sleeping outside for so long that he is here at all.

This has been going on a long time. I've wanted to sleep out under the stars ever since my cousin Maurice and his friend John Brown, both Boy Scouts, cycled from Warrenpoint and came to camp on the lough shore where we lived in Ireland. Such a thing had never been heard of in our quarter before. It was 1954, and Warrenpoint was at least fifty miles away. We greeted them with awe and curiosity and caution, as now we might greet a large silver saucer-shaped object full of little green men. Maurice and John in fact did look like little green men in their Boy Scout uniforms and the glamour of the knife stuck down the side of sock knocked me out. My heart still misses a beat when I think on it.

Anyway, there they were, handsome aliens camping out beside their small green pointy tent and looking at the stars and coming up to our house for milk. I yearned ardently, not after them but after their sleeping bags, their palliasses, the whole enviable accoutrement of the outdoors.

We were brought up, as most children were in rural Ireland in those days, to regard the countryside as a place where men worked hard and left outside as soon as possible. I conceived a passionate desire to be a Boy Scout, again not number one social activity in deepest Tyrone in the fifties when October Devotions in the little chapel were the high spot of the Season. I wanted to be a Boy Scout partly because of the knife in the sock but mostly because I wanted to sleep out in the open. It seemed as magic a thing to me as, say, having wings. Night after night I lay in my bedroom with the window wide open listening to dogs bark at each other all along the lough shore and wishing I was out there with them in the dark.

Then when I left home the opportunities for al fresco sleepings shrank. In London the men I was with tended, naturally enough, to be more interested in bed than in sleeping outside; and as time ran on whenever I remembered the old craving it was raining or freezing or I was in Hammersmith; or whoever I was with had slept under the stars on the slopes of Kilimanjaro, in the sands of desert, or beneath the vast canopies of the Steppes and was not even vaguely interested in a little rural excursion.

And then last year, the most beautiful summer ever, day after day and night after night of balmy delicious weather, I finally saw that there was nothing to stop me. Why did I not do it? Years slipping by and such a simple but fierce ambition unfulfilled. It was reading that extraordinary poem by W. H. Auden that I quoted at the beginning that galvanized me.

I pretended, even to myself, that I was going to do it alone in some secret tryst with my untamed soul, but I also knew fine well that at the last minute my husband would join me. Now there's a man who *has* slept out. We're talking here of a man who drove a train from Rondônia to Bolivia and slept on the footplate; there's not a continent whose open skies he doesn't know. So he wasn't exactly palpitating with excitement. In fact, I knew the whole idea filled him with a kind of mild horror. But he divined that at three o'clock in the morning in the middle of my beloved field I might not be as brave as I was at six in the evening in a crowded house. So, being the man he is, he gathered his singing robes about him and came along. Sorry, read grizzling robes there.

The moon rose, the dew fell. I hadn't known about dew. I thought dew was a light misting, a little spangled dampness for the grass overnight, one of nature's kindnesses. Here is the interesting bit. The dew is a large, dripping, cold face flannel laid heavily along the surfaces of the night. It's a large wet eel that slithers down your orifices no matter how tucked away they be. Dew pressed wetly into the corners of my eyes. Dew soaked my hair. Dew ran in runnels into my ears. And the more the dew fell the more the dogs barked, partly to shake off the tidal wave of wetness and partly because the night was alive with noise. From every corner came moanings and whinings and breathings and sighings. Things nestled, pounced, fled, squealed, went silent. And every noise made the dogs madder with excitement.

Mona, the white bull terrier, barked the worst, and at one point so desperate did my husband become that he braved the de Borgia-scissoring effect of his camp bed, reached out, grabbed her and pushed her to the bottom of his sleeping bag, where she hung deep, like a large suspended sausage, over the bottom rail. (At least she was silent, though I thought that might well be from suffocation.) We didn't sleep. We lay like the stone couple in the poem, staring at the studded scudding sky above and listening to the cacophony. We were dripping wet and frozen. The clouds came over and hid the stars and a keen wind sprang up. At five o'clock the birds woke up and began their thunderous chorus. 'Are you awake?' I whispered. 'Awake?' he asked incredulously. 'Am I awake?'

I said, 'Maybe we should go home?' With one bound we had flung ourselves out of the manky sleeping bags.

Mona crawled up from the depths of her pit, well pleased with herself, and turned around and around in a white spinning circle while we shook ourselves and shivered and began the long trek home. From a neighbouring field I saw an early morning farmer watch us with his mouth opening and closing and then turn and run on his little stumpy legs to try to get Mrs Farmer out to share the fun before it had disappeared. I could have told him he had plenty of time. We could only walk very slowly, like old clockwork toys whose joints have rusted up.

But, all the same, it was worth it.

Now, in spring and summer, I sleep out in a perfect compromise; or campromise, as my daughter calls it. I bought a gypsy caravan (or van, or wagon, as I now know I must call it – *never* caravan) in Ireland, and a man from Castleblaney with a cigarette in his mouth and fearlessness in his blood hitched it on to a trolley and ferried it across the water and bowled along the motorways of England to bring it here, pursued by police whom he shook off without a bother on him. It is painted and decorated and has a pair of lanterns and a place for a bale of hay and I sleep out in it most summer nights, watching out from under the hooped canvas, dry and snug but in the open air, as the moon rises. The dogs sleep on the ledges and steps, and being above ground seems to mean they can relax and can stop barking. Occasionally. The sheep sleep underneath and shift and stir in the dark. The cuckoo calls sometimes, an amazing sound in the night, and the owl and the wood pigeon hoot and purl.

Sometimes the air is torn by a dreadful fight between two creatures and the dogs are instantly alert. So am I. It sounds like blue murder. But I go straight back to sleep. I have become so accustomed to these strange sounds of the night air that they accompany me into my dreams. I think before I sleep of that old lough shore and the little green tent and Maurice and John camping and my longing to join them and to watch the moon rising over the water and see it climb all night. And as I drift to sleep I remember those Larkin lines I couldn't remember on that first disastrous night *en plein air* when the man I love loved me enough to share the dew and my dreams (or, to be truthful, the lack of them):

   . . . and to prove
Our almost-instinct almost true;
What will survive of us is love.

The Stag
of the Stubble

Let us now think about the hare. I don't know why it's called the 'mad March hare', since you are far more likely to see one in April, the fool's month and none the worse for that. Not that you are likely to see one. Stand up all those who have seen a hare, really seen one. Do you know what an Irish hare looks like? It has a yellowy orange fur, a rusty look, rich as a fox, not glossy but reflective of many shades of light; the tail is fluffy and white both in summer and winter; the furry soles of the feet are brownish. So. Now let me tell you that your chances of seeing one are rapidly diminishing because hares are too. If you are lucky enough to remember them from a rural childhood, then treasure the memory. Soon, I think, that will be all we have and if the hare does disappear from our countryside, we are diminished. It is too important a chain in the links that bind us together and keep us alive to disappear without affecting us all.

The hare is an archetype, one of the original symbols that man has used to make peace or come to terms with and explain his mysterious and often frightening environment. It has a place in myth and in story all over the world, from the beginnings of memory. In a thirteenth-century poem from the Welsh borders, written as a ritual to be recited by the hunter on encountering a hare, there are seventy-seven names for the hare, including: the way-beater, the white-spotted one, the lurker in ditches, the filthy beast, the scutter, the fellow in the dew, the grass nibbler, old Goibert, the one who doesn't go straight home, the friendless one, the stag of the stubble, the cat of the wood . . .

In China, they talk about the hare in the moon, not the man in the moon; in India, Egypt, Africa, the hare is a symbol of potency; Native American Indians had the Great Hare of the Algonquin and, in Europe, the cult of the hare goddess is perhaps the origin of the association between hares and witches.

Hares are the most magic of creatures. It is not just about superstition and folklore, this magic associated with the hare; it is about the old role of animals as links between man and his gods, through dreams, through worship, through symbol. They are celebrated, vilified, revered and hated, feared and looked on with respect. I have always been filled with awe and horror at the idea of killing them and, at home in Ardboe, when I meet the man who I know kills them on the aerodrome, I will turn back before I will pass him. If I could, I would not have him live in the same parish. Such men carry with them the true odour of bad luck and ill omen.

This superstition of mine – if that is the word for my magic belief – goes back not just to the regard I have for the enchanted, wonderful animals I saw as I grew up beside that vast, unwanted aerodrome that had been slapped down on top of the parish, and where, on the unhedged prairies between the runways that once sheltered small farms, the hares coursed and gambolled; not just back to the fact that behind me as I walked the aerodrome came that man who trapped every hare he could find, trapped them most cruelly so that, as they died slowly, they screamed, as hares do, like a woman, or a baby. Then he brought parts of his horrible booty into Cookstown where the taxpayer paid him for every animal he slaughtered.

No, it goes back to something far more atavistic, back to prehistory and our collective unconscious, back to our wonder at the hare's strange behaviour and strange appearances, back to what unites us in dread and in joy, back to when we believed in sacrifices and woodland deities, back to immemorial symbols, to beliefs buried so deeply in the unconscious of the human race that now we shy away from the knowledge, decry it or disallow it, anything rather than know again how powerful myth is in our lives and how, by avoiding it, we are disturbing the planet we live on. The hare in its seasonal abandon and appearances is the stuff of dreams and nightmares.

In Ireland I have seen men turn back, unable to continue their journey, because a dead hare lay on their path and to cross it would mean bad luck and misfortune; a pregnant woman would break her heart if she saw one, because she was afraid her child would be born with a harelip.

They are enchanted creatures and I have found them enchanting ever since, as a child, I spent hours watching them – not for the sake of it but because I was searching for larks' nests, which were made in the same terrain as a hare chooses for its form or shallow burrow. I was a good and careful child and tried not to disturb sleeping animals and nesting birds, but the hare would uncrouch before I got near its form and watch me; that ovoid, umber shape would suddenly twist and leap and land many feet away in order to leave no scent from the paws, then it would bound long and high, spinning out across the field in a subtle curve, again to leave no constant line of scent. After it felt out immediate range of danger, it would sit bolt upright, reconnoitring, its paws clasped in front, then speed off again. The ears would stay erect until the hare reached top speed when they would flatten back and she (I can't call a hare *it*) was travelling at up to thirty-five miles an hour. The hare never took a short cut; she knew she might be up against a greyhound or lurcher who could outflank her; unlike the rabbit which scuttles towards the nearest covert, a hare will run with great force across the open field, feinting and swerving without losing speed. As she runs, she makes what are called 'pups', little marks and indentations where the pads hit the ground so that after she had gone, you could follow her course. In those days, I did not watch the hare run but would keep my eyes fixed on the place from which she had risen and, when I reached it, would lie down in the form. A hare lies with her back to the weather, sheltered by the best wall she can make or find, and, as she so lies, the grass or the heather takes on her shape. I cannot describe to you, only a poet could, what it was like to feel the warmth left behind, electric, soft, sluttish, crackling with velocity and energy.

Lying there, I would watch the lark rise. We all know about the lark but who has seen it surging upwards? No matter how high it rises from that astounding vertical take-off, it never disappears. I would watch it drilling its way up into the azure transparency when its notes fell like glazed shavings of blue sound and bounced off my ear. I can hear them still. Wordsworth said he had been sprung into poetry by hearing the sound of a walnut dropping; such sounds are not heard by many people now and I was blessed to hear them. The year after I did my eleven-plus exam, it was over. I never heard nor saw nature like that again. The noble savage went to the convent school.

Now the hares are disappearing, harried out of existence. It used to be that, at the international airport on the shores of Lough Neagh, up to seventy or eighty hares would course alongside the aeroplane as it landed or took off; you wouldn't see such a sight now. Not a one.

They are chased for sport, week in and week out. I have never met a person who enjoys coursing or a hunt who wasn't a moral dunderhead. Some go so far as to tell you, solemnly, that animals enjoy being hunted. What planet do such people live on? I watched priests, those erstwhile moral guardians, at coursing events, and saw their faces distended with pleasure at the cruelty, and knew that the following Sunday they would have the brass neck to preach moral behaviour to their flock. For flock read sheep.

I have two hundred acres of land which ten years ago harboured the hare – the hopper of ditches, the cropper of corn, the wee brown cow, the pair of leather horns – the little leverets and their long-eared parents. Now there are none. We do not shoot or hunt; we do not use fertilizers; there are no tractors; we do not make silage; we farm as land was farmed a hundred years ago, cropping with the seasons – yet I have not seen a hare in three years. An organization called Hare Watch in England reports they are disappearing fast. Yet, not long ago, a syndicate in West Suffolk shot eight thousand hares on an organized shoot. Some experts think that in certain parts of the country hares appear to have stopped breeding. Given up, I shouldn't wonder, traumatized out of existence.

I won't let the hunt harass foxes to death on our land, or close up their hides, so that when the exhausted and desperate animal gets to its haven, he finds it has been stopped up. No animal would do that to another animal. I'm vilified for it and at many a dinner party in the country where the guests suppose their fellow guests to be like-minded, I have found myself sitting next to someone who tells me with relish what Those Anti-Hunt People are really like and what he would like to do to them. I know he is both a good hater and an angry, frustrated and impotent man and that's partly what his lust to kill is about. The ejaculation of death.

Some time ago the newspapers published a photograph of the Queen holding a pheasant by its broken wing and clubbing it to death. Have you, reading this, ever looked at a pheasant? Its iridescent plumage, spectacular colours, sheer beauty? Have you ever seen a hen pheasant tending her young, clucking anxiously as they stagger across the field? And why was the Queen beating the bird to death? Well, my dears, to put it out of its misery. Oh, that's all right then. But why was it in misery, this exquisite wild creature? Her husband had shot it, but not very accurately, so it was dying slowly. So she took out the little club she carries for such a purpose and, merciful as she is, beat it to death. The people I was supping with were furious: furious with the spies, the cameras and the media yobs who would embarrass the Queen like that. But she comes from good stock. In 1913 her grandfather led a hunting party which killed 3,937 birds in one day. He also shot twenty-one tigers on a hunting trip to India. Her father, George VI, on almost his last shoot, had a haul of ninety pheasants, seventeen rabbits, two pigeons and three mallards. On 5 February 1952 he killed a hare at full speed. It is recorded that he especially enjoyed this last kill. Soon after he himself was dead.

One of the arguments put forward by those who get enjoyment from chasing animals to death is that dogs will naturally chase hares, that it is part of their nature. William Cowper, during one of his long periods of sanity (he suffered from manic depression), kept hares. They became his companions and hastened his recovery. He wrote most tenderly about them and kept them for ten years. 'There is no natural antipathy between dog and hare,' he wrote, 'the dog pursues because he is trained to it.' Cowper's hares and his dog 'ate bread at the same time out of the same hand and are in all respects sociable and friendly.'

The struggle towards animal rights is a long one and will be over (perhaps) only when our grandchildren are watching videos of how it used to be: hares in a meadow, badgers in a wood, all disappeared into nostalgia and heritage parks. We are all part of a living entity that is the earth; and we are going to have to stop treating other things on this planet as though they were objects for our use. We are killing them and in so doing, we are killing our poetry, our souls, our imagination and ourselves.

Rooks

'They'll start building their nests tomorrow,' he said, looking out of the window at the constellation of rooks, watching their undulations, sinking downwards and then sheering up, flapping, shifting, settling, swaying on the edges of the tall old trees around the house in which I grew up, the family house, like crepe decorations on Dracula's flophouse.

'Why tomorrow?' I said.

'It's the first of March,' he said, 'their anniversary, and they always start then, except if it's a Sunday. They won't start on a Sunday.'

He was the sanest of men except when he was dealing with folklore, superstition and charms. And now we're coming round to believing in what he believed in, what so many of his generation and generations before him, reeling back into history, believed in, before we got so clever and so cynical, the magic that has nearly been lost, of the cures and charms which were intrinsic and corporeal in our lives when we were children and are now so rare as to be almost vanished.

The Charm was a gift, an attribute for a particular form of healing often passed down from one member of a family to another and the custodian of such healing gifts often possessed a seer's vision, knowing in advance what form of cure someone needed before they had made a formal request. When I was a child in my country district, as many people went to have their own illness or that of an animal charmed away as went to a vet or a doctor – and all the many children with warts at school had them charmed off. (But then again who has warts now? No regrets there, which makes a change for me.)

I went out to look at what preparations the rooks were making for this vast new nesting operation on the morrow but they seemed as impudently relaxed as ever, apparently undriven by any biological urge other than to behave like the hooligans of the bird world, raucous, bullying, swaggering on the wing.

In fact they looked and sounded as they always do, handsome scoundrels, small-time gangsters, hanging around the street corners of the sky, giving any passer-by a hard time and the once-over, and making a real racket about it. The idea of them starting to build a cosy nest the next day seemed fairly improbable.

'You should always tell the rooks any news that has come into the house or has happened in the house, you go down to under the rookery and talk up at them. For to tell them.' Willie said. Willie knows all the folklore; if he gets stuck he makes it up.

'Surely you mean the bees?' I said. 'You tell the bees.'

'Not a hait of the crack,' he said. 'You wouldn't tell themens anything, they'd sting the face off you as soon as listen. It's rooks you tell; if you don't and then the thing happens they'll leave and build their rookery someplace else.'

I tried to think of some vast exciting piece of news I could withhold from them, to occasion the sulk and the exodus.

'Rooks have schools,' Willie said. 'There's times when they'll all be perched on the branches sitting and not a peep out of them and that's when they're teaching the young.'

If those are schools, I thought, then they were not unlike the schools I sometimes see released on London for a day's outing – anarchic, heaving swarms of pupils, with defeated teachers, trying to make themselves heard, lost in the muddle.

'They say that if they leave a house it's bad luck,' my father said.

'That's the honest truth,' Willie said. 'There's not a house they left that's not derelict.'

I did not say that, as is so often the case, philosophy can be made to fit the facts and vice versa, and the sad raw history of Ireland is tied up with folklore and superstition. Only big houses in that land-hungry country had the stands of trees, the plantations necessary to support a rookery. And since many of the big houses had since the Civil War in Ireland suffered neglect and depredation, or had been burned or fallen into ruins, and the rooks had been frightened off or starved out, the dereliction had very little to do with them either coming or going. But this was wisdom after the event so I kept my peace.

'I would miss them if they left,' my father said.

I thought how much I wouldn't. That incessant cawing that had punctuated my childhood; the way they ruined the trees, tearing at the branches, and the muddle of fallen sticks on the lawns; the endless circling shapes against the sky, the vast flurries when they all poured themselves upwards at some internal alarum, the early morning hacking chorus.

And I thought, too, of how quiet the place would be without them and how lonely, and how much my father loved and celebrated them as he loved and celebrated so much, seeing interest and amusement in things that left to myself I would only find irritating. He could always shift the world a little on its axis by the nudge of his humour.

I was going back to England and I was frightened and before I left I went down under the trees and told them that I had no news and didn't want any news; all I wanted was that he would see them build their nests for a little while longer.

'You were down with them all the same,' he said, when I came back in. 'What were you telling them?'

'Nothing,' I said.

He looked at me sharply. 'Do you remember what your mother used to recite . . . "I climbed a hill as light fell . . ." He hesitated.

'"As light fell short,"' I prompted, the tears about to trip me.

'"Short,"' he said, pleased.

'"Short . . . And rooks came home in scramble sort; and filled the trees and flapped and fought, and sang themselves to sleep." Scramble sort. Whoever wrote that had looked their fill at rooks all right.'

To cover the moment, I said, 'You couldn't exactly call it singing.'

'I do, daughter,' he said. 'It's singing to me. I'd hate not to hear them singing themselves to sleep.'

The next morning. as I drove away, along the road by the lough shore, I saw one rook and then another and another, a kind of disconnected rosary of black shapes, fly to the top of the trees with twigs and straws in their beaks to start their nests. It was the first of March and it wasn't a Sunday, and I knew he would be at the window smiling.

I went back again this year, on a different kind of anniversary, and there they were, busily about their nests as though nothing had happened. I went down to them, perched in their trees, and I told them and I told them too that there was no one left who thought their noise was singing and as I watched their great black wings rising in scramble sort, I remembered those lines from 'In Memoriam': 'The last red leaf is whirl'd away, / The rooks are blown about the skies . . .' and their colour matched my mourning.

The Shadow
of the Oak

If I had a wish . . . and a wish, if it is to be of any use, must be extravagant, impossible, beyond dreams. (What's the use of wishing to win the lottery? You might do that anyway.) If I had a wish, then, it would be that I could come back in sixty years, just for a little while, on a fine day and walk under the trees we planted instead of peering down at them in their pink canisters. Five years ago, we planted eight thousand oak saplings and I want to see them fully grown. A mature oak is one of the most beautiful of all plants, in its dark verdant leaf, its crisp shape spreading so widely from its low boughs, not to mention the totally satisfactory feel and shape of an acorn. In sixty years, if the planet still exists – and increasingly, it seems as if it won't – my forest will look as it looks now in our dreams, a lost demesne.

We are hopefully working for the future, to make something that should last for hundreds of years, and I'd rather write a great poem, a new 'Ode to the Nightingale' or 'To Autumn', but since I can't, I will go along with Joyce Kilmer, who thought he would never see a poem lovely as a tree. We are also doing it because if we don't, who will? Then there is the sheer joy and pleasure that come from doing something so palpable, so seeable. Perhaps there is something else.

The art historian and epitome of white privilege Lord Clark (of Civilization, as he was known) once wrote:

> There is a fear which seems to take possession of Western man connected with the millennium, and known to historians as Chiliasm . . . Can we escape from our fears by creating once again the image of an enclosed garden? It is a possible way of life: is it a possible basis for art? No. The artist may escape from battles and plagues but he cannot escape from an idea. The enclosed garden of the fifteenth century offered

shelter from many terrors but it was based on a living idea, that nature was friendly and harmonious. Science has taught us that nature is the reverse; and we shall not recover our confidence in her until we have learnt or forgotten infinitely more than we know at present.

Nature in England is benign, healing and harmonious – no earthquakes, tsunamis, no shaking of her angry core, and the natural response to our restoring and planting has been a revelation. Everything flourishes and dances, though when we planted the first oaks in what was to be the oak forest, our fields looked like a pink cemetery – filled with memorials to dead fairies or fallen ballet dancers, or some cult that only wore pink. I think that the man who invented these pink containers, which are in effect mini-greenhouses, worked for a county council and never made a penny out of them; yet he has revolutionized tree planting. Without them our trees would be about ten inches high now; instead they are bursting up out of their seams. If he had patented his discovery, he would surely be a multimillionaire, since they have been used ever since by every council, park planner and motorway planting company, indeed by everyone who plants trees in any quantity. The only drawback is their appearance, but that is temporary.

There is nothing that makes me rise up more than hearing someone say the best custodians of our land are farmers. I hear it on the radio often, politicians parrot it, when in reality many farmers are greedy to the bone and behave like psychopaths towards our planet, a part of which they are fortunate enough to own. Instead of cherishing, they wring it to death to get a penny more subsidy. They ruin the scape of the land; flatten features, plough out landmarks, fill up dew ponds, dig out the hedgerows, cut down trees and ill-treat their animals. They nitrate and fertilize with chemicals that have decimated insects and the irreplaceable bumble bee, spray wild flowers, mow hay in such a way the corncrake is practically extinct, the hare has nowhere to go and our children will never hear the lark. By the time they are finished, the land is bleeding: it may look green to you but that green field is a nitrated desert. I speak from empirical experience.

I grew up along the shores of Lough Neagh alongside a superb and unique merging of land and water. It is utterly changed. For an extra rood or two of land, a farmer has rendered it extinct – the shoreline has been levelled, every boulder removed, the sally trees where the fishermen hung their nets cut down, the sedge and rushes and yellow water iris killed and where once the water and the land slid in a silky little rush towards each other in a fringe of grass and rushes and brown boulders, now there is a stiff line of virulent nitrated green growth, broken only where the deep rut of the tractor has been driven to draw water for the cows that graze what was always common territory and now has been annexed, without a by your leave, by him. That lough shore, like our pasture here, lay like a palimpsest of years of continuous uninterrupted verdant life. Gone, gone, gone.

All of our fields in Somerset we bought from farmers and all save one had been ruined, and that one I saved only by prostrating myself in front of the tractor to stop the farmer who had suddenly decided to spread nitrates and fertilizer on an old pasture. Why was he doing it in such a hurry? Because he had heard the Nature Conservancy people were coming to have a look at it and perhaps put a protective order on it and he was going to nip that in the bud, heh. And why did he sell? Because I paid him well over the odds and he took me for a fool.

I wish I could describe this foolishness; it is a field of such beauty that people fall silent when they walk into it, suddenly aware, as I was when I first saw it, of what we have lost. Just as those we live with grow older so imperceptibly that we hardly notice the change, until suddenly we are confronted with an image out of our past and are forced into witnessing what has transpired, so older men and women who walk this meadow are the most moved; they stand silent, entranced, appalled, knee-deep in the tangled, pied, thick beauty of the fields of their childhood, realizing it has almost, elsewhere, vanished.

This meadow which we hold in trust and have covenanted so it can never be ploughed (or, in Orwell speak, 'improved') is now a Site of Special Scientific Interest. Until the Second World War (Dig for Victory) it was only one of tens of thousands of such fields in Somerset. Now there are only about ten left in the county. It is like a multicoloured medieval tapestry or the background to a Botticelli painting, striped, flecked, spangled and eyed like a peacock. You wade through swards of purple and spotted orchids, brush past silverweed, devil's-bit scabious, cornflowers, yellow vetchling, bird's-foot trefoil, knapweed, ox-eye daisy, betony, cowslips, dyers, greenweed, timothy, sedges, vernal grass, rushes, horsetails, thistles, clovers, saxifrage, through one hundred and thirty varieties growing in a prodigal muddle and realize that those great *millefleurs* tapestries of hounds and unicorns and ladies in their paradise of flowers were not a dream representation of some Utopia but an accurate account of what the artist saw around him. And the noise! A million flying butterflies, grasshoppers, ladybirds, moths and insects, whirring away like a miniature busy airport of an evening.

Every so often we acquire another stretch of farmed dead land and start in: we know the finished picture in our imagination, and slowly we are bringing them back to organic life. We use manure from organically fed animals. When we bought in farm manure it had to be kept at the side of a field for two years to lose its toxicity. God alone knows what effect the flesh of the unfortunate beasts from whom this poisoned manure came has had on those who eat it. Every year we gather the seed from the pasture field, till another field, and spread the seed; every year more flowers grow. I won't see the end results – my lifetime isn't long enough. But future generations, if there are any, will wake within its leafy bounds and revel in it. Or so I hope.

Sometimes when I am in a despairing rage about what has happened in my lifetime (avoiding the burnt-out zones of Hiroshima, the Holocaust), and think long on the disappearing hare, the almost extinct corncrake, the increasingly rare cuckoo, the silence of the larks, I calm myself by rehearsing what we are doing. Very little, but something; about the big things we can do nothing except remember daily. The small things have big statistics and when I recite them, an unholy peace descends. Eight thousand trees, 1,800 tons of hard core, 1,000 tons of top soil, two dams (little dams, but dams), four JCBs (to restore the dew ponds the farmers ploughed over and to make paths through the forest that still lives in its little pink boxes). The JCBs wallow like yellow hippos, shifting mud around in the boggy little valleys, scooping out what I call lakes, my husband calls ponds and our daughters call lakettes.

Three delightful airy bridges, with the gossamer look of a half-finished spider's web, span these lakes and were commissioned from Richard La Trobe-Bateman, a brilliant furniture designer and engineer who started building bridges after he was asked to design a high table for an Oxford college. The problem was how to make a long table for all the many Fellows, their wives and guests without having to incorporate extra supports along the sides. When he had most elegantly solved the problem, he found he had in effect built a wonderful cantilevered bridge and after that there was no stopping him.

Our bridges are a vibrant mix of oak planks, wishful thinking and a slight edge of danger. The dogs run across them without thinking and I, too confident, amble across and some day will fall in; first-timers take a deep breath and walk gingerly, arms outstretched like Houdini. These lakettes and bridges fringe the new forest in the centre of which stands an urn. More statistics, gentle readers. Carved 1740; twelve foot high; two tons in weight; sold out of a great garden by a vandal who should have known better, but it was an ill wind. I now have healthy respect for people who build monuments on soil – the underpinnings are tremendous.

When we dug the pit for ours it had to be deep and filled with cement and hard core, and one evening I went down when the workmen had smoothed over almost the last layer of cement before the actual pedestals were laid; it was just hardening and irresistible and, with a pointy stick, I wrote: 'A & P caused this to be laid on 10 October 1990'. When I went down the next day, the last layer of cement bore the legend 'R G, mason, laid this on 11 October 1990'. The urn stands high, baroque, magnificent, dominating the little trees in what one day will be an encircling oak grove.

By building an enclosed and enchanted garden, though perhaps I cannot escape my fears, I can do what that great poet John Clare did nearly two hundred years ago, 'see the hawk hang in the summer sky, the kite make its circles above the wood, hear the wood pigeons clapping their wings among the oaks, hunt curious flowers in rapture and mutter thoughts in their praise.' And I can ally myself with poets and artists in this work and say, post-Hiroshima, 'I believe in the shadow of the oak.'

All the same, I would like to be granted my wish and live long enough to walk, just once on a sunny day, across our bridges over the now-fringed lakes and down the paths under a canopy of leaves to find the urn in its hidden grove, its perfect proportions in perfect harmony with the spreading trees.

Dublin Opinion

She said: 'Mum? When someone in Dublin says they're not a bit annoyed, not in the least, does that mean they're very annoyed?'

'Who's been saying it?'

'It doesn't matter. I just wanted to know the meaning.'

'The meaning depends on who said it,' I said, 'when they said it, why they said it and were they sober?'

'I dunno,' she said. 'But he seemed a bit annoyed before he fell over; what does stocious mean?'

'It means he was very cross indeed,' I said, 'and very drunk. Where were you when this happened?'

I was the more curious because, contrary to myth, manifestations of drunkenness in Dublin seem rarer than in London, say, although perhaps I lead a sheltered life here, officher. I do remember after a rugby match at Lansdowne Road Stadium one far-gone man with Rastafarian locks climbing contentedly enough into my skip on the assumption perhaps that it was his bed, or his car; I didn't enquire as to his thought processes but warned that it was not a good resting place if only because my neighbour John might at any moment retrieve him from the skip and hoard him in the cellar without much noticing. John and I could vie about skips but I know he would always win; he is a more obdurate elaborate committed obsessive hoarder than I am. I am dazzled by his retrieval skills; he is a maestro in the art of assemblage. He has even been known to salvage things out of my skip. Jeananne said the other day, 'I see John has sent Alix and the children away and has ordered a skip in their place; it won't last.'

Oh, Dubliners can be very droll.

This is my fourth skip. The man who delivers them is one of the most beautiful creatures I have ever clapped eyes on and has no absolutely no idea of his own beauty. He puts huge gloves on to clamp the chains and hooks into the side of the skip, lowers the great erect pulley, and lifts the whole big filled-up affair into the air – no wonder my little heart goes pit-a-pat.

How *could* this much rubbish come out of a small garden some 35 yards long and 15 feet wide? This fourth skip is not by any means the last. It is said (probably with truth) that one of the things that distinguishes our age from earlier ages is the amount of rubbish we have and make and buy and throw away; yet over the centuries my little front garden obviously became a depository for everything under the sun – as well as the Leisure Centre and Public Convenience for the local cats, who are put out (to say the least) to find that their territory has been taken over by black plastic bags, flowers, paving stones, cleaner-uppers and, worst of all, those she-creatures of the Devil, DOGS. They can't believe that such dogs as mine are allowed to exist and are in residence Next Door. The cats, frustrated, slink along the new Stalag fence, turning and twisting and dabbing at the wire mesh, determined to mark their boundaries (aka my garden), especially one huge scarred patriarch with a single greeny-yellow eye who puts me in mind of that poem which half-cut men would intone, tears in their eyes, in manys a pub of an evening: 'There's a one-eyed yellow idol to the north of Kathmandu . . . there's a little marble cross below the town, there's a broken-hearted woman tends the grave of mad Carew and the Yellow God forever gazes down.'

There's nothing that this big bad green-eyed cat would like to see more than a little marble cross bearing the names Pester and Kafka which Lulu and Yum-Yum have been rechristened as being better fitted to their characters. This huge tawny feral creaturecat and its partner have been rechristened Spoor and Spray by me, SS for short, and they teeter on the posts of the fence while Pester and Kafka keep constant vigilance willing these Don Corleones of the cat mafia to fall, arse over tit, into our garden, so they can savage them to cruel tattered death. They forget that when the cats did trapeze down to make their mark the dogs were well drubbed and came limping in, hair on end, noses bleeding, eyes popping, dribbling and yowling, to howl their defiance from the window. Watching them gibber and squeak I pondered on how anyone can buy into the deal that dogs are clever and can suss out what we are saying. If they had even a modicum of brain they would surely have intuited, after living with us for tens of thousands of years, that we don't want their great paw marks all over our yellow silk upholstered sofas. Talk about dumb friends. That UR-woman in the grass skirt who screeched 'Get off the bleedin' yak skin' has her descendant in me, but the dogs are still all over the furniture, shaking themselves dry and paddling wetly and adroitly across a clean floor wagging their tails at the Burglars with great, pleased grins on their goofy faces.

I leave the cats and the dogs and go for a walk and peer at a lovely chair in a shop window in Lower Pembroke Street, and a small sharp-faced, bespectacled man in the shop sees me admiring the chair and invites me to cross the mews to his wonderful workroom. I fall upon a tremendous elaborate gilt mirror, all harps and shamrocks and needing restoration and he says, amused by my curiosity and covetousness, 'You can have it for £150,000.' Perhaps not today, I say.

Looking at his glinty, intelligent face, his assurance, his shyness, I was reminded of *Dublin Opinion*, the humorous magazine which, when I was a child, gave me an idea of Dublin as the City of Laughter; it was a place populated by artful creatures, gamblers, would-be gents, dim-witted Anglo-Irish all intent on holding their own against certain citizens, i.e. Dubliners, who would always get the better of them simply by being cleverer and wittier and more worldly.

This was a man from its pages and within two minutes of conversation I could see he was a perfectionist about furniture. I told him about my Irish Regency sofa and its bad, mad legs and how I couldn't live with it any more. All I could see as soon as I opened the front door were its cabriole legs where they should be sabre.

'I can't go on,' I sobbed.

'You must,' he said, unmoved.

'*You* could change them,' I said, all artful.

'I could indeed,' he said, 'but I won't.'

I tried a different tack to lull him. 'Is that lime wood that mirror is made out of?'

He looked at me with more interest.

A voice behind said, 'It wouldn't be lime wood; lime is such a lovely wood it would never have been painted over.'

It was the voice of authority. The Knight of Glin, possibly the most knowledgeable men in all the world about Irish furniture and paintings, was peering at the wood. We kissed, mmmm, mmmm, air kisses, and the furniture man looked on fairly indulgently at such nonsense.

I said, 'I'm telling Mr Mitchell about my sofa, how I can't live with it.'

'And I'm after telling her she has to,' he said.

'I can't,' I said.

'She's right,' Desmond said. 'It's a mess. You go round, Tommy, and tell her what she's got to do.'

'The only problem,' I said, 'apart of course from the legs, is that it's beautifully upholstered.'

I did not say the yellow watered silk had cost a fortune, even with getting it wholesale through my friend Judy, but they both knew the subtext.

'I wouldn't touch it if it's upholstered,' Tommy said.

'You might be able to save some of the upholstery,' Desmond said.

'I wouldn't know about that,' he said, 'but I'll go round and see it on Monday.'

On the Saturday morning I went to Michael Conlon, one of the best dealers in Dublin, and certainly the most laconic. 'Don't go scratching any surfaces with your handbag,' he said. As I mentioned, they can very droll. Michael's furniture isn't scratchable; shabby chic isn't in it; it's scratched, scored and jagged, but the point is that the furniture he finds with his fine eye has seen better days and will again. Then my new friend Tommy Mitchell walked in.

'The sofa woman,' he said. 'She gets around.'

'She does,' Michael said.

'He's coming to look at that sofa,' I said.

Michael looked gloomy. 'The Legs the Legs,' he said.

'I've heard tell,' Tommy said, 'and I have my doubts. I'm not promising anything but I'm having a look on Monday. 12 noon.'

On Monday I was redd up and so was the house, waiting for Tommy, Mr Mitchell. The cats were stuck on the points of their posts, the dogs were dribbling at the window. 12:00; 1.00; 1.15; 1.16. No sign. And such a nice, precise man. I telephoned the shop and said in that irritated, righteous voice that only those who are habitually late themselves have at the ready, 'I believe that Mr Mitchell had an appointment with me at 12.45.' There was an awful silence. The voice said, 'I'm sorry to have to tell you that Mr Mitchell died today.' Time stands still at these moments and your priorities change. I sat on the sofa and grieved. I'd known him for about a day altogether, but I knew I'd met a man of great quality.

Later that day Mort came round to do the hundred horrid little jobs that seem to live in the corners of every house and creep out when you're not looking. When he was marking out where to hang the smart new magnifying mirror (why, *why*, I hear you cry) and pulling it in and out I saw him suddenly recoil. 'Maybe I should try it the other way around,' he said.

I held it in place for him as he pencilled in where the screws should go, and looking into its masochistic depths saw an appalling mad-eyed hairy image zooming out at me. No wonder Mort recoiled. I've bought a mirror that makes anyone who looks into it look like Corleone, the cat next door. Mort's full name is Mortimer, after the great Irish soldier, and it is perhaps the most exotic name of a Dublin man I've ever heard. You hear parents calling their children Gary, Lorcan, Jason, even Orlando for heaven's sake, or Fedlimid and Cuchulainn for all I know. (Incidentally, Standish O'Grady said that if he had known how to pronounce Cuchulainn or had heard it said, he would have interpreted the Irish Sagas in a different way. Apparently, he pronounced it Kuku lane. It comes of being called Standish. But then again, my mother, all her life, when she wanted a sofa covered would set off for the youfolsterers. You can *see* the psychological significance of the yellow sofa now, surely?)

It was pissing down rain, cats and dogs and cold.

'It used to be,' I said bitterly, 'that you could depend on a bit of spring in May. Now you can't; the whole climate has changed.'

Mort said, 'It's supposed to all be down to the . . .' He hesitated.

'The greenhouse effect?' I said.

'No, the Bible says . . . the end of the world . . . season will meet with season.' He smiled. 'I wouldn't mind,' he said. 'I'd rather we all went, all together.'

'I'd rather go out on my own,' I said, 'leaving people behind crazed with grief. But until then I wish I didn't have to go out at all, especially in this weather. Imagine that going to the shops for a pint of milk in May means you have to dress as if you were going on fishing excursion in November.'

I spend so much of my time whining and moaning as a comforting sort of background noise that it never occurred to me that Mort was listening. When he was leaving I suggested he borrowed an umbrella and he looked downright alarmed. My dad was the same. Maybe some atavistic memory of the first days of umbrella-users in Europe when they were stoned as children of the Snail Devil. The Irish have long memories. I think it was Terence de Vere White, that lovely man, who said that when an Irishman sees a leaking tap his mind hops back to the Flood. 'It's going to be like this all day,' Mort said, 'So I'll make a run for it.' He was soaked before he got to the bottom of the steps.

I went back to my interesting job of scratching the sticky label off a Chinese cabinet with a jagged fingernail. Why will most antique dealers use them? When creating an effect of Instant Heritage sticky labels are not a Good Thing; indeed, one might end up being like someone who bought all his own furniture, a remark made by Alan Clark in his memoirs, about Michael Heseltine, and surely one of the sublime moments of English snobbery.

The doorbell rang and Pester and Kafka hurled themselves out to where Mort, thoroughly soaked, was holding out a carton of milk. 'To save you going,' he said. 'No point to the two of us getting wet.' It happened in Dublin.

When the rain finally stopped I went around to Michael Conlon's, where you never see a sticky label, and bought two round granite balls, with carved straps. They were extremely large and heavy and by the time the men who delivered had rolled them into the garden they were exhausted. In the time lapse between the fourth and fifth skip the spheres became covered with more rubbish from the excavated garden and I asked the council dustmen would they take the rubbish away (don't ask if money changed hands). I saw from my window that they were helpfully attempting to drag the balls away as well, so I flung open the casement, stuck my head out like Barbara Frietchie and shouted, 'The balls, the balls, leave the balls, don't touch the balls.' 'Thank god for that,' a dustman shouted back. 'They're lovely balls but they could do you a mischief.'

An old lady was hurrying past. I remembered Bay's question: 'When someone in Dublin says they're not a bit annoyed, not in the least, does that mean they're very annoyed?' I wanted to show her what annoyed looked like, but by the time I found her the old woman had hurried out of sight, the dustmen had gone and only the feline yellow idol sat on the fence post, dreaming of two dead dogs and an empty garden.

Et in Arcadia Ego

The most beautiful interiors in the world can be the place in your mind's eye and mine is a sacred grove and it is to that spirit-place that I return most often in the inward eye that is the bliss of rare solitude.

It was the summer of 1996 and there's hardly ever been a summer like it except maybe 1976. High, blue skies, sharp-edged cerulean in the morning, a dazzle at noon and in the evening long, long shadows. I was staying in a castle on the very edge of Clew Bay in Mayo. There are supposed to be 365 islands dotted around that exquisite inlet and when you looked out of the windows of the castle you looked straight down on jagged rocks below. You could easily have dashed yourself on to them, no bother.

A small rough jetty led far enough out from the rocks to be able to dive into topaz water at high tide. When the tide withdrew, stealthily, soundlessly, innumerable small islands appeared in the distance with channels gleaming between long swards of sand.

On one of the bigger islands stood a ruin with a sacred look, an ancient oratory perhaps, and one morning at low tide I set out to walk across the sands to explore it. The bay was deserted. Anywhere else in the world such an astonishingly beautiful place would be crammed with gin-palace yachts and tourists, but the only things moving here were cows grazing on an island in the distance; apparently, they crossed to the island through quite deep water without turning a hair.

What made this day such a visionary one was the quality of the light. The limned colours all around made me look at everything as though I had never seen it before, like the flash of a kingfisher writ large, shocking sight into awareness. The light sculpted land, sand, sky, sea into a singing harmony. The sun emphasized colour and form rather than draining it, as vivid light often does. As the sun rose higher all became gilded. I walked as in a dream towards the isle with the abbey ruins but before I reached it I came upon a smaller island, a small hillock really, rising gently out of the water, the verdant grass all over it as close and smooth as any tended lawn. Even under the old gnarled trees it was a tight shimmering emerald. Furled ferns and ivies grew down to the shoreline and the whole was criss-crossed with the bleached trunks of trees lying like an informal trellis among large blanched and lichened boulders: the most beautiful natural garden I have ever seen.

As I drew nearer the reason for the groomed condition of the grass became apparent. The blanched boulders were sheep taking their serene ease in dark hollows in the shade of a grove. Some were busy about their grazing and as I approached looked at me mildly but did not move away.

I lay down near the exposed great roots of a tree, under the shade of its branches. To the right the trunks of two old trees had collided with each other as they fell, and the gothic arch they formed framed the ruined monument on the next island which had been my destination.

There were no sounds other than the sound of the sheep cropping; no insects; no human voice; and, oddly enough, no birdsong. At some point I lost consciousness of where I actually was and of time, but I was not asleep and I came to the idea that I was in a nether world and that by some miracle I had entered a Sacred Grove.

In ancient Greece the Sacred Grove was a place of contact between the divine and human worlds, a place of divination where the divine will was communicated to humans. Such groves are intrinsic to the idea of the Golden Age and most of the gods and goddesses had one dedicated to him or her. Homer writes of them as being the headquarters of religious worship, with an altar surrounded by shady trees and often with a spring nearby; certainly my tree-arch looked like the entrance to an altar and the sheep did well enough as votaries. There were mystery cults associated with Sacred Groves and rituals celebrated within them to do with fecundity, birth and death; and the Sacred Grove was sometimes seen as a twilight world between the upper world and the lower, a place where the soul might start its suffering journey in search of the revelation.

There was no excavation of my unconscious as I lay, which is the usual course of my downwards quest to the book of unknown signs that lie within us all, no direct request to the oracle that can, if it so pleases, tell me what is wrong, or what is up, or even what to do. But something happened, a shift in my perception, and I had my revelation that day in that heavenly garden in the Irish sun.

I would like to have lived by what I learned there about the world and its glories but, really, I am resistant to change and old habits die hard. Nothing eventful happened to me in terms of the material world. I rose from Arcadia as the tide began to rise and walked home through deeper water and a gathering dusk.

But the experience altered my life and I have tried to abide by what I learned, which included an apprehension of the meaning of Keats's great poetic dictum: beauty is truth, truth beauty.

A Christmas Miracle

I know what I'm getting for Christmas because I've already got it. Standing about four inches off the ground, and bat-eared, it looks a little like a tiny Chinese pagoda, and, if it has a mind to, responds to the name Loulou. It is my fourth dog – I mean I have four all at the same time. Don't even ask. My husband, god love him, says the only reason he married me was that I didn't like dogs. And now that even this reason is gone, he can't get away. I've trained Mona, the bull terrier, to tackle and pin him down if he makes even the slightest dash for freedom.

My third dog, Flossie, lugubrious and pessimistic as befits a dog from Yorkshire, reminds me of the Yorkshire man who, when asked how he had enjoyed the sights of Blackpool, said, 'It were all reet if tha' likes laughin'.' And what about Yum-Yum? I hear you cry. She has one eye and a broken tail and indeed I sometimes think if you melted all four dogs down you might get one complete dog. Might.

But all of this is mere preliminary to the Christmas miracle that happened to me and Loulou; it is also, I am sorry to say, tabloid testimony to a saint's sleaze. Indeed, St Anthony, the patron saint of lost things, could be a member of the Conservative government without any bother on him. The manifestation of the miracle started simply enough, on an ordinary day a week before Christmas.

I drove up one of the busiest streets in London, found a parking space (a miracle in itself) and took the dogs for a walk in the park and after they had pretended to kill all the squirrels, and I had scooped up their little offerings, we all headed back to the car and the dogs reluctantly heaved themselves in. I spotted Lorenza, weary after her day's work, carrying heavy bags. 'I'll give you a lift,' I said and the dogs began hurling abuse and flinging themselves about in the way they apparently must when they see any mortal being approaching the car doors. I told her to just sit down hard on all three – they soon get out of the way, except Loulou, who's like a mushroom and can push her way up through flagstones. So Lorenza sat down on them and as she did so said casually, 'Not as bad as usual; only two today.'

'No, three,' I said, 'three; I left Mona at home, but the others are all in here somewhere – Loulou, Yum-Yum, Flossie.'

'Polly,' she said, 'there are two dogs in the car.'

My heart stopped. 'Loulou?' I said. And then, my voice rising, 'Loulou?' She wasn't in the car. Six months old, a bundle of black and white, loving, idiotic, greeting everyone, endearing, ridiculous, with no idea about traffic and no name tag on her collar, no idea about anything, and she's not in the car. It meant that, if she had hopped out without me noticing, she'd be in one of the busiest, most dangerous streets in London.

At first I didn't panic, or, more accurately, my panic was so deep I was frozen into calm. Now I must say here that, if you are neither a dog owner nor a dog lover, you won't understand my terror. If you are, you will. Lorenza and I fanned out and called and ran about but it was hopeless – a thousand cars, a thousand people, a maze of streets, half-dark. People hurrying and nowhere for a little dog, never before separated from friends and family, to go for refuge. As I called and searched, getting more desperate, the bustling crowds and anonymous faces separated into individual kind people who stopped in their hurryings and helped in the search. The English really do love dogs.

By now all I could think was that if Loulou did survive, she would never again hear her own name.

I went back up towards the park but the gates were shut and I remembered my mother declaring that St Anthony was the greatest capitalist in heaven and the easiest to buy. 'Promise him money,' she said, 'and he's yours.' So I, from some atavistic hidden recess of my mind, or perhaps my soul, and I an adamant humanist, implored St Anthony in words I hadn't said in many decades to find Loulou. And I must suppose that I prayed, although it sounded to me curiously like a bribe.

I hunted on and finally, both hope and Lorenza gone, I began my miserable drive home. The other two dogs knew something was wrong. Yum-Yum huddled in the back seat. Flossie, of course, was in high good spirits. Life was just to her taste.

I took a different route home and there on Holland Park Avenue, picked out by the lights of the car, stood a tall man, isolated, on the side of the street, the rush hour traffic almost brushing him, and in his arms, Loulou . . .

I stopped the car beside him and he mouthed through the window, 'Is she yours?'

I put my head on the steering wheel and began to cry.

He opened the car door. 'I can see she is,' he said. 'I saw her in t'road and thought yon's a loved dog. I reckoned someone would be back, looking for her, no doubt breaking their heart, an' I were right.'

Loulou climbed on to my lap. Except for her little tongue licking my hand, she was rigid.

'She hasn't moved a muscle since I picked her up,' he said. 'And mind, she weren't an easy dog to pick up. She were right frightened. And there were a lady who wanted to take her home. She reckoned she were an abandoned dog. But I knew the dog were lost. I've always been a dog man myself.'

Where do you start asking a man about what motivates him to stand for two hours in the same blessed spot on a busy street in a city to wait and wait as the evening lengthens and darkens because he reckons the owner of a small, frightened, lost dog is out there somewhere, searching and calling? How do you start to thank him? You know you've come across a miracle and that the spirit of that other manger – not the one with the dog in it – but the one that makes Christmas what it is, still lives on.

You've met St Anthony in the flesh, down-to-earth, and what's so marvellous is that he's so down-to-earth easy to thank. You keep your side of the bargain as he has kept his and you simply pay up. The parish priest is still smiling and so, dear reader, am I. So – a Happy Christmas from Loulou and me and Mona and Yum-Yum. Flossie says: No Comment.

Thank You for Your Custom

She was off to Paris the next morning on a school trip and she was walking up the stairs well ahead of me and I was going after her, like a terrier after a bone, because I knew she'd borrowed my hairbrush, the only one that works on my hair, and she was denying it but laughing in that way that means 'I'm lying, Mum, but so what.' I love her and her nose ring and her vocabulary. When someone behaves really, really badly, so that I'm speechless at their manners, she says sweetly, 'That was well rude,' and I am calmed. She discovers three pieces of rotting chicken that Flossie, my neurotic Yorkshire terrier, has buried in her room against some famine day and as the smell hits her she says, amiably, 'Rrrank out.' I know a whole code of words and ciphers to do with her generation, but they change all the time, rather like the music she listens to, mooning, round-eyed, ears clamped with wires like something out of a 1950s sci-fi movie, and where she used to follow me home now I'm always a step behind her.

She was turning the top of the stairs, foot poised for escape, when I saw an odd flash. She moved. I saw it again. 'What's that on the soles of your feet?' 'Nothing,' she said. The only time she says nothing is when it's something in spades. The house is rocking, the roof is lifting, because she has forty friends raving away in her room. 'What are you doing up there?' 'Nothing.' She has dropped a tray with six glasses, four tin plates and a steel bucket. 'What fell?' 'Nothing.'

So, naturally, I made her show me the nothing on her feet. There were two huge holes in the soles. You could see the callouses on her skin through them. I was horrified. No mother who is even halfway at home in her head ever supposes that a child, any child, will mention that a garment, shoe, object needs mending. Maintenance in a family is sheer luck, intuition and a pathetic gallant attempt to make and keep appointments. You fix up the dentist's appointment a month from today, the earliest he can fit you in, and you always remember on the evening of the day you were meant to go. So I knew there was no point to scolding – not that that's ever stopped me – but what did puzzle me was why was she wearing these boots at all, since I knew she'd bought new ones in a smart shop just days before.

'Why aren't you wearing the new ones?' I cried, starting back. She looked shifty. 'They're not comfortable.'

'You're not proposing to wear these to Paris?' I asked. (Rhetoric becomes a weapon in families.) 'You couldn't. You'll walk miles in Paris, and you'll do your feet a terrible injury. What's wrong with the new ones?' I was getting quite fretful.

'OK, I'll take the new ones to Paris,' she said. It was her fast capitulation that made me nervy, suspicious. Normally it's skirmishes in the foothills and bodies on the mountain before she gives in.

'Well, then, why aren't you wearing them now?'

'I like these ones. They fit my feet.'

'But they're ruining them.'

'My feet are used to them. They're hard where's the holes.'

'But you paid a fortune for those boots – show me them.'

'Oh, Mum.'

It's the long-drawn-out wail of true despair. I know I've hit pay dirt. There is something wrong with the boots, and she doesn't want me to know because she thinks, quite rightly, that I will make a fuss. We find the boots in her room. That one sentence could be expanded into a prose poem on how we found them, under what we found them, where we found them, and indeed one by Theodore Roethke springs to mind when I creep into her room to do a cull: '. . . the little/Sleepers, numb nudgers in cold dimensions,/Beetles in caves, newts, stone-deaf fishes'. (Not that she's a zoologist, you understand: this is just how her room looks.)

I stared at the boots with rising anger: both heel mounts had collapsed, so that she couldn't even begin to get her feet in. She had saved for months, she had worn them three or four times and they were utterly useless.

'We'll bring them back to have them changed,' I said. 'This is a reputable company. Have you got your receipt?'

I knew the answer. Did you ever keep a receipt in your life before you were about one hundred years old? I could rehearse the scenario: the bland faces of the sales people; their refusal to take the boots back without a receipt, even though they were manifestly almost brand new, soles unscuffed, brand name blazoned all over the insteps. I couldn't face it, and so I phoned their head office and explained the situation. The woman there professed surprise that I might anticipate trouble even without a receipt and said she could guarantee I would have no trouble. So I cleaned myself up nice, found (oh, joy!) their original bag, routed out my daughter from the back of her cave and set out, eyes glittering, for the big, dark, chic shop near Sloane Square.

Inside, a few women were trying on shoes or staring hopelessly ahead, waiting for service. At the back, on a kind of dais where stood the gleaming counter and the paraphernalia of the computers and pay machines, two saleswomen watched us approach – and though I tried to suss out as I got closer who had the more sympathetic body language, it was like gauging which of the harpies would soften first. (You will recall that the harpies are a representation of the evil harmonies of cosmic energies.) I knew my daughter, hovering near my shoulder, was anxious that I shouldn't, at all costs, make a scene. (It's odd that almost the worst possible scenario for one's children is to say anything to anyone that isn't utterly placatory and mild. 'Oh dear, look, you've crashed into my car, but never mind,' is the ideal reaction to the lunatic who has pranged your car from behind when your children are with you.)

I explained to the nearest saleswoman about my call to head office, blah, blah, blah, and she said she should check with the manager. My heart sank. And when he came, nosing and blinking his way out of his little nest at the back, it sank even further: a sandy, ferrety creature he was, with sharp teeth showing in a sharp smile, and I comprehended when I saw him that I had already lost; this was not a magnanimous man, nor a helpful man; he looked like someone who got his jollies from wielding his tiny piece of power triumphantly.

I explained my case. He stared at me, enjoying my discomfiture, my daughter's unease, and sidestepped the issue of the receipt completely.

'I'll have to send them back to the factory for analysis, Madam,' he said.

'Well, do,' I said. 'But my daughter is going away tomorrow and she needs replacement boots today.'

'I don't think Madam heard,' he said. 'They have to go back to the factory to see what's wrong.'

'But I'm not interested in what's wrong,' I said, 'though I quite see why you are, faced with workmanship like this. We just need another pair of boots.'

'We can't give you another pair until we see what's wrong with these ones,' he said.

'But what does it matter what's wrong to me, the customer?' I said, trying not to sound like Mrs Gummidge. 'You find out, by all means, but we need boots that work; and these are the ones we've paid for.'

'I don't think Madam is hearing what I said,' he said, pointing his little teeth at me.

What did he think I was doing? Sitting like rhubarb under a bucket? But I knew I was defeated. He wasn't going to replace the boots: the best thing was to leave with my dignity intact, just cut my losses. So I said, politely, in order to keep everything low key because something feral and ominous was happening in my body: 'Fine. As soon as you find out can you send me a letter and a refund please?'

I put the boots on the counter, and as he bent down to take my name and address he did a foolish thing. He smiled a sly little smile of triumph to the assistant who had summoned him up from his lair.

Now I digress a little here to remind the reader that in Ireland the Devlins were known as the Hatchet Men for good reasons. Or maybe not so good. That old breeding lies dormant in our veins, but it's like a bullet in an unfired gun. Touch the trigger and there's trouble. Fortunately, the trigger is quite hard to get at and has been fairly swaddled by the restraint of civilized living. But his smile, his meanness, his way of dealing with me, as no doubt he dealt with many of the women who gave him his living, didn't just touch the trigger, it pulled it hard.

Before I even knew I'd moved, I'd lifted the computer monitor. It was attached to cables and power points and as I threw it a lot of debris followed in its wake. As it hit the glass display cases its interior exploded.

The harpies began to scream, the manager shouted, 'The police, get the police.'

So I lifted the phone and threw it at him. Then, still on the incandescent dynamic energy that rage of this calamitous nature brings, I reached the credit card terminal and threw it too and, finally, like Samson with the pillars, I pushed the cash register off the counter. It hung piteous and screaming.

'Give me back the boots,' I said to the manager. In a moment of spontaneous ordinary emotion, such, I would hazard, as he hadn't allowed himself for years, his little watery eyes blazed and he threw – nay, hurled – the boots at me. I caught them, one in each hand, and my daughter and I walked out of the shop. Then we legged it as fast as we could down the street and round the corner. She was smiling.

'That was well rude, Mum,' she said. 'I should think you done his head in.'

Why Are There No Great Women Artists? Give Me a Break!

She said, 'I've got this essay to write in a hurry, "Why are there are no great women artists?" Do you know why, Mum?'

Now we have to be careful here, no use rolling on the carpet, spitting tacks and biting dust and getting pointy teeth because the indoctrination is continuous, no use yclepting names and screaming blue murder about how we wuz robbed. I did all of this anyway while she watched and listened, unmoved, having seen it all before, and she then said, 'I have to do it quickly, so will you help me?'

'When do you need it for?' I asked.

'Tomorrow,' she said.

'They can't expect you to do an essay like this in that time,' I said. 'This needs thought and research and talking through.'

'No, it just needs remembering, Mum,' she said. 'You're always going on about it, I just can't remember it all. Anyway, they gave me the title a while ago.'

'How long ago?' I asked.

'Last term,' she said, all innocence. 'So will you help me or not?'

'NOT,' I said. 'Go and remember. And,' I called after her, 'examine who asked the question and why it has been asked.'

She came back later. 'It's an aggressive question,' she said. 'My tutor told me that a bloke called Wittgenstein said that a question which was not a true question could not be asked, and this isn't a true question. It's not a question at all.'

'It's asked all the time, though,' I said.

'Yes,' she said, 'but it's a well hostile statement; and its aggression lies in it pretending to be fact. There *are* great women artists and their work is there to be seen. So the question really should be why is it not recognized?'

'That's my girl,' I said fondly. I were fair blushing with pride. 'So what's the answer?'

'I dunno,' she said.

'Go you to your tutor,' I said, 'and tell her you need more time. And then get down to this essay; it's Important.'

Now I was at the time starting to read a fun book called *Death and the Enlightenment* by John McManners and to postpone the start was reading his acknowledgements, always a pertinent exercise. And just before *that* I had received a letter from a friend who was trying to do the research for her book while running her household, supporting her poorly husband and looking after her children. The people for whom she was writing made no allowances for her frenzied circumstances. It was her bed: the female bed and she must lie on it and meet the deadline.

The acknowledgements in the Death Book by Professor McManners included thanks to the British Academy for research grants; to a French Foundation for providing the hospitality of Hotel Chalon-Luxembourg so agreeably situated in the Marais in Paris; thanks to the Rockefeller Foundation for a month of agreeable retreat at Bellagio in palatial surroundings by Lake Como; thanks to various scholars for hours of lovely – sorry, read lively there – discourse in flats and restaurants in Paris and in Oxford, in Senior Common Rooms, at lunch in Christ Church; thanks to the astonishing forbearance of a woman scholar and her staff who apparently laboured for four years transforming his drafts into typescripts and in the process of interpreting his handwriting acquired skills apparently worthy of professional code-breakers and palaeographers; thanks to people who haunted him to hand over incomplete manuscripts; to librarians who devoted their weekends to reading same; to another woman who performed astonishing feats of copy-editing on unsystematic references; thanks to his editor, another woman – the most patient and encouraging of people – and, of course, thanks to his wife, who relieved him of the burden of compiling an index; and, I presume, of providing the occasional meal. I quote, you understand.

As I read the catalogue of care, the pampered existence of your scholarly male writer – and he is not untypical, I could quote others who have trays left outside their doors by their wives, whose telephone calls are intercepted, whose every need is answered, their energies conserved in order to create more eclectism – I thought of how any woman struggling to meet the demands made on her would surely be filled, if not with rage, then with envy; but I also reflected that no woman born would be at the receiving end of such babying care or accept it with such apparently orotund complacency. Pure privilege. And while I was thus reading of these differing circumstances in the lives of two writers I had encountered via the written word in one morning, my daughter was searching for the answer posed by her tutor as to why there are no great women artists.

She came back a week later. She said: 'Will you listen for once, really listen? I've worked out that the question or statement is not only aggressive and pretends to be simple but is also a paradox. Women respond to it in a way which almost answers the "why" of it. And the reason they respond like *that*' ('Like what?' I asked. 'Just *listen*,' she said), to the *why* of it is because women know deeply through the way they lead their lives the difficulties of becoming an artist, in the sense that to *become* it, to be recognized by a lot of work over a lot of years, needs time, commitment and a kind of luxury or maybe selfishness that has traditionally been given to the masculine way of life supported by a woman.'

'Quite so,' I said. 'Some day remind me to show you a certain set of acknowledgements I've just been reading.'

'Don't interrupt,' she said. 'One of the most interesting things about this question with its hostility built into it is that men seem to want you to answer it by naming women whose genius and work matches people like Rembrandt, say, or Michelangelo, who are really rare in the whole human race. They should ask why are there not more artists like Rembrandt or Michelangelo; when you think of how many advantages men have there should be more. Or else they shouldn't be taken as typical examples.'

'Quite so,' I said.

'Have you heard of someone called Mary Cassatt?' she asked.

'I have,' I said, 'but remind me.'

'An American painter; Degas thought she was one of the greatest painters of his time, but she was almost unknown throughout her life. But it says that the advice she gave to American collectors meant that many great Impressionist masterpieces went to the USA. She said that a woman artist must be capable of making the primary sacrifices. And she did, Mum. She lived alone in Paris, not that I think that's a great sacrifice, and she got on with her work. But do men feel they have to make primary sacrifices in order to do their work? Have you heard of Berthe Morisot?'

'I have,' I said. 'She's the beauty on the balcony painted by Manet.'

'You see,' she said, 'you remember that first! But she was a leading Impressionist painter but never fully rated; when she was young and trying to learn she was forbidden to work at the Louvre museum unchaperoned, and was also totally barred from formal training. And Elisabeth Vigée-Le Brun?'

'Yes,' I said. 'But remind me.'

'Her paintings are brilliant; many museums now would like to have a painting by her at any price, but when she was alive she could not get one institution to show her work. When Sir Joshua Reynolds saw two paintings by her in London someone asked him what he thought of them and he said they were very fine, as fine as the work of any painter living or dead, as fine as van Dyck's and finer. But for centuries people did not even recognize her name, never mind her achievements. Have you heard of John Ruskin?'

'Yes,' I said, 'but remind me.'

'God, he was a male CP, wasn't he? I wrote down some of his sayings. "The masculine intellect is for invention and speculation. But the woman's intellect is not for invention or creation but sweet ordering, arrangement and decision. Her great function is praise."'

'Well,' I said, cheerily, 'it's an opinion still held by many priests and politicians and we must battle against this sort of history; while men have been encouraged throughout time to expand their minds, to become great artists, women have had their roles planted elsewhere by men, generally looking after them and their interests.'

'It's true,' she said, 'it's true. 'Do you know Barbara Hepworth? She said once that she rarely drew what she saw but what she felt in her body.'

'I'd buy into that,' I said, 'and into that a woman's full awareness of herself as an entity, including her sensations and emotions, informs her work and makes it what it is . . . Though men may feel the same . . . who knows?'

'I can't use that,' she said. 'The tutors would say that we're using gestation metaphors and female biology to make a statement about art; or to make excuses.'

'Oh, great,' I said, 'we're kicked right out of the playing field before we even begin simply by being ourselves; we have to deny our femininity in order to be taken seriously.'

'If you go on like that you'll never be taken seriously,' she said. 'Do you know Frida Kahlo?'

'Hello?' I said.

'She was married to Diego Rivera, who was so keen on attention and praise that he almost gobbled her up and no one hardly looked at her work when they were alive; and now they think she's great. What I've found is that when you find the women artists, you see that they *are* great but also that they've had to be these amazing exceptional women in themselves to be able to leap all the obstacles mostly erected by men. You know that painting by Vanessa Bell you love? Well, her instructor, he was called Tonks, was lecturing on how a certain painting in an exhibition could not have been done by a woman; no female had the vision or technique to pull it off. And then someone pointed out that it was wrongly labelled and had been painted by her. But he wasn't even embarrassed, he said she might have copied it.'

'It's my turn,' I said. 'Do you know what her sister, Virginia Woolf, said about a room of your own?'

'I do,' she said, 'of course I do. Our other tutor got us to read that. But there's always odds against us getting the room. Do you like Georgia O'Keeffe?'

'Sort of,' I said. 'I never knew if she realized what she was painting or not. Not that it matters.'

'Oh, I really like her work. Great big flowers. Early on she realized that if she was to become what she knew she must become she had to change her life. She wrote – listen, Mum – "I can't live where I want to, I can't go where I want to, I can't do what I want to – I decided I was a very stupid fool not to paint as I wanted to – that was nobody's business but my own." So she took off on her own, on her own quest. That's what women should be able to do.'

'But it's a luxury,' I said, 'to be able to take off, to be solitary, not to have to deal with anybody else's business. If you have children you won't do it. Would you like it if I had left you for the sake of art? Women *have* to deal with other people's business – most women, even if they have a room of their own, the door has to be open so that a woman can hear what is going on – she needs to; the welfare of children mostly depends on that attention, but it makes for a split vision and a divided concentration and less time; and time is needed to produce art. You wouldn't have liked it if I had kept my door closed to write while you were a baby. I wouldn't have liked it either.'

'Don't lay any guilt trips on me, Mum,' she said. 'Anyway, it was often closed. Now are you going to help me write this essay about – here, hold on, here's some of them – Elisabeth Vigée-Le Brun, Artemesia Gentileschi – don't know how to pronounce that – Angelica Kauffmann, Mary Moser, Meret Oppenheim, Winifred Nicholson, Laura Knight, Rosalba Carriera, Berthe Morisot, Dora Carrington, Sonia Delaunay, Romaine Brooks, Frida Kahlo, Eileen Agar, Helen Chadwick, Helen Frankenthaler, Sarah Purser, Paula Modersohn-Becker, Louise Bourgeois, Kathe Kollwitz, Eva Hesse, Prunella Clough, Tracey Emin, Mainie Jellett, Sarah Lucas, Gillian Ayres, Elizabeth Magill, Alice Neel, Agnes Martin . . . or not?'

'Not,' I said. 'But now you know such a lot, go and read Germaine Greer's book *The Obstacle Race* and learn even more.'

I only just stopped myself saying, 'And go and tidy your room.'

Instead I said, 'And get that wonderful essay in.'

The Last Christmas Tree

The journey to buy it meant that Christmas was near – there was that feeling of flare in the air, the atmosphere spiked, a taut line behind the dark, sometimes snowy atmosphere – and it had not only to be a perfect shape but to be enormous, to stand high, twenty feet off the ground so that it almost brushed the ceiling of the Big Room. To choose it meant the adventure of an expedition to Longleat. You don't get many Longleats to the pound. We'd drive up to the Gate of Heaven entrance and every time we would come over all silent and open-mouthed staring in wonder at the great Elizabethan palace below shimmering in its vast landscape. Finished in 1580, it is one of the most spectacular sights in England and nothing gives more of an idea of the power, richness and peace of England in the sixteenth century than this magnificent and beautiful domestic house, the seat of the Marquess of Bath.

Then we'd reverse back to the forestry gate to pick out the tree.

Once it was got home it took two strong men, a clucking woman and a bevy of children to raise it high and when I think about us decorating it I go into another kind of reverse and see my children (long since disappeared into their own future) as in a film montage, frame by frame, their images age upon age, flashing and cascading past in the costumes they chose to wear for the ceremonies of the tree. Here are three small blondes entangled in the fairy lights, here a luminous tot in a tutu – yes, even in the winter – another solemn in a lilac negligee and Violet Elizabeth Bott style ringlets, here one caught up in the branches in her small and earnest reality wearing a nurse's white uniform with the red cross on the skewed cap. And here, whizzing past, is your actual adolescent, an awesome thing like something from Gormenghast with a ring in her nose staring out at you from under black hair with dislike; but still helping with the tree. That ceremony was the constant in the kaleidoscope of our lives.

I don't think any of us ever missed a Christmas in the house that we all made and loved together. The Raising Up and Dressing of the Tree was a ritual as ordained and set as any ancient tribal ceremony. Getting the tree skewered into the vast sinister-looking iron contraption (made by the local blacksmith when we first moved into the derelict house) was a delicate job involving much heaving and falling down and tenterhooks of one kind or another, and when it was solidly up the Disinterring of the Ornaments from their deep tissued boxes began. Ornaments isn't the right word, being a catch-all word for anything from coloured lights to tinsel to gaudy balls, whereas mine – ah, gentle reader, no words can convey the pristine and jewel-like beauty of these useless treasures that I collected over forty years, these rare glass and glittery objects of exquisite fragility and glamour, so utterly removed from the everyday hewn textures of our lives.

I would seek them out wherever I was at whatever time of the year; wonderful opal ones in Russia; in India: in Czechoslovakia as it was then, and best of all in July in New York and London in Bloomingdales and Harrods – July or August is when the cognoscenti seek them out, when the big glass beauties come in and are unpacked and laid out without fanfare. Later in the year, in October say, you only have the leavings; and as for buying decorations in December . . . well, spare me while I go and lie down in a darkened room.

Every single one is crystal or glass or silver – no other colour at all, dearie me no – and some of the glass balls are more than four inches in diameter, fragile as bubbles; the children unpacked these great globes from their tissues every year and never broke one, ever, or any of the icicles, five to eight inches long, spiral or straight, over five hundred of them, tinkling glass bells and elaborate three-dimensional stars. They came glimmering out of their boxes with the bloom of all the Christmases before clinging to them.

The stout stem of the tree was bound with silver glitter and every single branch was lit by tiny white bulbs so wrapped that no flex was visible, so the whole thing became a shapely edifice pinpricked with light, a glistening cascade falling from the wings of the American angel blowing her brilliant trumpet. Daisy always did the job of putting her firmly into her place and I see her in her gauntlets on a high ladder leaning perilously into space and then on the way down pinning back a recalcitrant piece of flex or hanging another icicle.

As the fire blazed and we each worked on our section of the tree we took it in turns to choose the music; it was an eclectic mix and over the years I got to know the difference between garage and house and long-gone arcane trends and sounds in music. When it was almost dark I would watch how the firelight illuminated the family as they delved and fastened fragility to fragility and talked and laughed and hit each other and the room looked like a Georges de la Tour painting.

It took two days to dress the tree and it could only be finished on Christmas Eve, never earlier. When it was complete in its glory the unspectacular joy of our Christmas was mirrored in this great totem pole and made spectacular. The image of life as a cornucopia became a reality for those few days while it was at the centre of our lives.

This year is the last time it will happen. We are leaving the house we have lived in for a lifetime; no new house will ever have a room that size again. My children have families of their own and want to make their own rituals and memories.

Memory makes enormous the surroundings of our youth; we are astonished by their diminution on our return. Not mine; the Christmases of my memory will grow bigger every year, as big as the Longleat tree. When we switched it on more than a tree was illuminated.

Home Thoughts in the Vernacular

How could we have sunk back into the vernacular so quickly?

It's the South of France and the skyline stretches towards forever; it's hot, foreign Provence: sunflowers, terracotta, the crushed smell of lavender, the look of brown skin and the feeling of well-being.

Suzanne, whose house this is, comes round the corner to where we are sitting drinking wine on the terrace and says, 'Yous is on the step.' No one else there could have any idea of why we both were so suddenly transported not just into peals of laughter but into another landscape, a place where people fell into sheughs and hoked in the back of presses and dressers, and caught themselves on and behaved like ganches, a place where boils and carbuncles of all sorts rose up and beeled (and beeling was a Good Thing – it meant the poison was drawing up; I remember the exquisite pain of the hot poultice of milk and bread applied to our beels), a place where people juked in and around corners and had quare consates of themselves and threw their caps at the cabinet, where you redd up the house before visitors came and the sink where you washed the ware was called the jar box. This shared shorthand of a place is one of the pleasures and rewards of coming from a small place which has held in some measure on to its dialect.

Of course all families have a private language, words stained by place and associations, a shorthand where you have only to say one word and the family seethes or collapses. All families have many such phrases: my sister Claire was walking down O'Connell Street in Dublin when she saw just ahead of her a smartly dressed woman with the back of her skirt tucked into the back of her knickers the way you can do so easy . . . Now, Claire has a sensitivity that is almost too finely tuned to ramifications and consequences, so she was in a turmoil about whether or not to tell the woman: would she welcome the knowledge or shoot the messenger? She decided that in such circumstances she would much prefer to be told herself, so she overtook the woman and told her as gently and tactfully as possible that she was walking through Dublin with her knickers exposed (although she didn't put it like that). The woman looked at her and said, 'What is it to you?' Ever since the phrase has only to be muttered within the family for a whole complex of ambiguities to be brought into play – together with a fair amount of laughter.

Anyway, back to the South of France: at dinner that night another guest, an American, confessed that he lived in dread that a certain woman was going to pursue him from New York; he did not want to see her and had tried tactfully to tell her so, but thought there was a chance she might suddenly turn up. To tell you the truth, all of us thought he was rather boastful and a bit given to wishful thinking – but, lo, while he was out trawling Mazamet for lavender oil and woven baskets and hand-milled soaps and long-haired goats' cheese your woman turned up in a taxi. We all jostled and shoved and composed our faces into earnest expressions of welcoming surprise.

'He has a hard time expressing his wishes . . . we all do, we Americans,' she said. 'He finds it hard to say to me, "I'd so much like you to be there."' We none of us looked at each other. She went out to sit on the white wall the better to surprise him on his return, and we busied ourselves at jobs that somehow needed doing well within eye and earshot of the moment when he would step out of his car with his ethnic treasure trove and no inkling. Suzanne said to me, 'He's going to get a quare gunk,' and we had to run off and roll in the grass, stuffing clothes into our mouths to stop the gurgling noises. Then he drove up and I saw his face, and I haven't, as they say in Tamnamore, cast the cool of it yet.

At dinner that night, sitting on the terrace, with France stretching scented into the azure distance and sounds of angry American voices above our heads, Tom told us of his visit to Egypt: while there he'd had a rush of blood to the head and bethought himself to have made a sharp and natty white suit (indeed, he was wearing the selfsame suit and, being long, thin and blond, looked wonderful). Maddened by his success, he decided that what was needed to complete the swank was a fez. These turned out to be difficult to find, not being wholly politically correct, but at last he found a man who could make one – scarlet with a gold tassel, a hat fit for a pasha or potentate. When he walked out of the little backstreet shop wearing suit and fez he found himself being followed by a crowd of children shouting, 'King Farouk! King Farouk!' Nothing fazed, he considered how many of his friends back in Bristol would love such a feeling as a fez gives and so he ordered half a dozen more and brought them home. He and his mates put on their fezzes and went down for a pint to their local Slug and Lettuce. As they came in through the door of the pub the landlord, without missing a beat, pointed at the door and shouted, 'No fezzes; no fezzes; house rule; no fezzes, out, out, out.' And they had to leave.

I drove back home to rainy England and almost immediately got an invitation to go back to lovely France. It was from a friend inviting us to her husband's seventieth birthday party – a Surprise Party. These are seriously good party-givers and the big Seven-O is quite a landmark, so I made happy noises, until my husband pointed out that there was a little local difficulty. The party was to be held in their house in the South of France, behind St Tropez (the house used to belong to Jeanne Moreau and is stunning). Now, I don't have the lifestyle, Latin or equipment to be able to make it extempore to the South of France for a dinner party, and so, reader, when my putative hostess rang to see if we were coming I said with genuine regret that we wouldn't be able to make it. Well, talk about throwing the bull over the bridge. 'What a pity,' she said. 'I was going to send the jet to pick you up.'

Then I said, being so sophisticated and all, 'But, Regine, you couldn't land a jet here; it's too hilly.'

There was another silence, this time the stunned one that comes from someone absorbing another's true state of ignorance. 'No, darling,' she said, 'we'd send it to Farnborough, which is only forty-five minutes from you, you'd land at Nice and we'd have had the helicopter bring you the rest of the way. I'm so sorry you can't come . . .'

'So am I,' I said glumly, well hoisted.

I shuffled upstairs to where my husband was writing. 'Guess what I've done,' I said.

He lifted the phone. He said, 'Regine, we'll be at Farnborough just whenever it suits.'

'Fine, darling,' she said. 'I couldn't be more delighted.'

Then they both laughed like drains.

It was, I'm happy to report, one of the best birthday parties ever, with a Cuban salsa band and a group from Glasgow, plus everything else, and a woman who warned me that I must never dive because diving shatters emeralds. I could get used to life like that. And then I went on to see Suzanne again in her house in Mazamet and she wasn't at home so I sat at the foot of her front door and she got out of her car and said, 'Yous is on the step,' and I knew that I was back at home.

Talking about home: a while ago, my little dog Yum-Yum was run over in Dublin and Mrs Tabiteau, my dear old neighbour, drove like the clappers to the Charlemont clinic, so that although Yum-Yum lost one of her eyes her life was saved. To say Mrs T. liked cats is like saying children like Christmas; at one count we reckoned she had thirty cats living in and about her small house and garden. She was a beautiful white-haired woman but tiny and in her car could hardly be seen over the top of the steering wheel by anyone outside the vehicle. I sometimes wonder what Dublin commuters made of a Morris Minor hurtling at speed across red traffic lights, apparently without a driver but with a mad-eyed, tear-drenched woman in the passenger seat holding a dog the right way round so its eyes would stay in place.

Alas, last month Mrs Tabiteau died and with her one of the last vestiges of the old proud professional Protestant Dublin folk descended from the Huguenots; when she died I inherited her two pugs, Archie and Jamie, which means that one way or another I now have seven small dogs. Both Archie and Jamie were subdued and quiet when I first got them – and who wouldn't be, losing the person they loved and who loved them, going to a new owner, a new house, and five terrible hostile watchful resident beasts to boot. Not only that but Jamie had run from Mrs Tabiteau's house soon after she died and was found in Clonskeagh – and how he crossed some of the busiest roads in Dublin without being killed I'll never know, nor will the angelic family who rescued him, and that adventure had shaken him up.

Anyway, they have, as you might say, settled in – almost to a fault – and Archie beats all. Soon after he arrived his eyes fell out (what is it with me and dogs' eyes?) and for a while after the vet had stitched them back in, Archie was made to wear a plastic thing around his neck which, although it made him look like a small fat fawn thing stuck in a colander or a small fat fawn thing wearing a lampshade, somehow didn't stop him sinking teeth in legs and hanging on to trousers and wellington boots (preferably inhabited). The postmen have threatened to stop delivering, the plumber turned and left, the greenhouse builders are still aloft.

One last little dog story and then I promise I'll never tell another. Last week a couple came down the lane in a car, with a beautiful little collie without a collar crouched in the back. It was very sad and cringey; they had found it wandering along a road miles from anywhere and asked if I would look after it till its owner could be found as they were going away the next day.

I hated it being so sad and frightened and remembered that one of the things that most distressed me when I lost Loulou was the knowledge that she might never hear her own name again. So I said to my husband, who – as you will have gathered – is bored patience itself, 'I wish at least we knew her name.'

'Call her Lassie,' he said. 'She looks like Lassie.'

'Talk about showing your age,' I said. 'I'll call her Bessie.' At which the dog stopped looking quite so woebegone and stepped across the room, waving her tail a little tentatively. 'Bessie?' I said. 'Bessie?' She positively glowed.

So Bessie she became. We put out the calls to the vets, the rescue centres, the media, and eventually a woman rang with that tremor in the voice I know so well and said, 'Have you got a little black and white collie?'

'I have,' I said. She burst into tears.

'She's a sweet dog,' I said, 'and I christened her Bessie. What's her real name?'

'That's her real name,' she said. And so we both had a sniffle.

When I related the story to Suzanne in the South of France to show my spiritual link with the animals, she said, 'You're a tarra,' and our friends watched as two grown women laughed till they cried. The Americans drove off in separate cars.

A B Special Incident

You can always tell when you are leaving a Protestant area in Northern Ireland and entering a Catholic one. The roads deteriorate. You are reminded at every jolt of old sores, they rattle back up to the surface as the car bumps along. Forty years ago, we had a car with running boards that we were sometimes allowed to cling to like barnacles. For years that car was the only one in the parish, save for the priest's Triumph Mayflower which, with its razor-sharp edges, cut through the parish like something out of *Jaws,* seeking to devour the sinful.

My father drove his Austin with panache. He was the son of the local JP, who was an erstwhile agent of De Valera's, his brother was the Doctor, and he himself was an athlete with county records to his name. Such things counted enough then to make him distinctive in our small province. But they counted for very little when we were stopped as we bumped our way home out of Cookstown, down towards the lough shore where our clan lived. Every time we passed the good land further inshore which had been ours before the thefts of the Plantations, we looked at it, though without rancour – our rushy pastures had their compensations for children, and my father had never said a bitter word. The rancour came later, a rank weed sprouting from seeds sown long ago and cropped as the Troubles.

Years ago, the security checkpoints were mobile and you never knew where or when they would suddenly appear. They came in vehicles, in force and in uniform – they were the B Specials, auxiliary police force organized by the UK government in 1920 and taken over by the Northern Ireland government. The B Specials were voluntary and organized on a county basis, with about ten thousand members, and they were 100 per cent Protestant and, Catholics believed, both 100 per cent bigoted and borderline bovine. That was a provocative and dismaying thing for a government to do – to arm and empower a voluntary, licensed band of men from one section of the community, hostile to the other. We believed they could sniff a Catholic in a car like rats round strange bread.

Every time they stopped my father, handsome, distinctive, driving one of the few cars in the district for miles around, they would haul him out of the car and question him as to his business, his identity, his destination. It was meant to be ritual humiliation and it never appeared to work. We kept quiet in the back of the car. We didn't know much but we knew enough to be frightened. After it had happened a number of times, and I recognized the same men asking him the same questions, I asked,

'But didn't they know you?'

'They knew me like a begging ass, daughter.'

'So why did they stop and ask you who you were like that when they know?'

'To put manners on me,' he said.

No man needed putting manners on less, but it was my first experience of the prejudice and discrimination that floated out from Stormont, shrouding Catholics in discouragement, reducing our chances, stopping representation by gerrymandering and chicanery.

The leader of the ruling caste, Lord Brookeborough, a man of near-absolute power, made no secret of the fact that he despised Catholics. This man, who was for so many years our prime minister and who, through a kind of lazy viciousness, did so much damage to the province, once bestirred himself enough to call publicly on Protestants not to employ Catholics. ('I have not one about the place' – though legend has it all the same that his cook was Catholic.)

Years later, under pressure from Westminster, the B men were disbanded, barrelled back to their corners, and there they waited. They knew their time would come around again.

And, indeed, it did. The violence that for so many years bedevilled the province made a fine smokescreen for rank anti-libertarian attitudes to flourish. In Northern Ireland, policemen could harass anyone under the cover-all of a question of security, when it had nothing to do with security.

On one day's driving through Northern Ireland I had a series of encounters which would not be countenanced anywhere else in these islands and which encroached on my liberty, and those who encroached were using official cars, were being paid by the taxpayer, were on official duty and behaved like thugs. I relate only one of these incidents here.

It is a fine Saturday in August and I am driving from Belfast to Warrenpoint, and I reach the village of Moy, near Armagh, once the fiefdom of James Caulfeild, Lord Charlemont, bibliophile, dandy, soldier, queller of insurrection in Ulster, and whose Dublin town house is now the Hugh Lane Gallery in Parnell Square (Rutland Square in his day). At the entrance to the town I am stopped by two policemen and asked to wait, as a procession is marching through the town. I pull in, switch off and wait. I don't know what I expected; small, solemn children in white dresses? Some kind of feria? Mummers perhaps, or pageants on floats? Then I remember: Lady's Day, 15 August, the Feast of the Assumption, is one of the two days the Hibernians march; I look forward to hearing the old tunes.

Then I heard the approaching noise and knew this was a different sound of music. This band and these marchers were something else. There was no gaiety, no laughter. Men dressed in bowler hats, dark suits and orange sashes colonized the day in a sinister fashion. If one had seen such a group in Albania, say, or in some fastness of Latvia, one would have been fascinated by the folkloric display. These were the Black men, the elite of the Orange Order, which is reckoned to have over a hundred thousand members and is a powerful political and lobbying force and acts as a focus for bigotry and extremism. Traditionally, to rise in the Unionist Party it was essential to be an Orangeman. The Orange parades often marched through Catholic areas for the sake of it. Here they were again. My heart sank. Decades on and I'm listening to the same harsh beat I used to hear every July and August throughout my childhood. The members of these bands practise an aggressive drumming technique, especially exponents of the Big Slapper, the huge Lambeg drum, beaten with curved Malacca canes.

It would be hard to feel any warmth or pleasure watching the members of an Orange band, their faces hard as the hobs of hell, strutting their stuff as though they owned the place. Which they think they do. Seamus Heaney described it in a poem:

The lambeg balloons at his belly, weighs
Him back on his haunches, lodging thunder
Grossly there between his chin and his knees
He is raised up by what he buckles under . . .
The pigskin's scourged until his knuckles bleed.
The air is pounding like a stethoscope.

I waited in my car, looking ahead. My little dogs flung themselves
at the windows. Other cars drew up behind. We all waited. The
march passed by, ugly in its triumphalism. I tried to drive off.
Behind me, the row of cars revved, but my engine seemed dead.
I slightly panicked, swore, tried again and then, remembering I
was driving an automatic, put the gear into drive. The car jumped
forward as though stung and lurched off, the other cars following.
A hundred yards further along the road I saw a police officer
step into the road, talking into his mouth mike and pressing his
earphones hard. He flagged me down, waved the other cars on. I
rolled down the window.

'Pull over to the side,' he shouted. 'Pull over.'

I heard him say into his mike, 'I have her here.'

He leaned in through the window of the car and the dogs
sprang at him in a frenzy of outrage. They may be the insects of
the canine world but they have bottle. He pulled back sharpish. I
tried to silence them.

'What's wrong?' I asked, above the barking.

'You're being detained,' he said.

'Detained? Why? What for?'

'For shouting and cursing back there.'

'For *what*?' I couldn't believe my ears.

An unmarked car screeched up and a big policeman jumped
out and came running over. I had seen him and his like before.
Forty years before. A B man. Same look, same manners, same
dislocated anger.

'We'll soon see about this,' he said. 'What's wrong with you?'

'There's nothing wrong,' I said.

'Oh aye, there is, Miss,' he said, 'cursing and shouting at the
marchers back there. I seen you. I seen you. Miss Madam.'

'I never got out of the car,' I said. I was bewildered and, I have
to say, frightened. 'I don't know what you're talking about.'

He ran across the road and back again, manic, his hands frantic.

'You were in yer car,' he said, 'and you were seen to curse and swear. What's your date of birth?'

I was so stunned by this *non sequitur* that I told him. He ran to the back of the car, demented, shouting, banging on the boot, and I started to get out of the car.

'Get back,' he shouted. 'Get you back in.'

I climbed back in hastily. The two other policemen stood at each side of the car as though it was a mad animal.

'Where's your licence?' he said. 'We'll soon see about this, we'll soon see about this, cursing and shouting at marchers. Where are you from?'

'I live in Somerset,' I said.

'I see that,' he said, snatching the licence. 'I can read. I can read: But what I read is not where you're from. Your name is Devlin, Mrs Devlin, and that's not from Somerset. I know where you're from.' He banged the top of the car again, which set the dogs off like smoke alarms.

'What's this all about?' I said. My voice was weak, placatory, cowardly. 'What did I do? I haven't done anything.' I was so upset that I was nearly in tears.

He turned away, his face distorted with rage, and ran back across the road to where his colleague was presumably gathering data from his car's computer. I thought of my father, the number of times they had stopped him for no good reason just to show him who was boss, and I remembered his mannerliness, his intrinsic courtesy, and I took a deep breath and calmed myself. Across the road the policemen conferred on the radio. They kept looking across at me. The waves of anger were almost palpable. Why? Because someone in the march hadn't liked the way I looked? Because someone hadn't liked my demeanour as I moved off? They were still talking into the radio. Northern Ireland has the best security system in the world. In a matter of milliseconds they know who owns the car you are driving and where it's from and, for all I know, where you are going.

I don't know if I have conveyed the levels of anger and hostility surrounding me, but all I could do was wait and shiver and stroke the dogs, as the big, uniformed men terrorized a single woman in a car for no reason whatsoever, other than she had not smiled and waved as a band representing everything that is hateful to her marched past. The men were still at their car radio or computer or whatever they have in their patrol cars, but now they were looking over at me and conferring . . .

Now, I have an OBE (for services to literature, since you ask, and no laughing at the back of the class), an honour presented by the Queen. This, though not on my driving licence, is always used on letters sent to me from the Northern Ireland administration. Perhaps the police computer has this Establishment-friendly information on it, or perhaps the computer told them that I had a connection, however tenuous, with the press. Whatever; something did the trick. From being one of Them, I became one of Us. The big officer came back from his information centre with a different demeanour.

'What's your occupation, Mrs Garnett?'

'I'm a writer,' I said, angry with myself for parleying with him.

'That's some job you have there,' he said. 'Maybe you'll put me in a book sometime.' He looked at me consideringly and banged the top of the car with his hand, but more gently this time. The dogs leapt up like missiles, howling horribly.

'Good wee watchdogs, Miss,' he said. 'Go you on now. It was a bit of a mistake. All the best now. All the best.'

Now, I know I should have taken his name and number but hindsight is easy after an event. When, shaken, I reached Warrenpoint and told friends of the harassment, the questioning, the threats in the course of an ordinary morning's motoring, they were sympathetic but unsurprised. It happened a lot.

Back in England, someone who should have known a great deal better said, when I related the story, 'You lot brought it on yourselves.' Blame the victim because to look at the aggressor involves too thorough an examination of the system in power.

Sunshine and Incense

I was brought up in a household where no one walked if they could possibly help it. My mother would have been a walker – she was a great naturalist, knew every bird and flower, but she was too exhausted (full-time teacher, seven children, gambling husband) to have time for anything much other than to run to catch up; and my father would have driven the car to his breakfast table if he could.

I walk miles through woods when I am in the country and although it is a visual pleasure – a bluebell wood in the spring, a place of gloomy Sendak enchantment in the autumn – the floor of the forest never dries out and I plunge and slurp along dragging my boots out of Flanders-field-like gloop, using a boring amount of energy.

Now for many years I have wanted to walk the Camino de Santiago pilgrimage route, to Santiago de Compostela in northern Spain, the alleged burial site of St James.

I conceived the yearning when, years ago, standing in the exquisite cathedral square in Santiago, one of the most astonishing and felicitous arrangements of buildings in Europe, I saw how pilgrims, plodding into the square, suddenly became exultant and light-footed as they looked up at the beautiful and indecipherable architectural masterpiece that was their destination. They rejoiced and sang and hugged and threw their sticks in the air and I thought: 'What is that, I want to do that.' I was with my sister who lives in Asturias and speaks perfect Spanish and she described the pilgrims' routes and history with great feeling.

So I began to read the history and origin of this devotional walk which attracts people of all faiths and humanists from all over the world. During the Middle Ages half a million pilgrims annually walked the Camino, and the numbers are soaring again, including many young people and a lot of the elderly. Everyone just keeps going, each for their own reasons and each doing their own mileage, but it seems that everyone is uplifted and changed by the experience.

My favourite book about the walk is Cees Nooteboom's *Roads to Santiago*, a personal meditation, a delve into the magma of Spain and a terrific guidebook. I read of the miracle of St Dominic and the innocent pilgrim Hugonell in Santo Domingo de la Calzada and of course the hens. I rear hens myself and felt a proprietary interest. When Hugonell rejected the advances of a scheming temptress of the fourteenth century, a servant girl in a hostel, she filled his sack with stolen silver. (You might have thought he would have noticed a lot of jangling goblets in his backpack but there you are: men thick and innocent as ever, even then, and women as sluttish and devious . . . *plus ça change*.) The law pursued him, arrested him and hanged him. When his grieving parents came to cut him down from the gibbet they found him not dangling dead, but lively as you like, more or less sitting in the palm of St Dominic's hand, which thus prevented him dropping. The judge, told of the miracle while he was tucking into a meal of roast chicken, refused to believe it and swore if it was true then the chickens in his dish would reassemble themselves. At which point – you've guessed it – the cockerel and hen leapt out of his plate fully feathered. To commemorate the event, ever since a pair of immaculate white fowl are on display in a pretty hanging coop in the church. When I saw them – and I was thrilled – they were clucking and preening and reciting Larkin-like poetry. (Hen lovers relax; the shifts are replaced regularly.)

So the road to Santiago de Compostela played a vivid part in my imagination and figured immutably on that list we all carry about of Things We Must Do Sometime. When I was living in New York, I thought: if I don't go to Santiago soon I never will; and was further fired up to hear that my nephew Paul had walked all five hundred miles of it and, not content with that, turned northwards and walked till he fell into the sea at Finisterre; but he has forty years on me and I could only do it in the way I could do it. Taking refuge here and there with a hot bath in a hotel.

I'm not a Christian and I didn't walk the walk as a religious exercise, but that didn't stop me feeling that the love, the hope, the yearning that pilgrims must have carried with them as they walked the sacred route must somehow have been imparted, that the air is suffused by their desires and hopes, that a lingering miasma of good intentions and aspirations hangs there to be breathed in.

As I walked along the crest of the north of Spain through golden fields with the sound of tinkling cow bells and skylarks around me, not a soul in front, not a soul behind (though I knew there was a group of pilgrims less than half a mile behind and if I walked a mite faster I would come on others) – I could see across on every side thirty miles of glimmering deserted uplands and I felt exaltation.

I kept up around four miles an hour down shady paths, through woods, across enormous plains and vast landscapes where small villages lay against their churches for warmth. At times the route lay alongside a busy motorway or an A road thundering with traffic. Sometimes I was filled with happiness and sometimes with tears; sometimes with exhaustion, sometimes with a new energy. Everything daily dropped away. (Though not my appetite, alas. I have never eaten so much. Walking makes you hungry.)

When I finally entered Santiago, it was all I had hoped it might be. I participated in what Rebecca West called 'the paradox and mystery of the great churches . . . built by the grimness of supreme love' and I joined in the Pilgrim Mass. Many hundreds of us listened while our names were called out, and we clapped and cried as the great Botafumeiro (the largest censer in the world weighing eighty kilograms, filled with embers and incense and needing eight robed *tiraboleiros* to pull its ropes) swung above us in a dangerous silver arc, cleaving the air at some forty miles an hour and showering us with the symbol of what we had all done; and my heathen soul soared with it.

The
Longest Day

Once upon a time, a year and a bit into the twenty-first century, I – like the rest of the world – experienced one of the most memorable days of my life, a day full of darkness and light, grief and incredulity, hopeless terror and – in my case – overwhelming relief.

I was then living part of the time in the Waterloo Road in Dublin in a lovely Georgian house I had bought some years earlier for £142,000 (and I remember being pointed at, as a mad and obviously insanely rich person, because such a high price had never been heard of in that road). Then I began to write a guidebook to Dublin, because I discovered that, really, I knew nothing about the city.

Brought up as I was in the glum North of Ireland, Dublin had always seemd like Paris in the 1950s to me, the exotic bohemian art-filled city, a place of decadence and delight. Then, when I was a student, I had hitchhiked from Belfast down that endless gyrating single lane main road with its Long-John-Silver-type black spot posted at the corner where there had been once been a fatal accident, and when I finally reached the glamorous centre – Nelson's Pillar – I got a fair eye-opener. The city was run-down, the B&B cost £1 a night and was downright dirty, and the glorious squares of Georgian houses were being demolished. Where had I got this idea of glamour from? Certainly not from the books I'd read – James Joyce and Anthony Cronin and Brendan Behan didn't dress it up – but the putative city of light seemed as repressive a place in those days as Belfast on a Presbyterian Sunday.

There was one magical day during that visit in 1962 when I managed to get myself to the opening of the Joyce Museum in the Martello Tower at Sandycove and sat beside the famous founder of the Gate Theatre in Dublin, Micheál MacLiamóir, but I was too shy to speak to him. He was the first openly gay person I'd ever seen – I hardly knew that such a form of sexuality existed. He was wearing make-up and I was beside myself with judgemental provincial amazement and disbelief.

Years went by and for some reason the theoretical enchantment of Dublin still held me in thrall, so I bought the house. And when the guidebook was finally published there was nothing I didn't know about Dublin, its history, its hidden places, its legends (except, of course, the essence of the city itself). Having cracked the sights and sites of Dublin I thought to do a guidebook to Ireland and I drove around Ireland in search of it.

Anyway, this particular exploration began with a drive with a friend from Dublin to the coastal town of Portmagee in Kerry. I've always been a bird-watcher – not a twitcher, I don't care a toss how many birds I see, I just love looking at them going about their beguiling busy business – and I was heading for the Skelligs, those almost mythical, perpendicular and spectacular islands, Gormenghasts of the ocean, which look as though they are still rearing out of the sea, shaking water off their flanks as they blast off nine miles out in the Atlantic. Besides being one of the great sights of the world – never mind of Ireland – and now a UNESCO World Heritage Site, the two small islets are inhabited by huge colonies of seabirds and peregrine falcons and choughs. Little Skellig is home to thirty-six thousand pairs of gannet, the second-largest colony in the world.

Getting to the Skelligs is always a bit problematical, as the journey depends on the weather and the boats can't go out if it is stormy or threatening, which it is a great deal of the time.

There is hardly a way of capturing the spirit and sight of such a place as the Skelligs. More than twelve hundred years ago monks lived in beehive huts on the summit of Skellig Michael, the bigger peak, and these primitive shelters still survive. They are touching monuments braced with history and you can't help but marvel at how the monks endured living there on this wind-lashed pinnacle and on such paltry fare as they could come by all the year round.

We arrived at Portmagee in the early morning, and by good luck the sun was shining and a few of us (from all over the world) set off in the doughty Casey boat for the 45-minute journey. Seeing and hearing the twin peaks with their plumage of birds, making the most extraordinary clamour as they wheeled around, was heart-stopping; but, in the event, I never did reach the monastic settlement because when I started to climb up the steep ridge with the rocks falling steeply to each side I was overcome with such vertigo that I could go neither up or down.

If you don't suffer from vertigo you cannot imagine the terror and nausea: the knees go to water, the stomach is gripped by fear, and in my panic I knew the only way down was to throw myself into the sea, far, far below. My friend saw what was happening and scrambled back, eased me round, sat me down so that, eyes closed, white-faced, holding her hand, and with other people holding my feet, I could inch down on my arse.

Once down on a piece of flat land I crept on all fours round to the back of the island where a small blessedly level area of grass bounded by a low wall overlooks the deep chasm where the land ricochets back into the dark sea. It falls steep for about two hundred feet so it was as though I was on the top of a skyscraper, with the seabirds strafing the walls below, dive-bombing with such velocity that I thought they must surely dash themselves, kamikaze style, against the cliff and die; but always at the last moment they did a pyrotechnic turn and darted off again.

I did not know it, I could not know it, but I was watching a rehearsal, a metaphor for what was happening in New York that day on another pair of unimaginably high twin peaks but inhabited by people.

As happens after a dramatic personal incident – and I had felt very close to death up there on the ridge – one reviews precious life. I thought about my children. My youngest, Bay, living downtown in New York, had just sent me a photograph of her standing on the top of the World Trade Center, which had made me shudder. My second daughter, Daisy, was at that moment flying into New York from Los Angeles. I knew she'd ring soon after she landed, to quell an anxious mother's fears.

We set off on our return journey in the chugging little boat in the early afternoon. The sea had risen a bit and the skipper had his radio on in the cabin. Apart from him, and my friend and me, there were two other people in the boat, young German men. I kept hearing windblown staccato snatches of panicked news from the radio. I went into the cabin. The captain said: 'There's something bad going on in New York. A big bombing or something.' The more we listened the more it became apparent that something massive and terrible was happening and I said to my friend, 'It's Osama bin Laden . . . a terrorist attack.' The reason I was so prescient was that not long before I had read an article in *The New Yorker* predicting an attack on the American mainland by Al Qaeda. No one official seemed to have taken any notice of this warning.

Then, to my horror, we heard through the crackle that the targets were the Twin Towers of the World Trade Center and the weapons they were using were passenger jets. No one knew how many. The two young German men whooped and clapped with pleasure.

I hope never again to have a journey like that. The little boat ploughed on slowly through the choppy waves. The ocean became the Styx. My friend held my hand as I rehearsed over and over again how close Bay lived to the World Trade Center, how often she went up there for breakfast, that Daisy was on a plane that even now was heading for New York.

When we landed at Portmagee we watched those horrific images now scorched forever into our minds and watched too as those living near the World Trade Center ran up the whitened streets pursued by a living choking cloud of debris like a monstrous succubus. For all I knew Bay was in there, running for her life. I was in shock, gibbering. There was no way of getting in touch with anyone.

All over the world people were trying desperately to find out what I was trying to find out, but all communications were down. We began the wretched drive back to Dublin and then my mobile rang. To my incredulity, my friend Tessa Dahl had miraculously got through to me from New York – how did she do that? – to tell me that Bay (indeed one of those people running away from that sinister cloud) had reached Tessa's apartment uptown. Daisy's plane had been diverted to Kansas.

One day, 9 September 2001. But that day lasted longer than many a decade.

A Room of My Own: Manhattan

I love New York. I hate February, always have; it's neither here nor there; hated it in Ireland, hate it in England, hate it in France. Not too keen on March. So, I spend them now in Manhattan. People say, but it's so cold there. Yes, but it's crispy cold and sometimes with deep transforming romantic snow, and then click, it's over, the streets cleared, Central Park stops being a ski resort; the heating works a treat and it hardly ever rains, at least not on my parade.

I teach here from January to May, and though I mind something terrible missing the spring and I try to go back once in the semester to catch it (might as well try to catch a moonbeam), I couldn't be happier (except of course for missing the family – who are quite pleased to see me go).

It's such a thrill for me. To be offered an interesting and rewarding job in a big cosmopolitan city for a while at a time when a person might be well set in her olden ways, or thinking of giving up anything even vaguely intellectual as she searches yet again for her keys, seems to me a gift from the gods.

I seem to do more in a week in New York than I do in six months in London never mind in Somerset where I spend a good deal of the time. There, my teeth blacken into stumps, my hair somehow seems to give itself a 1950s perm itself all of its own accord, my wellies are melded to my stout legs and my flowered pinny covers the vast monolithic bust. My fancy hens and geese who can't be arsed laying – too cold – fall back clucking and cackling when they catch a glimpse of me. No human being sees me except for my husband and children and people who have become accustomed to the apparition. And I haven't a thought in my head. Yet I am busy, busy, busy, doing the lord knows what. It's what the country does to you.

Then I come to Manhattan. As I walk into the building and the doorman greets me and seizes up my luggage, the teeth whiten up, I become blonder, thinner, funnier and much, much richer and my footwear is Manolo. All right, all right, strictly speaking I don't and it isn't, but that's how I feel. It's a tonic, better than any health farm, better than any therapy. Paris is the love of my life, Manhattan the lover, a bold philanderer. I know that some day the lover won't be around any more but I'll make the best of it while the sap is rising.

What is it about New York that so quickens the blood? God knows I love Paris and Venice and London but nowhere do I get the sheer exhilaration that I feel when I hit the streets of Manhattan. My whole demeanour changes involuntarily – my depression vanishes, my energy levels rise and I become a wastoid without a care in the world. The air is filthy, the streets are canyons where if you stop for a moment a crowd bumps into you, muttering imprecations, the subway is noxious, yet you feel – or I do – as if I am getting great gulps of oxygen and my whole being is aerated.

In Manhattan I am surrounded by things that make me want to change my habits: the seriousness of style and its exclusivity; the non-compromising absolute importance of being thin in a city filled with fat people; the intensity of salesgirls in the beauty departments of the big stores who are determined to make you look good. They treat every customer as if they were their first or last and that *les petits soins de la personne* are the most important quality of character. I compare them to the lackadaisical salesgirls in London stores who lean against their counters as I scurry by in my ramshackleness, whereas these Bergdorf and Henri Bendel salesgirls do a flying tackle on me. I'm like raw meat to hungry lions in those futuristic aisles. At nine in the evening I can get a manicure or a pedicure and as part of the madness I immediately get impossibly long gel nails attached to my fat little digits so my hands look as though they have arrived from an alien planet looking for a leader and have attached themselves to me by mistake. I think they are madly glamorous and can't help looking at them with fond pride like those animals who adopt another species and don't know the difference. (God love the same nails when they get back to England and find themselves deep in potting compost. That'll put manners on them.)

Then. too, something else happens here which doesn't happen to me elsewhere, which is that I meet up with my friends a lot. A lot. Everyone is always arranging something: a lunch date, a night at the opera, a trip to the theatre, a museum (and there are so many museums on this small island), a new yoga place, a restaurant to try out, a lecture, a symposium, a dance class. How do they do it? if I'm not teaching and I go to, say, Balthazar – a little bit of Paris in lower Manhattan where I can get my fix of France – with someone for brunch it is absolutely seething on a weekday morning with a long line at the door. Why are these people not working? They can't all be skiving teachers like me – professors, as we are known here. Sniff.

I'm not panicked with busyness and things to be done here, though I have my timetable and my students' work to respond to – much more actual graft than I do in England. Yet I have time to do stimulating things. Great theatre and some of the best music in the world is near at hand, and there's almost always a ticket to be had. I'm out walking on a Sunday afternoon, see a tethered barge on the river in which a chamber concert is just beginning; on a side street on the Upper West Side there's a notice pinned to a door, I climb the stairs and in a panelled room three distinguished Proustian scholars are dissecting a knotty paragraph from *The Sweet Cheat Gone.*

And then, too, the joy of Central Park! One of my dearest friends is on the Women's Committee of the Central Park Conservancy, an association dedicated to its restoration and which has, over the years, raised hundreds of millions of dollars. When I first lived in Manhattan forty years ago the park was the Badlands, with the monuments derelict, the grass bald, and the buildings graffitied and boarded up. The joke doing the rounds at the time was about a tourist who asks one of New York's finest how long it would take to cross the park. The cop answers, 'I wouldn't know. No one's ever made it.'

Now, it's perfection. It's Manhattan's back yard and front garden, its ski slopes, aviary, pug-walking place, roller-skating rink, and concert hall, jogging and snogging space. On a sunny day it's Utopia. I have a passion for Central Park.

But it's something more than the realities and opportunities and atmosphere of this stunning city that changes my life and my character and my everyday outlook. It's not just that I have rewarding work. I love my students and they work their butts off. They also assess their teachers publicly at end of the semester – a system I think should be adopted everywhere. (I *still* want to tell the deadbeats who taught me what I think of them and their cruel dereliction of duty.)

It's not just that there are marvellous or mad things on all the time, everywhere, at all hours. When I sit down and think of why my life and my attitudes should be so different here, I realize it is because I am free, a single woman, free of responsibility other than to my job; free of the maintenance of house and animals and people. Free of rushing here and there and attending to the myriad details that constitute any woman's life whether she works outside the home or in it.

When Virginia Woolf wrote that seminal and stirring essay and talked of Shakespeare's sister, she was referring to every woman's need for time and space and the personal liberty to create art. 'A woman must have money and a room of her own if she is to write fiction,' she wrote. But a woman must have money and help and (if she has a family) to have finished rearing her children before she can have a room of her own in which to live her own parallel precious life.

We all need a wife but only men have that option. No, a room of our own is a long way away for most women. It took me a lifetime and a voyage across the Atlantic to find it.

The F Word

I always have to bring everything back home. The proverb says home is where the heart is, but my heart has no idea where it is meant to be (though it has often been on my sleeve). Home for me is a place where I can trust and feel safe. What happens to many of us leaves us so damaged that we can hardly trust anything. I'm talking feminism here. The paradox is how many women who live in our open society and are not trapped by circumstances refuse to call themselves feminist.

Every woman I know is a feminist to her inner core. Yet a February 2019 poll found that only 34 per cent of women in the UK (and fewer than one in five young women) said yes when asked whether they were feminist. When one considers those continents of women who are not liberated and cannot be, and would give thanks to the skies above for the chances we have – one feels like using a cattle prod.

'I wouldn't call myself a feminist, because I'm not anti-men,' a high-powered businesswoman in her mid-thirties, the boss of many men, tells me. 'Though,' she adds hastily, 'I *am* pro-women.' She is? Did she think I might doubt it?

A twenty-nine-year-old barrister: 'I get the impression that many women don't like to call themselves feminists because it has become a bit of a dirty word, conjuring up images of hairy legs and militantism.' It does?

A mother of three who works in the City: 'Feminism for me is something rather aggressive and militant; objecting to men standing up for you on a bus . . . A hater of men.' It is?

A forty-something gay art dealer: 'The term feminism is hideous. It brings to mind the old-fashioned political correctness of the 1970s that doesn't apply to our society any more.' Doesn't it?

And, from a musicians' agent: 'If being a feminist means equal rights for women, then, yes, I am a feminist. But I still want my men to help me with my coat, pay in restaurants and open car doors for me, so in that I suppose I am not a feminist. If my man helps with something or takes care of me, I melt at his feet.'

The archetypal anti-feminist, for me, is a woman – Margaret Thatcher. She pulled the ladder of equal opportunity up behind her, and the concept of positive action was anathema to her: 'No, a woman must rise through merit. There must be no discrimination.' (Well, yes – but many of the men in her Cabinet seemed either stupefied or simple-minded?)

Did she ever talk about disparity in wages? Hello? She sneered that the word feminism simply wasn't in her lexicon.

I cannot tell you how many women tell me that they aren't feminists because personally they haven't encountered sexual discrimination. Haven't they? Lived in a bubble, have they?

Women! I want to cry, we are all feminists! It doesn't mean you are anti-men or anti-dressing-up or that you think feminists want to be like men – our differences should be celebrated.

For me, it is simple. I am a feminist because I believe that women should not suffer discrimination, suffer abuse, suffer anything, on account of their gender. I was never a member of any active feminist organization, and wish I had been – dozy dork that I was – but, yes, I am a feminist to my angry heels.

Women are being abused in every way all over the world. We don't need to go to a bus in India – or a back room full of trafficked women in London, or Dublin, or Saudi Arabia – let's look at Afghanistan, say, where the West has spent a fortune trying to help the country and its society. Or that was the big idea. Hamid Karzai, the erstwhile Afghan president, endorsed a religious ruling that states: 'Men are fundamental and women are secondary.' Sound familiar? Are we shocked? I'm not shocked. It's what many men in our society believe.

Feminism is also deeply entwined with self-esteem. For so long we have been bullied and indoctrinated to stay in our place – a corral administered by patriarchs and priests, fathers and brothers, sons and tyrants, male didacts and philosophers and missionaries, where punishment was swift for transgression, and self-esteem was hard to come by. Without self-esteem it's hard to stand up for yourself.

The wonderful Gloria Steinem, prototype feminist leader, is an example to us all. Her depressive mother, although often out of it, loved and valued her children 'exactly as we were . . . She performed the miracle of loving others even when she could not love herself.' So her mother managed to break the pattern of her own upbringing and pass on to her children something quite different – the feeling that they were unique and worthwhile. That conviction of being loved and valuable *as we are*, that validation of our intrinsic worth regardless of what we do, is the beginning of core self-esteem.

I grew up in a society where men were fundamental and women were secondary. And second-rate. I was reared within a coercive and pervasive idea of female domesticity. I may shudder at the idea of my granddaughter growing up in a society where she has to wear the burqa and obey Sharia law, but I went to mandatory religious services every Sunday – no question of missing Mass or Benediction – and we had to cover our heads. In the pews at the back older women still wore black shawls that concealed their hair and their bodies effectively. Remind you of anything?

In our dispensation, *The Pilgrim's Progress* was a bad book, on the Index, which it would be a sin for a good Catholic to read. (Can you imagine?) Anyway, I contrived to find the book in my Protestant aunt's bookcase and found out a wonderful thing – Giant Despair was married to Madam Diffidence. Well, what a turn-up that was. We'd been taught that diffidence, which for me was just another name for modesty, was one of the Cardinal Virtues. Yet here in this book about virtue she was the big bad embodiment of a big Bad Sin. It was a relevation that one didn't need to be diffident, since it had been hammered into us that if you were brave and confident you were a Bold Girl who would come to No Good. (Thank goodness I came to No Good.)

In the dispensation that held in Ireland for centuries until recently the social life of women was severely curtailed. You rarely met a woman out walking unless she was going to Mass or to do the messages, as they were called. The only women who walked for pleasure in our district without incurring notice and surprise were my mother, who had a certain status as the teacher, and was anyway a blow-in; and an old eccentric beauty called Lizzie, who didn't give a hoot what anyone thought of her. There was no question of a woman going out alone to have a drink in a pub, and courting was a furtive affair.

Women's place in Irish society has changed so much that some of the young think the achievement was a fairly painless process; but it took enormous nerve and courage to stand up against patriarchal, priest-ridden, respectable Ireland; women were ring-fenced by the Establishment and the union of Church and State and the invidious legacy of the narrow-minded, benighted, obtuse Taoiseach Eamon de Valera, cut off by law from the liberation and change happening in other parts of the Western world.

From the altar priests continued to read out the letters of St Paul as Gospel truth to us . . . For example, First Letter to Timothy:

> Women should remain silent in the churches. They are not allowed to speak, but must be in submission, as the law says . . . I do not permit a woman to teach or to assume authority over a man; she must be quiet . . . women will be preserved through the bearing of children if they continue in faith and love and sanctity with self-restraint.

No mention of men's lack of self-restraint. Many women in the poor parish where I grew up had ten, or fifteen, or twenty children and were worn out and wearied to early death.

All this only began to change because pioneering women – and a few brave men – put themselves on the line, wrote and marched and defied the wicked conventions of the day and demanded contraception, the right to divorce, the right to abortion, the right to control their own bodies. Writers like Nell McCafferty, Mary Lavin, Edna O'Brien, Nuala O'Faolain – and John McGahern – wrote honestly about Irish society, and were condemned and censored for it. One woman we owe a huge debt to was Inez MacCormack, a Belfast Protestant who rose above her family's Unionist background to become a powerful activist on civil rights, women's rights and fair employment. (Meryl Streep, who played her on stage, said she felt 'slight next to her, because I'm an actress and she is the real deal'.)

The passing of the abortion laws was a cause of huge celebration in Ireland and effectively marked the end of the control of the patriarchy of the Catholic Church which had kept their faithful so repressed for hundreds of years.

But, all the same – Irishwomen are still faced with negative attitudes, discrimination and even dismissal because of their roles, actual or potential, as mothers and carers. The lack of paternity leave and flexible working, plus a culture of long working hours, mean that women pay the penalty. Ireland's Employment Equality Act was supposed to provide it with one of the most far-reaching equality laws in Europe, yet women still make an average of 17 per cent less than men (though women without children have a good chance of earning rather more than mothers).

There were four events, aside from marriage and motherhood, that made me realize how doubly and deeply colonized I was as an Ulster Catholic, as well as a woman, and how troubled.

The earliest I didn't know about till I was nearly an adult and I still haven't come to terms with it, so really the first moment which impacted consciously happened was when I was fifteen, cycling home from the chapel after confessing my meagre sins to a horrible man, and I suddenly realized what a cod it all was and how I had been brainwashed from birth.

The second event was reading two books, the third, meeting one remarkable woman, the fourth, a photograph. My daughter Daisy interviewed me for a magazine and I have just now reread her article.

My mother rails, still, and rightly so, about how domestic duties threaten, unchecked, to suffocate women's creativity. She always, always stands up for herself. In my head, therefore, she's always been a feminist *extraordinaire*. I telephone her . . . to confirm this. 'No,' says my mum, to my surprise. 'I'm a feminist to my bones now, but when I first arrived in London from Ireland I hadn't heard of feminism. I was steeped in the old lore that said men were powerful creatures that had to be pleased. I sucked up to men. It was meeting Gloria Steinem that changed my life. She was feisty and beautiful and not timid. *She* was the eye-opener. Listening to her changed my attitudes.'

And the books? *The Female Eunuch* with that famous iconic cover of the female torso as a sad sack with handles (designed by a man – John Holmes), in which, with rage and revolutionary energy, Germaine Greer revealed – or to me it was revelation – among so many other things, that men hate women, though we don't realize this and are taught to hate ourselves. (We have only to open the newspaper to see in our own society the terrible subjugation and torture of women, the everyday occurrence of women battered to death and children killed, by their husbands and fathers.)

She demanded the freedom to be a person, with dignity, integrity, nobility, passion, and the pride that constitutes personhood. 'Freedom to run, shout, talk loudly and sit with your knees apart. Freedom to know and love the earth and all that swims, lies, and crawls upon it . . . most of the women in the world are still afraid, still hungry, still mute and loaded by religion with all kinds of fetters, masked, muzzled, mutilated and beaten.'

The other book was *The Bell Jar* by Victoria Lucas and I still have that first edition, a rare find now. I was properly startled by it, like coming to a standstill in front of an unexpected mirror. A young woman suffering from depression is starting work on a women's magazine. 'If neurotic is wanting two mutually exclusive things at one and the same time, then I'm neurotic as hell. I'll be flying back and forth between one mutually exclusive thing and another for the rest of my days . . . I was supposed to be having the time of my life.' Which I was. And I was so unhappy. When it became known that it was written by Sylvia Plath, already dead by then, I thought I would try to be happy. (By the way, William Blake said we had a duty to be happy – that was yet another mind-opener for me.)

The photograph: when I was working on American *Vogue* in the 1960s it published an erotically suggestive double-page spread by the legendary photographer Irving Penn, of Marisa Berenson lying naked, one knee raised, trussed up with jewellery like a kind of female turkey, ready for devouring. I found this image deeply troubling – I hated it. Coming to feminism made me interpret the photograph as an aggressive act of male colonization – such as I might have expected of *Playboy* but not of a magazine entirely directed towards women, which paid lip service to women's equality, and for which I worked.

It is still true that women who appear in public are expected to appeal to men's desires and if they don't they suffer. Look at Mary Beard, the erudite Cambridge professor with long grey hair in her own slightly rumpled style who was bombed with sickeningly misogynist emails concerning that same hair and her teeth – among them sadistic rape fantasies. She inspired such particular fury, one analyst commented, 'because long hair is typically associated with unrestrained sexuality, while grey hair is associated with being past it. If you are bad at processing complex information the combination will fry your brain.' Whose brain? What brain?

Not long ago a CBS news correspondent, Lara Logan, thought she was going to die in Tahrir Square in Cairo when in full public view she was sexually assaulted and tortured by a mob of two to three hundred men: 'For an extended period of time they raped me with their hands.' An interviewer (on the BBC World Service) asked her 'Did no one help?' 'No,' she said, 'I could hear the people in the street laughing while I was being tortured.' 'Why do you think this is happening?' the interviewer asked. 'It is political and social,' she said. 'By attacking me they are frightening everyone, so we have to stay home – and then men don't want their women to be attacked so they do the same to women who *do* go out so we learn we can't go out.' Eve-teasing is a euphemism used in India and Bangladesh for public sexual harassment or molestation of women, including many frightful rapes and murders. Women are rising up in India because of it – but it is unlikely that anything will change soon, since the laws already in place to prevent Eve-teasing are rarely enforced.

We learn by example and our children must learn by our example – because by god they won't learn from the masculine porn-based damaging tech society they are growing up in.

The late great Nora Ephron, whom I met when I first went to New York and instantly fell in love with, said in an address to her alma mater.

> What I'm saying is, don't delude yourself that the powerful cultural values that wrecked the lives of so many of my classmates have vanished from the earth. There's still a glass ceiling . . . Don't underestimate how much antagonism there is toward women and how many people wish we could turn the clock back. One of the things people always say to you if you get upset is, don't take it personally, but . . . please, I beg you, take it personally. Above all, be the heroine of your life, not the victim.

In her book *The Whole Woman* Germaine Greer writes: 'Women have come a long, long way; our lives are nobler and richer than they were, but they are also fiendishly difficult . . . The contradictions women face have never been more bruising than they are now . . . It's time to get angry again.'

Isn't it? Isn't it.

And Gloria Steinem, practical as ever, gives an exercise to help us find our courage, our self-esteem, our feminism, and to re-parent ourselves.

So. Write down on a blank page, in whatever order they come to you, the things you wish you had received in your childhood and did not.

You have just written what you should do for yourself.

Intricate Rented World

Dear Poll – I walked up Broadway after your place and the cold outside me and the champagne within turned me purple on top of my other aesthetic shortcomings. However, the apartment was charming and our hostess, a distinguished Englishwoman who runs a workshop here on Dickens as a volunteer among other cultivated things – she'd made a huge cottage pie and a veggie thing with noodles and aubergines and a salad and hot bread, and another Hungarian, an architect I was seated beside, had brought a chocolate and ground poppyseed cake he'd made himself and there was also rhubarb fool and whipped cream. . . . So, though I hate going to people's houses and hate dinner parties that's just in principle and I did of course thoroughly enjoy myself and went home in a good humour . . .
love, Nuala

A little while ago – ten years now but a lifetime of loss – I went to a concert in the Carnegie Hall to hear Schubert's *Death and the Maiden*, a piece to which there is paradoxically no end. It is unfathomable. Schubert was nearing the end of his life when he wrote it and he knew what was approaching him in all its ineluctable dread.

I was there with my funny, intemperate and beloved friend Nuala O'Faolain. She had been in Ireland getting radiotherapy for her cancer and I was in New York but nevertheless in the middle of this horrible time she had flown over to say goodbye to her friends in New York and to hear this music one last time. One last time.

At the best of times you listen to live music with attention. But you cannot sit beside someone you love who is dying by inches in front of your eyes and listen to the *Death and the Maiden* without being affected beyond words; so I will say no more about it.

I will, though, say more about her. I loved her. I never met a truer or keener intelligence. She was a polymath – a writer, filmmaker, academic, teacher, book reviewer and brave pioneering feminist. She wrote brilliant columns for *The Irish Times* and was a political correspondent covering the American elections. She made groundbreaking television documentaries which won awards, was a brilliant broadcaster, and was famous throughout Ireland. A publisher thought to publish her columns and asked her to write a preface to the collection. She was not enthusiastic – she thought they were too ephemeral and time-sensitive, but started in to write a sort of introduction. She didn't stop. The resultant work was published as *Are You Somebody?* and became a bestseller around the world, selling over a million copies.

'I sneaked out my autobiography when no one was looking,' she said later. 'My unconscious recognized a chance.'

Yet she was so chary of her own talents, this brilliant writer, and refused to recognize their extent. She could be wide-eyed about the most ordinary of social things – she always insisted she had no social graces and loved any arcane example of ritual behaviour and was gleeful at social pretension (her stay among certain women in County Down in Northern Ireland gave her much pleasure in that direction), but she always trod a thin wire between despair and joy; and, alas, grief ran taut throughout her life.

And how she could write:

The way country lanes are in Ireland at this time of year came into my head when I read that John McGahern was dead – such a beautiful time, with life bursting out through the flowers of the blackthorn and the vigorous singing of the small birds, and the earth and ourselves moving forward, the great round starting off again. Except for the dead, who have to stay behind. John's funeral procession will make its way through a landscape of newly green little fields. He'd have known every detail of them. He was one with the place where he lived as few people are. And he was a man, to paraphrase Hardy, who used to notice such things . . . Yet when I think of him I think of the rainy, shadowy, dark grey Dublin of his youth and mine, where the golden light from pubs was almost the only light along the quiet streets.

There were many women in her life who were more important to her than me – her sisters, and many others, and I was never her lover, but I warrant no one loved her more. She was funny, impatient, demanding, alchemic; going shopping with her, which I often did, was a nightmare and there was much flouncing and screaming and then the calm that passeth all understanding when she found – or, more often, I found – something that she liked.

There was no one more generous, with time, with affection and care and temper, with money – I don't think anyone really knows, for example, what she did for women and children with Aids in Africa, paying to provide them with shelter and care.

She was so ironic. She deflected emotion, she couldn't bear compliments, she had a way of ducking her head when she was told she was loved – as if to say, ah, don't, don't say it. She didn't see herself as the world saw her. She didn't perceive her own beauty yet saw it so fast in everyone else.

She was straight as a die and had a fantastic critical mind. I would ask her – say – about Henry James, or I'd ask have you read Colm Tóibín's essay on Hart Crane, and she'd burst to a halt quivering with excitement and pleasure to tell me her opinion.

We spent time together in isolated places and away from people, or, rather, isolated from our usual daily lives and loves and friends: a week in Aspen in Colorado at a literary festival, the snowy mountains towering above us, was the first time I found how active she was, how much she got done. Lord, how she could bustle. Left to myself I would have walked around the town or gone to a concert or read. Not Nuala. She did all those things, too, at breakneck speed, but also hired bicycles and we cycled for miles discovering lakes and forests; and all the time there was her talk – evidence of that original true mind of such raving intelligence and integrity.

We spent six weeks together at the McDowell Writing Colony in darkest, snowiest New Hampshire and I have a vivid memory of her running down Peterborough High Street in the snow with tiny steps like a geisha, in a red woolly hat (why was there so often snow around?).

We went to visit Willa Cather's grave in a deserted New England graveyard covered in snow, twenty-seven inches of it, as I found out when I climbed over the wall to reach her monument and fell down into the drifts. 'I'm in it up to the oxters,' I called to Nuala and she laughed so much she fell off the wall on top of me and we had to haul each other up from the depths and then we both fell down again like children.

We were together in New York, always for the spring semester, from January through to May – she teaching at Bennington or Hunter College and me up at Barnard – and in all these places where we saw a lot of each other I have endless images of her larking about; no one could do larking – or despondency – better, or being apocalyptic, joyless, joyful . . . It was often extremes. I'd have a glass of wine; she wouldn't. 'I don't see any point in drinking unless you drink too much,' she said, dead primly.

We hired bikes – again – and took a fast ferry to New Jersey for forty-five glorious scudding minutes, with Manhattan receding under the Verrazano Bridge to Sandy Hook, where the criminals and the insane were landed before being allowed to go to Ellis Island, and where she set part of her book *The Story of Chicago May*.

It was a little bit of dreamy, lost, archetypal America, and we were cycling all innocent alongside the ocean in the sunshine when the weather came up over the horizon without warning and slammed us off our bikes. Freezing hail and ripping wind tore our clothes half off; in the space of five or six minutes we were wet through, our knickers and bras sopping wet, our shoes gushing, our bodies streaming water. We had brought plastic macs, and Nuala got her head stuck in a sleeve, like a pink condom, and I couldn't get her out of it; you couldn't see much through the rain but I could see her two desperate eyes staring out of the pink sheath and her lips under the plastic shaping the words 'For fuck's sake get me outta here.' But I had got myself lost in a big brown poncho and looked like something DHL had dropped out of the back of a van, and in any case we were laughing so much that we couldn't help each other, that hysterical laughter that incapacitates. We pushed back with real difficulty to a clam house where there was no heating and wrapped as much of ourselves as we could in towels, hoping not to break the decency code or frighten the horses, and hung our clothes out to drip on the wet porch, where they got much wetter. I had my first steamed clams – one of the best meals I've ever eaten.

Dear Poll,

I hope you are well and reasonably content and smothered in beautiful daughters and that you have at least access to a dog.

How would you feel about lunch on Friday? We have the whole of this city to choose from. I know a hole-in-the-wall in Chinatown with good food, or we could meet at the Met Museum and eat there, or there is a very gemutlich cafe in the Austrian gallery there on the Upper East Side – I am looking for somewhere with a huge collection of cheap lampshades – or the Noho Star or whatever you're having yourself (title for a cookbook?). I am trying to find some small parchment sconce lampshades.

Or you could get the F train to Brooklyn and we could walk in the beautiful park?

All this is sheer time-wasting, but I'd like to be with you and I'm not writing.

xxxxxxxxxxxxxxxxxxxxNuala

We both loved dogs and missed ours when we were away; she wrote about her beloved mutt Molly's reaction when she got home to County Clare.

It was enough to make me weep, she was so beside herself. I got out of the car and whistled and she hurtled up the lane, and she's a fat little thing, but her little muddy legs blurred practically and then she wouldn't leave me. Even in the shower she sat outside looking through the glass . . . I face 5 months without her. I don't know how to bear it.

She used to fret that Molly would outlive her, but Molly died a year before her.

Nuala had a great sweetness of nature mixed in with general fury. She also had extraordinary intellectual capacities, but she wore her learning lightly and was never didactic. I've never met anyone who was so well read. And she could be hysterically funny. She brought such vivid apprehensions of daily life, such energy, quickness, delight, profound knowledge of the arts, literature, music, passionate feelings, surprise and pleasure to living and to life. You could never be bored for an instant with her around (though you could be alarmed by a freakish change of mood).

She wrote to me not long before the diagnosis of her illness:

Maybe it's the season but black anxiety wakes me up too. Though, like you, I know how fortunate I am and can count all the things up. and I try to pray.

I think it becomes too hard, the whole thing, Poll. I think time loads too much on us. And we have to negotiate our way into grey hair and dumpiness and of course that breaks a woman's heart . . . The only answer I know is to turn out from ourselves. Work is part of this, and you have such a family, and friends, such opportunity.

One night we were having supper in her apartment in New York and I saw that she was walking oddly and asked her what was wrong; she said she had been exercising too much and I laughed fit to bust because Nuala never exercised. But she insisted no, no, she had turned over a new leaf and knew now, for the first time, that what she wanted was a beautiful old age with cats and dogs and Proust, and to spend time in County Clare and Dublin and Brooklyn with her friends and with her partner, John.

The next day both her arms and her legs felt funny and she went to the emergency department of NYU Hospital and they pulled her in immediately. John phoned me from the hospital and I got down there in a glaze of panic, all our lives changed by a sentence. Six weeks to live, a sentence told to her without care or tenderness while she sat in her meagre hospital smock on a high gurney so that her legs dangled like a little girl's, her blonde curls tousled, her little round face pale.

We had such plans: to go to Colmar to see that most terrifying of all masterpieces, the Isenheim Altarpiece by Grünewald; to Paris, where she was teaching, in July, and to Vienna for the opera.

She went to Sicily with her family just before she died and to Madrid with her friends Brian and Luke and told me in excitement that Luke was making her read everything about Velázquez; 'And you wouldn't know, you wouldn't know, Poll, how much I have learnt.'

And on top of it all she was a most wonderful and felicitous writer. She finished that obituary of John McGahern with these words:

> He had embarked on a life of heroic honesty. He already knew what he meant by being a writer. He gave me, what he could ill afford, a copy of Rilke's *Letters to a Young Poet*. Now, I see that John, for all that he was shabby and provincial-looking and unregarded and about to incur the hatred of the deathly Ireland of that time, had already absorbed Rilke's advice: 'That you may find in yourself enough patience to endure and enough simplicity to have faith; that you may gain more and more confidence in what is difficult and in your solitude among other people . . . And as for the rest, let life happen to you. Believe me: life is in the right, always.' No more life for John. But there was a distance from experience in him from the start – the distance he used, I suppose, in the making of his art – that prevents me from pitying him even for his death. He had pieced his broken heart together after he lost his mother. He had made himself into a true stoic. I don't think I've ever met anyone who so fully accepted the way things are. In the simplest way, he was always ready to die.

She knew what she was writing about but I don't think she ever pieced her heart together. She wrote to me from Clare a year before with terrible presentiment:

> I am okay but uneasy, very uneasy. And my first-ever boyfriend, his obit was in the paper, it is as if the grim reaper is at the edge of the field sharpening his scythe . . . Goodbye for now, not for long xx Nuala

And now it's for ever. I don't know what I'll do without her.

The Last Time
I Saw Paris

So, who's adorable then?

The last removal van has gone. Only in Paris could you stick a bollard, nicked from Chiswick (and, oh yes, returned), at the bottom of a street, sling a hand-painted sign saying *fermé* across it and not have one driver or person object – cars reversed obediently, the gendarmerie walked past, the street was ours. The drivers of the removal vans, all rookies in Paris, were amazed – in London they would have been fined and given points and moved on within five minutes. Here, in the busy Ile Saint-Louis, they stayed much of the day.

M. Kieken, who owns the antique shop opposite and who became such a good friend (and who had found me the apartment in the first place), watched with anguished relish as the furniture – much of it French and to his taste – was ladled into the vans bound for London. He had watched it all arrive over the past few years, always on a Saturday.

This is germane because the only way I can furnish a house is by trial and error, by putting Thi*s here* and That *there*, then shaking my head – it doesn't work – but since the This and That were in another country entirely, things got a leetle complicated. The Channel intervened for a start. Eurotunnel and myself are like *that*. The Effort! The Miles! The Pas de Calais, the most boring landscape in the world! Picardie! No roses blooming ever! The AutoRoute du Nord! Aargh. The Paris *périphérique*! I could do it in my sleep, like an old horse. And I adored ever minute.

But the thing is M. Kieken had only seen the stuff going in – he doesn't work on a Sunday so he never saw a stick coming out and thus must have become persuaded of one of two things: one, that I had bought the whole block and was gradually furnishing it; or, two, the more likely, I was one of those people one reads about in the silly season when police and social workers have to carve a way through mountains of mouldy detritus to get to the body of the person finally mired under her hoarding habit, her face gnawed by the cat.

The last of the pictures was carted down, the last carpet rolled, the last bit of dysoning done and I was alone in a place where on and off for five short and idyllic years I had fulfilled a dream.

I walked round the empty apartment. The French windows – well, they would be French – were open, and the courtyard lay in its spring glory, every window box abloom; on the street side the Seine glittered at each end. The apartment still looked lovely and I suddenly wished I was a minimalist and could live in bareness.

I walked over to the Left Bank to stay with my friend Diane Johnson, who lives half of the year in California and half in Paris. Tough, tough life, but she bears up well. The most unobtrusively intelligent conversationalist I know (and good conversation is an art hard to come by in England, believe me), she is also the wittiest writer – if you haven't read *Le Mariage* and *Le Divorce* go buy them now, not only for a cracking good story but also to get a perfect outsider/inside look into the workings of French high society, usually impenetrable to the stranger.

The next morning, my last as a resident of Paris, I did something I have never done. I sat down to have a long luxurious morning coffee in a cafe sidewalk on the rue du Bac. Paris was intent on giving me a good send-off, intent on punishing me for leaving her. Enchantment in the air, and not just driven by pre-nostalgia and incipient yearning. The sun was beaming down; the sky was that intense cerulean blue that Paris mornings have in late spring; the markets in the rue de Seine and the rue Mazarin were buzzing; an old lady in a pink Chanel suit tottered by, tugged by two Bichons Frisés, which will give you an idea of her size, and at one of the tables on the sidewalk a couple with a small nippy Jack Russell sat down opposite me. They would have given Robert Doisneau a run for his money. Both beautiful: she like Juliette Greco crossed with Rachel Weisz – and with a smouldering Gauloise; he like Bernard-Henri Lévy, only with a kinder face.

They smiled at me. I smiled at them and I asked if I might pet their adorable little dog. *Oui alors*, they were 'appy, but I must not on any account feeed 'im. I restrained myself and frolicked a little with the dog and went back to my table rubbing my nipped fingers. At the next table a young Japanese beauty and an American man were having coffee. He was smoking and trying to break the habit; she was unhappy that he smoked and I asked him if he had ever tried an electronic ciggie. He avowed he had not and never would and I said, wiping mine on the soiled paper tablecloth, that he could try mine. This he did and declared himself converted – anything to shut me up – but the Japanese girl hugged me and thanked me because she said she hated the smell of tobacco and it literally was coming between them.

A party of elderly women, very American, very black hair, very red lips, very big bags, came along looking for wherever to sit. There was only room for four within the cafe so the fifth one loitered a mite disconsolately and I said you why don't you sit at my table. She sat down gratefully because her feet were tired, they were a party from Pittsburgh, they had never been to Paris, they were walked off their feet, they adored it, it was so good of me, was I English, she didn't think the English spoke to strangers, just goes to show. I said, 'I'm not English, I'm Irish and the English don't speak to strangers, they don't hardly speak to each other. I've been married to one for over forty years and he still hasn't addressed me.'

She squealed with laughter and regaled the others with what I'd said so loudly that everyone stared at us and the Parisians passing by rolled their eyes at what Paris had to put up with. A couple of well-groomed women came and sat at the last vacant table to my left. They were neat and pretty; could well have been French, with *les petits soins* so much in evidence, but they were English from Yorkshire. Diane and Anne. Anne had moved to Florida to be near her daughter but her son-in-law wasn't all that pleased; Diane had lost the love of her life a few months before and was grieving; and they had come to Paris to be happy. They looked fifty and I was astounded to find they were over seventy, so vibrant they were, so full of life, so optimistic, all adding to the gaiety of the morning with Paris at her most seductive and everyone around, Japanese, American, English, Irish chatting and laughing.

I noticed that the pretty girl with the dog had left and the man was sitting by himself. He smiled at me with a sweet smile. For me, one of the wonderful things about getting older is that you are never on the pull. In fact, women over a certain age are invisible, but in Paris they are not and it is good for the spirit. There was no hint of flirtatiousness in his smile, however, nor in my returning one. It was simply two happy people – though I was filled with sadness too – basking in a spring morning in the *joie de vivre* of the city of light. Which I was leaving of my own accord. I finished my coffee and was preparing to take my leave when a shadow loomed over my table. Anne, Diane and I looked up. The beautiful Frenchman was leaning over my table. He took my hand. He kissed it.

He said, *'Vous êtes adorable,'* and walked off into the market.

I sat goose-fleshed with pleasure and romance.

Anne said, 'Is this a set-up?' They looked around for the cameras. 'No, no,' I said, 'I'm as stunned as you. More so.'

'Do you know him?' Diane asked.

'No,' I said. 'I never saw him before in my life.'

They looked at me with utter absorption and, I have to say, puzzlement.

Diane clapped her hand to her open mouth. 'You think it only happens in the movies. Or bad advertisements. But however it came about, happen it's the most romantic thing that I ever witnessed.'

'It is to me too,' I said, completely pink with pleasure and feeling like Audrey Hepburn in any old film. 'But I can never tell anyone,' I said. 'No one would ever believe me. And anyway, my friends, and especially my daughters, they'd hate me for telling it and start pushing each other over.'

'We'll bear witness,' Diane said, and wrote down my email address.

But I didn't hold much cop by that.

So, I left Paris on wings, given the most tender and beautiful of send-offs, utterly unsolicited, by a good-hearted handsome stranger who knows what Paris and sad women are all about.

Epilogue
An email from Diane

Hi, Polly – I just wanted to say I really enjoyed meeting you at Smith's Bakery in lovely Paris. I was the Englishwoman with my friend (small, blonde hair, big appetite for muffins & hot chocolate) whose mouths dropped open when the gorgeous Frenchman greeted you and kissed you as only a Frenchman could! We went on to have a lovely day in the Parisian sun and for a few minutes I too stepped out of 50+++ invisibility! Whilst strolling in the Place de Vosges, one of the artists took a shine to me and wasted no time in demonstrating that his intentions were far from honourable! It may have been part of his sales technique but do you know, I don't care! For a few minutes I felt fabulous, something I haven't felt since my lover/friend died. Altogether a fabulous and very memorable day.

Best wishes, Diane

The Cranes
are Flying

I've always loved cranes, the avian kind, their odd slightly prehistoric look. I'd never seen them in real life and the most telling images in my mind were the marvellous Japanese prints of cranes flying around Mount Fuji – draughtsmanship and aesthetics at their best.

Then this summer someone mentioned that at a certain place in Hungary up to sixty thousand cranes passed overhead in a matter of a few days in October. I tried to visualize it. I thought of the cranes as passing through some sky chasm above Hungary, those grey, elegant, crepuscular, elongated, etiolated ancient bodies skeining in fine trails across the sky.

I also thought of the passenger pigeon, a native of North America, of how at the beginning of the nineteenth century as the birds arrived for nesting, people spoke of flocks a hundred miles wide, of billions of birds, of the day being darkened as they flew over state after state.

To the American pioneers the birds were for food and sport. They were hunted by bands of professional shooters, used as bait in trap shooting, persecuted relentlessly, yet even in the 1880s, after endless butchery, they still numbered millions. Then, quite suddenly, they died. They needed those enormous flocks to create the conditions for continued life. The last known passenger pigeon, a bird called Martha, died in Cincinnati Zoo in 1914.

I know that there are fears that the same collapse of bird numbers may well happen to many bird species soon: fertilizers, land improvement (oh weasel words), has meant the loss of habitats within a few years. So I wanted to see the cranes while they were still flying in their great numbers.

I've always been passionate about birds, and I can quote the terrible statistics that are turning us into birdless Britain. I listen to farmers and the Countryside Alliance prate about their love for and protection of the English countryside and I want to hammer them upside down into hard soil. One hundred and thirty-seven British bird species are on the danger list. The population of skylarks has declined by 75 per cent, the house sparrow population by nearly 71 per cent in the last thirty years; lapwings have declined continuously on lowland farmland since the mid-1980s, because changes in agricultural practice have led to their breeding productivity dropping below a sustainable level; swallows are endangered and the corncrake has almost vanished; corn buntings are down by 77 per cent, the linnets down by 56 per cent, reed buntings by 59 per cent, grey partridges by 75 per cent. All perishing through horrible and prevalent farming practice.

On our land we sowed spring cereal, restored dew ponds, cut tramways for owls, left the hedges high, and planted trees; none of it too difficult, all without subsidy, but too difficult apparently for farmers subsidized to the hilt. The birds have returned, including barn owls and partridges, and the place is now crawling with bats (also on the decline) but the acreage – two hundred – is too small to make an appreciable difference to the overall picture of doom. So the idea of going to Hungary, a country as yet unravaged by bad farming practices, and seeing unlimited number of birds seemed a gift too great not to grasp.

In Hungary I made an astonishing entry into a parallel universe. Three hours hard driving due east of Budapest to the back of beyond to a national park called Hortobágy near the town of Debrecen, brought me into the vanished realms of childhood, into a vast simulacrum of the lost country where I grew up and as it had been for a millennium before. There, in Ireland, it has vanished.

But first, the size of the place; the great national parks are immense (and there are many like Hortobágy where we were based, staying in a hunting lodge straight out of a Charles Adams cartoon). They stretch across hundreds of thousands of acres – imagine Salisbury Plain, or half of Norfolk, endless epic vast spaces flat as water, with few inhabitants, no hedges, or any kind of pylon or pole, and you begin to apprehend the size. Empty long roads with few cars skirt the plains with their autumnal clumps of trees along waterways. These rich plains are only fertilized by sheep, horses and cattle and so are still covered with an immense diversity of plant life, weeds and grasses which look as beautiful as anything we grow so proudly in our gardens. A rare and discreet convolvulus twines about, and a lovely white flat flower looking something like a gardenia, as well as abutilon and myriad others grow lavishly.

In the distance one sees an occasional homestead, a rickety wooden house, the traditional long barn, looking like something painted by Andrew Wyeth, in bleached wood, silvered by the weather; the profound silence is broken only by the call of birds and the distant tinkle of a bell tied around the neck of an animal.

In Hortobágy there are enormous fishponds, hundreds of acres in size, dug out by Russian prisoners of war, which have become havens for birds. Great white egrets in their hundreds congregate here, grey herons, teal, avocets, tern, geese, reed warblers, ducks; even the secretive bittern – I couldn't believe I'd actually seen a bittern – all standing and feeding so near by you hardly needed binoculars. (Well, not the bittern – he silently disappeared.)

Although everything is quiet, untouched, a few high viewing platforms which reveal stupendous panoramic views have been built in the national park. Through binoculars one may see a herd of sheep three or four miles away cropping the dense rich pasture while a good half a mile further on their shepherd lies fast asleep, a coat over his head, his dog alert by his side, doing his own and the shepherd's work.

From these platforms one also sees an astounding variety of birds. In one sweep of the telescope I saw three white-tailed eagles high in the sky, harriers, merlins, falcons, all circling in different holding patterns in the crisp cerulean air. I felt like calling them in to land from the control tower. On the ground and on the stretches of water, dotterel, curlew, lapwing, plover, larks, ospreys, herons, snipe, wagtails, buntings and geese fed in their hundreds.

One morning Dr Gabo Kovacs, a famous bird expert and a keeper in the national park, with eyes that made Paul Newman's seem muddy, came to help find the great bustard. They are noble birds, big birds, bigger than storks, with wonderful markings, extremely wary and shy. For over an hour we watched these lovely remnants of an older world, grazing and stepping delicately only two fields away.

The cranes were less obliging: morning and evening we went to where the famous skeins of thousands of cranes were expected to come flying in, and morning and evening we would sight them miles away, struggling along. It transpired that for the first time in years they had separated and were flying erratically in different small groups and on slightly different routes. Sod's law, but by this time I didn't really care as the whole thrust of my Hungarian adventure had changed and I was experiencing – or re-experiencing – something that jolted me so profoundly that I found it hard to recover.

But then one morning I was woken by an odd noise, pervasive clamouring but subdued, which I couldn't identify – some kind of muffled calling, circles of noises in the distance. The Cranes! The Cranes! coming in to land on their feeding grounds before setting off on the long journey south. That first sighting as they came in low across the rising sun, marking the sky like celestial writing, was heart-stopping.

But what moved me most profoundly was the look and feel of these Hungarian plains and their people. I was back in Ireland sixty years ago, tumbling without warning through time into that extraordinary shaggy old place; wrinkled aged women with crumpled faces and headscarves and enormous bosoms in flowery overalls and long skirts; fierce men, black-browed, big-nosed, moustached, unkempt, intense, alive, in old dungarees and grey trousers thick with oil and sweat, and wearing hats.

'Anglo-Saxons are a lot tidier than Hungarians,' a Hungarian man remarked, which is something I never thought to hear. But we have become so homogenized in Western Europe in the last few decades that our characters seem to have been scrubbed out of our faces. We have indeed been tidied up. The people in the small villages in eastern Hungary were like the vanished people I grew up among in rural Ireland. They seemed made of sterner stuff, literally – their features more craggy and hewn, their expressions more intense and curious, their skin more wrinkled, weather-beaten. Their clothes were quite different too – older, duller, more worn, more layered and more preserved because scarcer. There wasn't much of anything and what there was had to last. This is how it still is in this part of Hungary.

On the main roads there are cars, but between the small villages there are still horses and carts and on one of few busy roads, between two villages, I saw a sight to make the heart stand still – a tiny foal in its harness, 'learning the route', out for the first time in the shafts of a cart with her mother the mare, pulling a big wagon facing the oncoming traffic, the little thing wild-eyed and quivering with fright, trying to get to her mother but the reins and shafts preventing her. I'd forgotten the reality of that, of horse and cart, the smells, the leather, the uninsulated makeshiftness of it, how the weather and countryside closed around you, though for the first years of my life it was an intrinsic part of that life.

We've forgotten now what it is like to see a town or a village without any cars at all. Streets look totally different without any markings or any parked cars. Nothing is regimented. The gardens of the houses dribble into the street and nearly every village house has a self-sufficient smallholding around it, filled with hens and geese, haystacks, wood stacks, apple trees, onions.

These are the last relics of a dispensation that lasted millennia, has already vanished in Western Europe and will vanish here within ten years. I grew up in such a dispensation, I watched it vanish as I thought for ever, so suddenly to find myself back in it stabbed me to my heart. I looked into faces that I thought I would never look on again. These were people who have never heard of plenitude, of skin care, of a culture of grooming, of any kind of pampering. The beautiful skinny groomed girls of Budapest and Debrecen have no place in this, the deep country, in the villages and hamlets where time is spent in wresting a living from the land.

For most of the time while there I was in a state of almost painful, attenuated feeling – to be back in time, to that other place so long vanished, not in memory, but in sensory feeling – to be able to see it, touch it, smell it, breathe it, was a profound shock to the system. I had gone for the birds, to find the cranes, but what I found were the lost domains. A.E. Housman country . . .

That is the land of lost content,
I see it shining plain,
The happy highways where I went,
And cannot come again.

Not that they were all that happy. But I loved that land.

Look Back in Wonder

January Make resolution not to lose my temper so quickly. I've lost it every day since. That will teach me to break my resolution never to make a resolution. I read a sentence in Flaubert that makes me laugh, so well does it describe my current state. 'I go from exasperation to a state of collapse then I recover and go from prostration to Fury so that my average state is being annoyed.' Resolve to do better. I also make a resolution not to get any more dogs and my addiction is soothed by daughter Rose getting a white miniature bull terrier called Aggie. Not the brightest spark in the fire but so delighted with life that she doesn't notice when she hits her head against a wall, just bounces away like Gatsby's gold-hatted lover. Then my life suddenly changes – my husband gets a chest infection leading to pneumonia, and the threat of kidney failure. When the doctors said he wouldn't last the night the pain for all of us was cellular. A week later when he is sitting up drinking coffee and eating biscuits I realize he is from Planet Krypton. Then my happiness is tempered by hearing about the wonderful Caroline Walsh's death. She was the literary editor of *The Irish Times*, brilliant and passionate and a marvel – everyone loved her and she was at the centre of Irish literary life. I deal with it by not believing it. I find incredulity to be my best weapon now against the ravages of time.

In **February** I go to New York for a day. This is one of the most glamorous things I've ever done. An amazing suede-lined jet takes me to a small airport in Upper New York State and from there I whizz in a helicopter along the Hudson Valley, low enough to be able to see all the great mansions above the bluffs – the houses that Edith Wharton and her ilk lived in and wrote about it. I have lunch with friends who commit to loving me as they know

I am leaving again the next morning. Afterwards I go up to the university where I sometimes teach and dig out all the stuff I left behind after my last teaching term. Last year I arrived in New York for three months, at the beginning of the semester, with two suitcases and some papers and when I left I had accumulated six suitcases and seventeen boxes. I have no idea how it happened. I'm like an old ship steaming through water with endless barnacles attaching to her hull all unbeknownst to the upper decks. And since I couldn't afford to take the junk home on a commercial flight I stored it in a tolerant friend's basement.

The owner of the jet is an old friend who spent twenty years of his life struggling to perfect a product, risking all, mortgaging his house, with banks refusing him credit and people stealing his ideas, but perfect it he did, so that it now it is the leading product of its kind all over the world. He loves his success. I confessed to him about my guilty secret cache. When he saw the actual amount I had collected being piled out on the tarmac to be loaded on to his plane, he said with a fairly sardonic gleam in his eye, 'So I'm just your private DHL?'

In **March** I travel on Eurostar to Paris with my husband. I am wearing a beret to humour him as he still somehow sees me as the young person he first met who was wearing a beret and a very short kilt with that big pin in it. It hardly bears thinking about. Anyway, two goons in a random security check come along the carriages to look at our passports – and they stare long and hard at mine. Well, I can't blame them – in my passport photograph I look as though I've recently escaped from the specimen room of the Natural History Museum. They give it back to me – really quite reluctantly – go along the carriage for a few yards, stop, confer, come back and ask for my passport again. One asks, 'Madame, how old are you?' I simper, as any girl in a beret should, and my husband rises to his feet (metaphorically speaking, as he can't do such a thing any more). 'Well!' he says,'I can hardly believe my ears. That any man, and especially a Frenchman, should ask a woman such a very ungallant question.' The Frenchman has the grace to blush. 'Monsieur,' he says, 'before you judge, please have a look at your wife's passport.' He looks. I have taken my youngest daughter's passport.

In **April** I fly from Stansted to Cork with Ryanair. Everyone is always grumbling and complaining about Ryanair. Why? It does what it says it will do. It's always on time, the staff are pleasant, the planes are clean, the fares are cheap. What else do the complainers want? If they want more, pay more and fly first class with someone else. (Not that there is first class on short haul flights any more.) Anyway on the plane the young attendant, very fit (I'll come back to that phrase later on), is intoning the usual safety mantra about the brace position and oxygen mask – which I can repeat word for word now like the Hail Mary, I've listened to it so often – when I hear him say, 'This is a non-smoking flight and anyone caught smoking will be asked to leave the plane immediately and I will help push him or her out the door. It's only an 18,000 foot drop at this point.' I look around to see what effect this interesting extempore take is having on my fellow passengers. Not a thing. No one has heard it because no one was listening. On the way back my cosmetics are in that small stupid statutory plastic bag. The girl at security won't let me through because, she says, the bag is 2 millimetres too big. To think that could happen in Cork! Remember my New Year resolution about temper-losing and bite my lip.

Back in London I interview Yoko Ono for *Vogue*. I first met her forty years ago and one of my treasured possessions is a *Box of Smile* made by her and given to me by John Lennon. How good is that. I'd forgotten how tiny she is and I am amazed that someone who is nearly eighty hasn't a trace of cellulite anywhere on her body – and there is a lot of the same body showing as she is being photographed in hot boy shorts. Not a moment's inhibition. 'How do you do it?' I ask, amazed and put out by her flamboyant and seductive response to the camera, her radioactive self-assurance; how to reconcile the rather shy person I know her to be with this feminine ferocity. She looks at me as though I am mad and says, astonished, 'Because I'm a performer. I just do the performance.'

Paris on a **May** morning. I am leaning out of the windows with the net curtains slightly billowing in the mild wind watching Paris awakening. The cliché is alive and well. Behind me a Beethoven late quartet is on the radio, full of pain and sweetness. The sky is celestially blue, M. Kieken is taking down his shutters and an old man is carrying a half-wrapped baguette home for breakfast. Somewhere I can hear the rhythmic creaking of a bed – a couple making love. Ah, Paris! Ah, romance! There is a smell of contentment in the very air. After half an hour I begin to be amazed by the stamina of the couple. Then I realize the rhythmic sounds are coming from the radiator cranking along in my bedroom. *Tiens!* Sad disillusionment.

In **June** I'm walking with my dog through a park and see a young bearded man doing push-ups on a park bench. Many, many push-ups. I start to count as I draw nearer . . . forty, forty-one . . . and as I look back see him still at it as I round the corner. His energy makes me feel like a two-toed sloth. After a while the dog and I turn back home and, lumme, there he is still, pushing and humping and just as I pass him, he stops and sits panting, on the bench. 'You're very fit,' I say to him. Well you've never seen a man skedaddle faster in your life. When I get home, a daughter tells me gently what the word 'fit' means now. I go into a darkened room, put a wet dog on my forehead. I dread meeting him again and resolve to buy a balaclava.

In **July** I rent a house by the seaside so I can have all the family around me, boating and shrimping, bathing and surfing. Actually, I hate renting. I like having my own things around me and am so territorial, it hurts. How can I be this age and be so immature that I have to be on my own turf to be happy? In theory the place is wonderful; three miles of crescent-shaped long golden sands (they filmed *Chariots of Fire* there), men in deckchairs, with rolled-up trousers and spotted handkerchiefs tied in knots on their heads, and kiss-me-quick cards and shouts of 'I've lost my little willie'. But this year the weather is disastrous. I get free exfoliation treatment every time I go out the door and the wind and rain are so constant that they whip the sea to a raging froth. There's nothing to do but read. In *The New Yorker* I read a solution to the problem that as we age, our faces lose volume and fullness. 'This deficit can be corrected by draping a naked newborn baby over your head and using a Sharpie to draw eyes and nose on the baby's bottom.' The writer also suggests that the most flattering outfit one can wear is a smile and a gun and the question, 'Now do you think I'm pretty?'

(Thinking of baby botties I remember reading in Brendan Behan of how as he was walking through the Daisy market in Dublin he heard a stallkeeper say to his wife, 'Keep the baby's bottom off the butter.') Then for two glorious days the sun appears and I have the holiday I dream of, though I work harder than I have ever worked in my life keeping the whole lot fed.

In **August** I visit my friend Suzanne in France and go for a long walk up small hills where I am surrounded by an amazing profusion of wild flowers. Very hot, dazzling blue sky, green vines and this exquisite conglomeration of flowers everywhere. There are no people but many fascinating old buildings and the remains of what looks like an ancient village with crumbling limestone foundations and a beautiful stone igloo. I call in for lunch in a cafe near the Canal du Midi and the woman who runs it tells me her extraordinary story. She and her husband used to run a bigger restaurant nearby and very well they did it too. Then one day when he was in McDonald's in Narbonne a madman came in and buried an axe in his head. I don't like to ask what a French chef was doing in McDonald's.

When I come back to England to my sorrow I realize summer is over before it has begun. The best thing I've ever read that captures that heart-piercing feeling of the nostalgia and sadness of this time, the gloaming of summer, is in Elizabeth Bishop's poem 'Song', which begins:

> Summer is over upon the sea.
> The pleasure yacht, the social being,
> that danced on the endless polished floor,
> stepped and side-stepped like Fred Astaire,
> is gone, is gone, docked somewhere ashore.

I put away all the swim suits and sarongs and beach balls. Next thing I know I will be hauling out the drifts of spangles for Christmas.

September A friend from Northern Ireland invites me to dinner in the House of Lords. One of the other guests is a bishop, a pompous, didactic man who lives in a bubble of self-esteem. As we walk down a long corridor we glimpse an old man in a large chair at the end. A woman comes out of a nearby room, crosses over to the cove on the chair and kisses him. The bishop gives a sentimental sigh and says words to the effect of how sweet to see a married couple behave like that. I snap to attention as I realize that the sweet couple is Ian and Eileen Paisley. I look at them with rage and disdain. These two people, who I think did so much harm to my kind, who helped fan the flame of prejudice and hatred in Ulster, who should be ashamed and ostracized, are lolling about in the Upper House, honoured with peerages, flown back and forth from London to Belfast, put up in style and paid a huge amount of expenses (£305 a sitting). I look at them, in their horrible complacency, and wonder if they have any idea or realization of how much harm they have done to our society and how much they are hated. As I pass the philistine pair I realize that nothing will ever penetrate their heads other than their own base opinions and beliefs.

In **October** the best thing happens. I have been in a state of tension for months because Daisy, my beloved daughter, who has not had a good history of pregnancy, is expecting again. It soon became apparent that the new baby was also at risk. It used to be that when that happened the mother-to-be was sent to bed for six months. Now it's the opposite and she is made to keep going as busily as possible. Since Daisy moves at the speed of light at the best of times this meant that all I've seen of her was a blur. Then in late October Charlie Ray comes barrelling out – he takes only an hour to be born and a whole new life begins and already he is the light of my life.

A week later I go to Belfast to give a talk under the aegis of Queen's University. The audience is great and seems to enjoy it well enough – afterwards people come up and talk and are generally appreciative. As I start off for lunch with my friend Tess, who has organized it all, a small ferrety man I have seen hovering rather ominously corners me. 'Can I be frank with you?' he says. My heart sinks. Everyone knows that these words herald rudeness. 'I'd rather you didn't,' I say. He takes no notice. 'I have to tell you I think you're a bad lecturer,' he says in that particular righteous Ulster accent I find so intolerable. I am somewhat startled but also amused, though I wouldn't dare show it. 'Don't take umbrage,' he says. 'I'm a vicar, in the Church of Ireland.' 'That wouldn't stop me taking umbrage,' I say, 'but I'm not taking umbrage, I'm taking my leave. I want to go to lunch.' 'You might have given a good lecture,' he continues, quite cross by now. 'People seemed to be liking it well enough but not me, for I couldn't hear hardly a word you said. I'm deaf.'

November It's my birthday – a significant one – and at the party which my husband gives for me, my grandson George says to me somewhat wistfully. 'I wish I'd known you when you were new.' As a birthday treat I go to Vienna and am given the chance of a lifetime by being allowed to look closely at the Dürer drawings and watercolours in the Albertina Museum. It is hard to fathom how he, the greatest artist of the Northern Renaissance, did these drawings. Apparently he did not use a magnifying glass, but you need one to tease out the details in these exquisite, epic drawings. Their visionary intensity leaves one breathless. The image of the bird – *Dead Blue Roller* – is inexpressibly sad and expressively beautiful. Actually touching the original drawing of *A Young Hare*, knowing that he had drawn these lines, was a highlight not just of the month, or the year, but of my life.

December Almost my favourite month – but then every month is, more or less, for Pollyanna here. January resolution gone to dust, I adopt a new dog – an old one, actually, who has been a stud, has sired about a thousand puppies and is now on the junk heap. I am frightened that he may terrorize my dear little cat and so far am keeping them apart. I adore Christmas and always have and it's my joyous annual decorating deal, perhaps a bit Beckettian – all that trouble for such short glory – but so worth it. But have you noticed how time is snapping back like taut elastic whereas it used to stretch? Not much point to putting the tree away. It will be December again in a minute.

But January with all its wonderful promise will wing its way in before that and we must celebrate that we are all still here. So Happy New Year and may each month bring fresh happiness. And I'll repeat what Emily Dickinson said and which I tell myself each year: 'We turn not older with years, but newer every day.'

Realms of Gold

I taught myself to read when I was three and I remember my mother not believing that I had read *Daddy-Long-Legs* in one night when I was eight; but who could not have devoured such a book at one sitting? I have always read voraciously, and you might say vicariously, almost as an antidote to reality, but lately and to put it simply I seemed to have no time to do something that for most of my life has been as essential as breathing.

I am a fast reader but no matter how fast I couldn't keep up with what flooded in, drenching me in words and images. The magazines, the newspapers, the supplements, the emails, the catalogues, the reviews . . . I think it was Margaret Drabble who said that as a young woman she understood the meaning of mortality when she realized that she would die before she had read all the books she wanted to read; now that she is a certain age she realizes mortality means that she will die before she reads all the books on her bedside table.

My dilemma exactly; but, worse still, I wasn't even able to finish all the piled-up *New Yorkers* throbbing reproachfully. I think of *The New Yorker* as required reading for anyone living in the slipstream of the world, but each issue takes three weeks to read, drat it (never mind the *London Review of Books*). And piled behind them are Must Read books from years back, plus newer, seductive-looking ones because I continue to buy them – I can't resist a good chubby dust jacket (oh, well named) – I even buy special ones from private presses like Simon Lawrence's glorious Fleece Press. In some the typeface makes an s look like an f and fo where the bee fuckf becomef quite rude.

Now the paradox is that, for all my early reading, I avoided the stuff called the classics. They seemed too grand, unreadable, unreachable, as if written in an unavailable language, and had attained classic status through being beyond the ordinary reach. Dickens, Tolstoy, Homer, Virgil, Woolf were literally closed to me.

I read Joyce early on because I never thought of him as a classic writer, and Jane Austen, George Eliot and the Brontës because they wrote such cracking good stories. Shakespeare's sonnets I knew, and *Julius Caesar* we read at school – but his great works I only knew from going to the theatre when I came to London.

So I hadn't travelled much in the realms of gold except for poetry; I always read poetry and learnt it from an early age (and paid my daughters £5 each if they learnt a Shakespearean sonnet, that inspired and precise work of art – this at a time when a fiver was real money). Jeanette Winterson wrote that she reads a poem on waking every morning and I adopted the practice. It does rev up the mental energy and the spirit life, and often gives a new perspective on the day ahead. Or it can cast you down . . . Auden's poem 'The Shield of Achilles' (*read it!*) is downright depressing but timely, timely:

> That girls are raped, that two boys knife a third,
> Were axioms to him, who'd never heard
> Of any world where promises were kept,
> Or one could weep because another wept.

I learn from poetry, and get that frisson of pure satisfaction when I recognize what is happening in the poem, the poet's ability to make it happen, a transformative process which nudges my life into a deeper channel. Put it like this; it does me good.

I am badly educated and I hold no brief for the Catholic Church; but my, did they teach you language! Here is what I was reading once a week when I was seven or eight years old. 'Set a watch before my mouth and door around about my lips that my heart may not incline to evil words to make excuses in sin. May the Lord enkindle in us the fire of his love and the flame of his everlasting charity.'

And we recited by heart every week these words about the Virgin Mary, the virgin who was also the mother of God, God help us: Cause of our Joy, Spiritual Vessel, Vessel of Honour, Singular Vessel of Devotion, Mystical Rose, Tower of David, Tower of Ivory, House of Gold, Ark of the Covenant, Morning Star . . . We murmured responses in Latin and sang Latin hymns.

What I learnt I learnt at primary school – forty-two of us in a smallish room with one amazing teacher – and then I went to a convent boarding school until, like many an adolescent, I became anorexic, was beaten by the nuns for my pains and was transferred to a Dothegirls Hall day school – one of the worst schools in Ireland. I was so unhappy I left it at seventeen and so didn't go to university. It has always has been one of the great regrets of my life and I get cross when I hear people decry those three or four luxurious years when they were able to read what they wanted and listen to more or less learned people lecturing about Coriolanus and T. S. Eliot and Auden and Donne and Montaigne and Whitman and Moby Dick and Herrick and anything else under the sun. I remember an upper-class Englishman who took his privileged sojourn at Oxford as an entitlement (although if his IQ had dipped any lower you'd have had to water him twice a day), saying to me when he'd worked out I hadn't been to university, 'Shame on you.' So I was a very happy woman when, in my sixties, I was asked to teach at Barnard College at Columbia University and became, thus, a Professor.

Then one day I was talking about how not long ago it was required that one read the classics, spoke French, played the piano, and painted watercolours before one could be called civilized; and I was whining about this when someone I greatly respect said – laughing, but serious nonetheless – 'Nah, to be civilized you must read Racine in French.'

Well! I'd never even read the said Racine in English, so I set off to classes at Birbeck College and, lo, there read *Phèdre* and then lost the run of myself and began to read Ronsard and the first thing I read was this: 'Quand vous serez bien vieille, au soir à la chandelle/Assise auprès du feu, devidant & filant . . .' and as I read I heard in my mind's ear, 'When you are old and grey and full of sleep, And nodding by the . . .' Eh? Hello, I thought – Yeats's great poem is a translation? (albeit one that transcends the original) and I was filled with such delight at the discovery that I couldn't wait to tell my friends – many of whom knew it already. (They'd been to university, hadn't they?) So that was the first step; I began to read Homer and Christopher Logue's inspired translations and couldn't believe how accessible and terrifying and compulsive it was.

So I tried my hand at translation and came up with a perfect rendering of a famous couplet in *Phèdre*: 'Ce n'est plus une ardeur dans mes veines cachée: C'est Vénus tout entière à sa proie attachée.' It's all there in a pop song sung by Connie Francis.

> Stupid Cupid, you're a real mean guy.
> I'd like to clip your wings so you can't fly.
> I'm in love and it's a crying shame.
> And I know that you're the one to blame.
> Hey, hey, set me free.
> Stupid Cupid, stop picking on me.

Read Cupid for Venus and it's done and dusted. Perfect. (But I didn't leave the day job.)

Then my sister Helen gave me Virginia Woolf's *To the Lighthouse*. What she doesn't know about English literature isn't worth knowing, and I knew if she had gone to the trouble of buying me a special edition of a book, I must read it. Of course, I knew what Virginia Woolf wrote – like, say, I knew the North Pole: I knew everything about the place but hadn't been there and would prefer not to enter that icy place with its quivering icicles and chilly purity; instead I entered a world glittering with prose fireworks and glory and generosity.

It had all come so late; will I now have time to read it all? Never, never, never. But I plod happily onwards making inroads on the great tradition that I had skated over, scudding along the surface, the murky waters of ignorance beneath, and I'm so happy and delighted with what I read. A great writer can use the simplest images and deliver an entire reality. Tolstoy describing 'a prince as round and green and fat as a cucumber'. Or Anna when Vronsky first claps eyes on 'her shining grey eyes that looked dark from the thick lashes, the suppressed eagerness which played over her face and flitted between the brilliant eyes and the faint smile that curved her red lips'. Shakespeare having a high-spirited girl say, 'I will do anything ere I'm married to a sponge.' Juliet saying, 'Give me my Romeo. And when he shall die, / Take him and cut him out in little stars. / And he will make the face of heaven so fine, / That all the world will be in love with night / And pay no worship to the garish sun.' And then the use of the word 'thickens' . . . 'Light thickens, and the crow / Makes wing to th' rooky wood. / Good things of day begin to droop and drowse . . .' Thickens! It does, it does, as I've watched them make wing to the rooky wood. These are no longer cold classics but glowing truth. A world, solid, miraculous, a place we can enter into.

Think of how much poorer the world would be without literature. Think of a heroine like Cinderella. Before Perrault wrote her down, she didn't exist. Now she's in all our heads for all time and through her we were taught a good deal about life and enchantment and disappointment and jealousy and love even when we were very young. It's a simple story and a wonderful piece of writing.

Swift was once told by an admirer that *Gulliver's Travels* was a very simple book. 'Of course,' said Swift. 'Once you've thought of the big man and the little man, the rest is easy.' No, it's not; and it's our blessing that these artists pulled the chair up to the table and got started and kept going in their art and their life.

As I read I can see behind me a long golden perspective into the past glowing with thoughts and words and ideas moulded into art. Those men and women who toiled over pages to commit their thoughts to paper over the centuries have bequeathed us a treasure trove – and I owe them the honour of opening and reading them.

What Makes a Marriage Last?

I've been to so many weddings lately I've lost count. This is the second wave; the first was when my friends got married. Now, astonishingly, it's the children of my friends who are marrying. Whoa! Hold on there for a minute. How can this be? I only looked away for a nanosecond to get on with my life and those children smiling up at me from their prams or bawling in the supermarket or scowling from behind their gothic fringes are grown up enough to be married? How absurd, I think, and then: how absurd to think they can enter the universe of marriage without having been married and learnt what a place and state it is, like going to the moon without oxygen. But there they are happily taking off into the thin air with only lovely onionskin love to sustain them. I tremble for them. I was married for nearly fifty years but could I tell them how to be married? Could I carry back real knowledge to give them? Not on your life. I'm still stunned by surprise. Could I tell them what it takes to make a marriage last? Not a chance. Every marriage is its own creation, touch and go, built minute by minute, vast repositories for memories, for love, anger, despair, depression, joy and hope for the future, for something ever more about to be.

And if I could tell them would they listen? Get away! Advice has such little reality, such little value until after the event. But some do ask what is the point of a piece of paper and I tell them olden things. Marriage has nothing to do with a piece of paper. Marriage is a sacred mutual state. It's a bond. We don't use the word sacred much now but it means regarded with, or entitled to, the kind of respect or reverence which attaches to holy things; it is meant to be inviolable, protected by sanction and when you get married you enter into that state. But being sacred doesn't make it a safe place.

Nearly all the long-lasting marriages, the stable relationships, that I know have had this in common. They have had a divorce point and they have got over it. People who aren't married or whose marriages have broken down think that other marriages have somehow avoided the breaking point, the divorce place. Generally, they haven't. Observers do not see the fissures and chasms and abysses into which partners in a marriage at one time or another have fallen and hauled themselves out of, leaving pieces of themselves, flayed skin and bone and conscience down there in the rag and bone shop of the heart. In most long-lasting marriages one partner has, at one time, rescued and redeemed the other. A wife or a husband may take a risk and try to join the raggle-taggle gypsies. Many a wife is, at one point, Guinevere in the castle and her husband a raggle-taggle gypsy; and many a wife becomes a raggle-taggle gypsy and her husband must become a King Arthur waiting back in the castle. This is an intricate and dangerous drama. If the timing is wrong and both are fleeing to play in the woods, the marriage is over; but when King Arthur and the Queen find that home isn't a fortress, that there's no drawbridge, that wherever they are that's where their marriage is, it works.

I remember saying to a stiff-lipped grand English friend who found it distasteful to show any emotion or to make any declarations, 'But, George, you really love Camilla, don't you?' He winced. Camilla looked at him. I waited, placid, having well stirred it. He said, 'She suits me down to the ground.' I thought it one of the most romantic declarations I'd ever heard.

Marriage is about suiting each other, accommodating each other, putting up with things – even how he or she eats toast or an orange – getting through the thick and thin of it, having a companion of the first resort, as well as having a walking almanac who, when you say to it wonderingly and impatiently: who and when was that man with the cheesy face by the blue house in that hot place by the sea, will reply: Geoffrey, Porto Ercole, 1966; or he won't, because you've been droning on as usual and as usual he has cut out, but if he listened he'd know what you were on about. No one else in the world would.

When I chose my mate so many years ago – god alone knows why he chose me – as well as everything else I wanted someone who would stand at the mouth of the cave and fight off all comers; it never occurred to me that I'd try to creep out when he was scanning the horizon for marauders like what I'd told him to do. But that's marriage all over: betrayals and avowals and forgiveness and starting over. Over and over. Marriage is such an intricate choreograph of role changes, intimate dramas, beat and counterpoint.

I want so much to say to young people: forget being in love; forget plain sailing; ahead lies falling out of love and into currents and storms and wreckages, as well as the occasional blue lagoon. You have to work hard at that inviolability I mentioned earlier, and one of you will have to stand fast. My husband stood fast. Falling in love with someone else is no reason to end a marriage, though it is used as one; falling in love and consequent infidelity is an affliction which can be got over. So long as, at a profound level, each partner wants the marriage to last.

And the foundering points are not always the avalanche of an affair; they can come by attrition, through boredom and shrewishness and disillusionment. I won't get on to the huge question of how children can take the romance out of marriage because of course they bring so much more.

The big question the young do actually ask is how can you not be bored being with the same man or woman for so many years? The answer is, you can't; we're all bored with each other from time to time. Doesn't your best friend bore you shitless at times? Or your sister? Or your parents? (And then again, try not being so boring yourself, for a start.)

Many marriages undergo severest stress not after those famous seven years but after about fourteen years, if only because women in their late thirties often become very sexy again. How do you deal with this? I was once told by a therapist to imagine I was in Paris and my husband had bought me for a night. I told this to same husband rather than play-acting it and the profound laughter it aroused in both of us was a tonic, though I don't think it was laughter the therapist meant to be aroused. If your partner can still make you laugh, you're on to a winner. However, if you don't fancy making a Toulouse-Lautrec spectacle of yourself, do something, anything, to trace and treasure and surprise that person you married rather than the familiar you see through the diurnal haze.

The wonderful thing is that if a marriage grows stronger as it grows older the love grows stronger and becomes a wiser love. Happily married people grow to love their spouses more than when they were first married. Observe the verb: grow. One of the many things long-married couples agree on – and I suppose this is the very nub of any marriage – is that they can neither of them imagine being married to anyone else.

Thoughts on Seamus Heaney

It was a sunny day in July and Daisy, my second daughter, who had just been christened, looking touching in the lace confection that her great-grandmother had worn in 1866, was in her pram outside Bradley Court, the house in which I lived then – an Elizabethan house in Gloucestershire enlarged in the Jacobean period and then in Georgian times, the sort of house you might find in the Irish countryside behind high walls – and the irony of that was never lost on me. Noisy peacocks strutted up and down yew walks and allées as though they owned the place, not knowing I could have wrung their necks and longed to. My sister Marie and her husband, Seamus Heaney, had just arrived from one of their many trips abroad and Marie was worried they hadn't had time to get Daisy a christening present. 'Go you and write a poem,' she said to Seamus – that that was what he was like then – on demand, as it were, he could extemporize a poem, profound and delicate, strong and sub-texted, glowing with observation and truth. He went upstairs and began the poem and halfway through writing it we all went for a walk, me pushing Daisy in the pram, and we came on a fallen peacock's feather. Seamus went back and finished the poem immediately – 'A Peacock's Feather for Daisy Garnett'. He was shy enough about it – his modesty was part of his character – but now it has became a much-loved part of his canon. It begins:

Six days ago the water fell
To name and bless your fontanel
That seasons towards womanhood,
But now your life is sleep and food
Which, with the touch of love, suffice
You, Daisy, Daisy, English niece.
Gloucestershire: its prospects lie

Wooded and misty to my eye
Whose landscape, like your mother's was,
Is other than this mellowness
Of topiary, lawn and brick,
Possessed, untrespassed, walled, nostalgic . . .

It ends, and I could cry when I read it now:

So this is a billet-doux to say
That in a warm July you lay
Christened and smiling in Bradley.
While I, a guest in your green court,
At a west window sat and wrote
Self-consciously in gathering dark,
I might as well be in Coole Park!
So before I leave your ordered home
Let us pray: may tilth and loam
Darkened with Celts' and Saxons' blood
Breastfeed your love of house and wood.
And I drop this for you, as I pass,
Like the peacock's feather in the grass . . .

He could and did give the gift of his talent not only to the world but also to individuals, with warm and smiling generosity. When my first daughter, Rose, was married he wrote and read a beguiling epithalamium which contains (in the cleverest treasure-hunt way) references to signifiers of importance in her life – and, indeed, her parents' lives – and it had us in a fervent mix of tears and laughter on that golden wedding day.

Once, by chance, he was working on *Beowulf* in my little office and as I walked in, interrupting him, he looked up, smiled and said, 'So'. No question mark. 'So,' I said back and the word carried everything we both knew about our lives and humour and Tyrone and Derry, just as the words 'your man' do to any Irishman. He had just solved the enigma of the first word, the magic beginning of his epic translation. 'So. The Spear-Danes, in days gone by . . .' I promise you, this is true.

Days gone by and gone for ever. I was on Martha's Vineyard, off the coast of Cape Cod, when I got the news of his death in the middle of that dark night. A friend texted, 'The world is a darker place without him: the brighter the light, the darker the shadow.' But that was as gibberish to me, because obviously it was a cosmic tragic mistake. He couldn't have gone. It was if a void had opened up and where there was goodness, genius, warmth, the knowledge that we could learn how we wanted to live; of what that most fabulous of beasts, language, could do; of words speaking to the springing spirit in all us, there was instead a galactic silent cold. As he wrote himself about a death,

> The morning tiles were harder, windows colder,
> The raindrops on the pane more scourged, the grass
> Barer to the sky, more wind-harrowed.

His death caught all our hearts off guard and blew them open; we never knew how much we loved him or much he had given us until he had gone. How did he do it? He carried our hopes and aspirations and our longings for a better and more truthful life and he carried them so lightly and with such grace. 'If poetry and the arts do anything,' he said, 'they can fortify your inner life, your inwardness.' He did fortify me; not just with his words but with his generosity of spirit, never mind his and my sister's embracing hospitality in their daily lives.

I would avoid sentimentality because Seamus had nothing to with that and everything to do with sentiment; but that crowd at the All-Ireland football final in Croke Park Stadium in Dublin – eighty thousand people clapping for two full minutes in slow tribute to their poet – is an extraordinary thing. Can you imagine, in any other country in the world, the death of a poet bringing football spectators to their feet, in a sports stadium, in a spontaneous tribute?

Everyone he met was made to feel an individual worthy of his attention. The moment Seamus walked on to the stage it was as if a dear friend had arrived; but people who had never heard him read, or never read his work, greeted him with pleasure as he went about his daily life. The number of people who have told me over the years of how he remembered them, of how he took the trouble to write to them, is innumerable. Wordsworth wrote: 'The face of every neighbour whom I met/

Was as a volume to me'; and Seamus too read every face and responded to it.

It is many years ago now since Marie first introduced me to him and I knew at once that their relationship was serious. I was honoured – but of course didn't know then how deeply honoured – to read his poems at the Belfast Festival at one of his first public readings – was it 1962? – and did I read the wonderful poem about his walking out with Marie along the Lagan, with her scarf à la Bardot? I was mystified not just by the breadth of the content, but how he wrote, at that age, and what he wrote – about life as we knew it, in the everyday, in the vernacular. And he created this living world with such complete mastery and technique and insight, with an ability to put the most tremulous feelings into words . . . to make words coil round and round and back again making something solid out of a fluster of a soft supply, like the straw rope in his poem 'Sugan'.

I was so lucky to be his sister-in-law. I never saw him but my heart jumped with pleasure, I never met him but he didn't welcome me as though he had been waiting to see me; and I know of no one who did not feel the same.

And we have come to the end of a dispensation with his passing. Who has seen how a coulter breaks ground behind sweating horses? Who knows what measling shins look like? Or has put a greath on a horse? Or what a scoop sunk past its gleam in a meal-tin looks like? That's what life was like – sitting too close to an open fire coloured your shins like red marbling; in the grocery/haberdasher nothing was packaged – sugar, meal, hen mash were measured out with a brass scoop out of round tin barrels – big caddies – into a paper bag and weighed with circular iron weights. Seamus not only knew to his bones these country ways and vanished words that resounded with usage; he used them as echo chambers, made them necessary memories. He wrote once about not using the word 'wrought' in the sense of struggling with something because although it came easily to his lips to use it would be kind of self-conscious harkening. He is often written about as a country man, a man of country ways, but he was enormously sophisticated, a cosmopolitan animal, with a ravening intelligence and a sensibility that was the finest I ever met; so down to earth, so ready to be made to laugh, so full of humour, so appreciative of the good things in life and yet so fine-grained that I feel he was like William Blake, who, when he stared at knot of wood in a tree, became frightened. I was beside him once when he walked into a hospital room and saw the corpse of someone we all loved and his knees buckled and Marie just caught him as he started to fall. His whole being became supersensitive – as when he went to Aarhus: 'I had a sense of crossing a line really, that my whole being was involved in the sense – the root sense – of religion, being bonded to something, being bound to do something. I felt it a vow; I felt my whole being caught in this . . .'

To read his prose is to read something worked at the highest level. He was a brilliant critic (although the word critic, with its hostile implications, seems inappropriate). His essays – the results of his incomparable close readings – are alive with insight, analysis, care and energy. I have to get up and walk about after I have read Seamus writing on Burns, for example, or Robert Lowell, just to burn off the excitement, the electrocuting power of his mind.

The thing that has always puzzled me was how did he find the time to do all he did. He was true to his muse – a hard taskmistress, she, and a full-time job; obsessed by his vocation as a poet, up all night to finish a poem; he taught at Harvard for years; was Professor of Poetry at Oxford; fulfilled thousands of other engagements in response to what he saw, I think, as his civic duty to respond to the public demand to give voice to his poetry at festivals and readings all over the world; always travelling, paying homage to dead poets and their places. On New Year's Eve 2001 we stood frozen amid the yews about Thomas Hardy's grave at Stinsford Church in Dorset, the wind howling, the snow blasting down, as Seamus fulfilled a vow he had made years before that he would read aloud, over Hardy's grave, the poem 'The Darkling Thrush' which Hardy had written exactly a hundred years before. The worst snowstorm in England and Ireland for years closed all airports but somehow one flight took off from Dublin to Bristol with Seamus and Marie on it and we made it to Dorset through the high drifts and a cold coming we had of it. I was never so touched as when he read that most confounding of autobiographical poems:

An aged thrush, frail, gaunt and small,
In blast be-ruffled plume
Had chosen thus to fling his soul
Upon the growing gloom.

He read more than anyone I knew – writings from all over the world; did superb translations, wise reviews, broadcasts, talked in schools; wrote about Virgil, and Dante, and Homer as readily as crossing stepping stones at Broagh, and, with Ted Hughes, compiled witty, erudite and charming anthologies for schools. It all seemed to come so easily to him but it must have been backbreaking, exhausting work. He didn't let on, or not to us on the outside. Sometimes one got an echo of the cost, especially in that frightening poem 'An Afterwards':

Why could you not have, oftener, in our years
Unclenched, and come down laughing from your room
And walked the twilight with me and your children
Like that one evening of elder bloom
And hay, when the wild roses were fading?

I remember when I first read the new-minted words in 'Blackberry Picking' (we were all so young then, these were poems fresh out of school): 'I always felt like crying. It wasn't fair.' What a thing it was to read such an apparently simple line. It opened a door into the light for me, where you could write what you thought and not what you thought might be poetry. But nothing will match the effect of one of his most famous poems, 'Sunlight Mossbawn'. It's so well known now that it's hard to describe what it was like to come on it, still rising as it were. He made a poem into a madeleine. It's easy to skip the extraordinary first line – 'There was a sunlit absence...' what absence? whose absence? And as you read, the small domestic happening is happening – just as Vermeer's beautiful woman is forever writing that letter – just wait one moment and she will raise her head and smile, and Aunt Mary will tap the scone and turn it while you are there quietly waiting.

There is breach where he was. A living bulwark against the degradation of words and of society has gone; as the poet Simon Armitage said, 'He was just part of the landscape. Now he's gone.

It is like you get up one day and somebody has taken one of the mountains away.'

His concluding words on Elizabeth Bishop's poetry apply to him – 'Continually managing to advance poetry beyond the point where it has been helping us to enjoy life to that even more profoundly verifying point where it also helps us to endure it'.

I remember Keats's marvellous line 'The hare limp'd trembling through the frozen grass', and I think many of us limp'd trembling the day he died and will do for a while to come.

Two Parakeets
and a
Blackthorn Tree

I am standing in front of a blackthorn tree. Something miraculous is happening. The whole process of trees is miraculous – their 'yearly trick of looking new' is something that makes my heart sing – but there are two trees in particular that outshine the rest. One is a magnolia outside my window which I look out at from my bed. In fact, I am practically nesting in it, since my bed is on a level with its high branches. See, my room is high and my bed stands at five foot tall so I have to climb up into it and this I do by way of a small set of gothic steps. I may sound ripe for pseuds' corner but hist – because, as I point out to anyone who sees the bed and will listen (though not many do, because they are staring), fairy stories tell of how the princess *climbed* into bed – not that she fell down into it. I don't understand the concept of low beds. You're so vulnerable down there just above the floor. Laugh if you must, I say, but what happens if a scorpion or a snake slithers into your room at night?

The laughing stops when I ask that, you can see they hadn't thought of this, and I expect gratitude.

My grandchildren adore my bed because it takes them five minutes of leaping and pushing each other up to get into it and then there is the element of acute danger once they make it.

Anyway – from my window just after dawn when the air is full of bird music I observe daily, in intense detail, the tiny buds on the black spiky magnolia branches unfolding themselves into a tornado of ripeness and blossom; and as a result, time s-l-o-w-s down. *Obviously* it is only for a short time in the morning and only in spring, that I lie there observing the minute unfurling of leaves and blossoms but it has brought me to a new apprehension of time. (Not a new understanding of time – I simply can't get over how one minute it is April and the next December; and sometimes I think of how long time must have seemed for the people in the planes going towards the World Trade Center – a lifetime of terror.)

And the other is that blackthorn. For some five months of the year it is a bleak apology for a tree, a bit gnarled, skeletal, planted in a dismal park. But on this spring morning it is a spangled explosion of whiteness, perfect symmetrical petals with a black centre, flounce upon flounce, creating a Bridal Tree. There it is, prodigally displaying the staggering beauty of the world we live in and which we so often don't notice (as I witnessed this morning when I watched people walk past it, eyes cast down, headphones clamped, never once glancing up at the beauty being proffered).

I learnt a poem at school beginning 'I think that I shall never see,/A poem lovely as a tree' (no contest there for me) written by Joyce Kilmer, who I took to be a woman (didn't you?). But no, he was an American soldier killed in the First World War and, according to his neighbours, before that he spent most of his time chopping down trees, pulling up stumps and splitting logs, so that the most distinguishing feature of his property was a colossal woodpile outside his home. I even more remember Pádraig Pearse's heart being shaken with great joy in his poem 'The Wayfarer' – 'The beauty of this world hath made me glad,/ This beauty that will pass.' Neither is a great poem but both were embedded in my consciousness at an early age and when I murmured his lines to my sister as we gazed at the blackthorn tree she murmured, 'Sad – it made Pearse sad. Not glad.'

I was so shocked. How could one not be glad at the coming of spring, the resurrection of our lives and hopes? And I was happy too that as a child I had edited the message in my head from melancholy to hope.

So – back to where I am, standing open-mouthed, like a half-wit, deliriously looking at a tree, on this dancing spring morning when – just like that – out of the blue darted two glittering green parakeets. They alighted among the furbelows and lace and started the most extraordinary ritual. I know nothing of the habits of parakeets, such exotic birds, now native in this London landscape and I wish they weren't, but I suddenly saw where the term love-birds come from; the smaller bird sat close beside but just below the male and he puffed up the feathers on his head and throat in a manly manner and began to make a soft chirping noise – his courtship song. And he kept – well, I can only use the word kissing – he kept kissing her and then looking away bashfully and then turning his head around and kissing her again and again. Well, if a red ladybird upon a stalk had made Pádraig Pearse sad, then surely two green living loving jewels in a white tree would have caused him to drop down dead, through sheer grief. When I got home and read up on them I found that he was tapping her repeatedly with his bill; but it looked like kissing to me.

Well, all of this is leading to time and its control – because for years I wouldn't and couldn't have been able to take the time to stand and stare. (Oh, I feel another poem coming on – I'm reciting from memory here . . . 'What is this life if, full of care/We have no time to stand and stare/No time to stand beneath the boughs/And stare as long as sheep or cows.') But to stand and stare, as W. H. Davies wrote, is one of the best things you can do. I did carve time to go and lie in my meadow when I lived in the country, but that was scheduled into my timetable. What I did with the blackthorn and magnolia tree was to capture the moment. Doing this as a distinct exercise is called mindfulness now; trying to make the most of every minute, experiencing the time you are in, making the most of your day-to-day life. It makes such sense and it should be so easy but how our mind wanders, how cross we get when we are kept waiting, how we drift away from the moment into the past or the future or carry on severe rehearsals of dialogues in our minds. Then, too, many of us suffer from an unspecified anxiety all the time – and feel that time is getting out of our control. It can have tragic consequences – think of Virginia Woolf, who wrote: 'I agree it's tragic about time and space. I no longer try to make them go my way.'

You don't need me to tell you that rates of depression and anxiety are rising all around us. Mindfulness in theory is simple: pay attention to the here and now, pay attention to your breathing, but in fact it is hard to develop the concentration to be able to stay with yourself, with the moment and with your breath – your mind races ahead. I, more often than not, am like the man Tolstoy wrote about who was 'so busy for whole days together that he had no time to reflect that he was doing nothing'. Paying attention to the magnolia and the blackthorn has taught me a lesson.

Look at what nature is doing around you, minute by minute. It doesn't have to be a blackthorn tree. Springtime is your own.

And – take your earphones out and listen to the murmurous haunt of flies on summer eves.

Index

WRITING HOME

Acknowledgements

First published in *The Gloss Magazine* Gloss Publications Ltd
'Flight Path' ©Polly Devlin Gloss Publications October 2007
'A Family Christmas' ©Polly Devlin Gloss Publications 2012
'The Millstone' ©Polly Devlin Gloss Publications November 2012
'Portrait of the Artist as a Young Interviewer' ©Polly Devlin Gloss Publications January 2013
Guess Who's Coming to Dinner ©Polly Devlin Gloss Publications March 2012
'On Blondeness' ©Polly Devlin Gloss Publications February 2011
'Sunshine and Incense' ©Polly Devlin November Gloss 2008
'The Longest Day' ©Polly Devlin Gloss Publications September 2011
'A Room of My Own: Manhattan' ©Polly Devlin Gloss Publications March 2008
'The F Word' ©Polly Devlin Gloss Publications March 2013
'Intricate Rented World' ©Polly Devlin Gloss Publications June 2008
'The Last Time I Saw Paris' ©Polly Devlin Gloss Publications 2009
'Realms of Gold' ©Polly Devlin Gloss Publications 2007
'What Makes a Marriage Last?' ©Polly Devlin Gloss Publications
'Two Parakeets and a Blackthorn Tree' ©Polly Devlin Gloss Publications April 2012

First published in *Image Magazine Ireland*
'Initiatory Drawings' ©Polly Devlin *Image* September 1996
'The Quality of Women' ©Polly Devlin *Image* May 1995
'Sunday Morning in the Country' ©Polly Devlin *Image* September 1994
'The Stag of the Stubble' ©Polly Devlin *Image* April 1995
'Rooks' ©Polly Devlin *Image* 1994
'The Shadow of the Oak' ©Polly Devlin *Image* October 1995
'Dublin Opinion' ©Polly Devlin *Image* June 1995
'Et in Arcadia Ego' ©Polly Devlin *Image* 2004
'A Christmas Miracle' ©Polly Devlin *Image* December 2005/January 2006
'Thank You for Your Custom' ©Polly Devlin *Image* June 1994
'Why Are There No Great Women Artists?' ©Polly Devlin *Image* February 1995
'Home Thoughts in the Vernacular' ©Polly Devlin *Image* November 1996
'A B Special Incident' ©Polly Devlin *Image* March 1995
'Look Back in Wonder' ©Polly Devlin *Image* 2013

Other
'The Road to King's Island' © Polly Devlin, first published in *Celebrating Boglands*
   (Irish Peatland Conservation Council), 2002
'Tinkers' © Polly Devlin, first published in *Cheap Date* magazine (ed. Kira Joliffe and Bay Garnett), 2004
'Tumbleweed at *Vogue*', ©Polly Devlin, first published in *Vogue* 2006
'Diana Vreeland: Wrists, Mists and Poets' ©Polly Devlin, first published in *The World of Hibernia*
   magazine 2004
'An Oddity' ©Polly Devlin & Andy Garnett, first published in *Memories of a Lucky Dog*
   (Turnham Press), 2011
'A Child of Dominica: Jean Rhys' ©Polly Devlin, first published in *Vogue* December 1979
'Stacking the Linen' ©Polly Devlin, first published in American *Vogue* 2000
'Deceived by Ornament' ©Polly Devlin, first published in *Cheap Date* magazine
   (ed. Kira Joliffe and Bay Garnett), 2005
'Camping It Up' ©Polly Devlin & Andy Garnett, first published in *A Year in the Life of an
   English Meadow* (Frances Lincoln Ltd), 2007
'The Last Christmas Tree' ©Polly Devlin, first published in *You* magazine (*Mail on Sunday*),
   December 2008
'The Cranes Are Flying' ©Polly Devlin, first published in *The Independent on Sunday* July 2001
'Thoughts on Seamus Heaney' ©Polly Devlin, first published in *The Guardian* 14 December 2013

The lines from the poems of Seamus Heaney ©Seamus Heaney on pages 26, 87, 157, 111–12, 213 and
216 are quoted by kind permission of Catherine Heaney and Faber & Faber. Thanks also to Faber &
Faber for permission to quote, on pages 67, 105 and 109, lines from the poems of Philip Larkin ©Philip
Larkin. The lines on pages 26, 104 and 206 from the poems of W.H. Auden ©W.H. Auden are quoted by
permission of Random House Inc. and Curtis Brown Ltd. The lines on page 200 from 'Song' ©Elizabeth
Bishop are quoted by permission of FSG/Macmillan. The lines on page 206 from 'Stupid Cupid' by Neil
Sedaka and Howard Greenfield are copyright © 2000–2019 AZLyrics.com.